The East Asian Model

AF763507

Hyungkee Kim analyzes the model of East Asian development as it existed during periods of high growth and how it was transformed by pressures from both the Washington consensus and its own internal contradictions.

Many have discussed the successes and failures of the East Asian Model, but Kim is concerned rather with the story of its transformation and its long-term sustainability. He uses a Five-Sector Model, which focuses on the state, corporate, financial, labor, and foreign sectors to identify the core of East Asian Model and examine the variants in Korea, Japan, and China. He also outlines the distinctions between the East Asian Model and Western development models, including the Anglo-American, Rhine, and Nordic Models. He analyzes in detail the institutional changes such as marketization, privatization, liberalization, and flexibilization that have transformed the East Asian Model. Highlighting the major problems that emerged from the transformation of the East Asian Model, Kim assesses its prospects for economic, social, and ecological sustainability and proposes an agenda for institutional reforms.

An essential reading for scholars of East Asian political economy.

Hyungkee Kim is Professor Emeritus of Economics at Kyungpook National University in Korea. He studied at Fudan University, UC Berkeley, and Harvard University. And he taught at Kyoto University. He published books and articles on economic development and labor economics. His recent researches focus on the East Asian economies. Major books include *New Political Economy* (2001) and *An Alternative Development Model: Beyond Neo-liberalism* (2007). Major articles include 'A Solidaristic Knowledge Policy for Sustainable Human Development', *International Critical Review*, Vol. 1, No. 3, 2011.

Routledge Contemporary Asia Series

76. Transnational Civil Society in Asia
The Potential of Grassroots Regionalization
Edited by Simon Avenell and Akihiro Ogawa

77. Whole Person Education in East Asian Universities
Perspectives from Philosophy and Beyond
Edited by Benedict S. B. Chan and Victor C. M. Chan

78. Air Pollution Governance in East Asia
Edited by Kuei-tien Chou, Koichi Hasegawa, Dowan Ku and Shu-Fen Kao

79. Authoritarianism and Civil Society in Asia
Edited by Akihiro Ogawa and Anthony J. Spires

80. Asian Sound Cultures
Voice, Noise, Sound, Technology
Edited by Iris Haukamp, Christin Hoene and Martyn David Smith

81. Indigenous Reconciliation in Contemporary Taiwan
From Stigma to Hope
Edited by Scott Simon, Peter Kang and Jolan Hsieh

82. Memory and Fabrication in East Asian Visual Culture
Ruinous Garden
Dennitza Gabrakova

83. The Geopolitics of Health in South and Southeast Asia
Perspectives from the Cold War to COVID-19
Edited by Vivek Neelakantan

For more information about this series, please visit: https://www.routledge.com/Routledge-Contemporary-Asia-Series/book-series/SE0794

The East Asian Model

Transformation and Sustainability

Hyungkee Kim

Routledge
Taylor & Francis Group
LONDON AND NEW YORK

First published 2023
by Routledge
4 Park Square, Milton Park, Abingdon, Oxon OX14 4RN

and by Routledge
605 Third Avenue, New York, NY 10158

Routledge is an imprint of the Taylor & Francis Group, an informa business

© 2023 Hyungkee Kim

The right of Hyungkee Kim to be identified as author[/s] of this work has been asserted in accordance with sections 77 and 78 of the Copyright, Designs and Patents Act 1988.

All rights reserved. No part of this book may be reprinted or reproduced or utilised in any form or by any electronic, mechanical, or other means, now known or hereafter invented, including photocopying and recording, or in any information storage or retrieval system, without permission in writing from the publishers.

Trademark notice: Product or corporate names may be trademarks or registered trademarks, and are used only for identification and explanation without intent to infringe.

British Library Cataloguing-in-Publication Data
A catalogue record for this book is available from the British Library

ISBN: 9781032365763 (hbk)
ISBN: 9781032365770 (pbk)
ISBN: 9781003332725 (ebk)

DOI: 10.4324/9781003332725

Typeset in Bembo Std
by KnowledgeWorks Global Ltd.

Contents

Figures

Tables

Acknowledgment

I started this study on East Asian economy while I stayed at Harvard University as a visiting scholar in my sabbatical year 2013–2014. Before going to Harvard, I stayed for three months at China Center for Economic Studies (CCES) in Fudan University. During the stay, I studied Chinese economy and discussed the economic issues of China with the professors who were affiliated at the CCES. The Director of CCES, Professor Zhang Jun, who invited me as a visiting professor, gave many useful information about Chinese economy. When I stayed at the Korea Institute in Harvard University, I studied intensively on East Asian economy, including Japanese economy, Korean economy, and Chinese economy. I prepared a working paper, the title of which was 'The East Asian Development Model: Transformation and Sustainability'. The Director of Korea Institute, Professor Kim Sun Joo, gave me an opportunity to present my paper at a lecture of Kim Koo Forum. My lecture was co-sponsored by Korea Institute, Reischauer Institute of Japanese Studies, and Fairbank Center for Chinese Studies. During the lecture, Harvard professors and scholars, including Professor Richard Freeman and Professor Carter Eckert, gave me valuable comments and suggestions, which were benefitable to improving my paper later. This working paper was actually the origin of this book. After returning to Korea, I upgraded continuously the working paper with a goal to publish it in a book. In July 2017, Professor Uni Hyroyuki at Graduate School of Economics in Kyoto University invited me to a class lecture. The title of the lecture was 'Comparative Studies on East Asian Economic Development'. I gave eight consecutive lectures to graduate students. The contents of lectures were eventually developed into a draft of this book. In early 2018 before I retired as a professor at the School of Economics and Trade in Kyungpook National University, I received a grant to publish a book from the Korea Research Foundation. I completed the manuscript of this book after three years' research. After reviewing my research result, the Korea Research Foundation gave me an approval to publish it in a book. In the end, I was lucky to publish my book by Routledge. Here, I would like to thank the committee who decided to publish my book. Finally, I would like to extend my thanks to Professor Dwight Perkins, who kindly sent me a recommendation message after reviewing my manuscript. During my stay at Harvard, I participated in the book launch of Professor Perkins. He published a book, the title of which was 'East Asian Development: Foundations and Strategies'. I owed much to his seminal book on East Asian economic development. I contributed a chapter on the transformation of the Korean economy in the book edited by Robert Boyer et al (2012). The Regulation approach adopted in the book that analyzed the diversity and transformations of Asian capitalisms was a useful reference to my research. And I also contributed a chapter on the impact of financial liberalization on the East Asian Model in the book edited by Lim et al. Professor Hyun-Chin Lim, who has served as a Director of Seoul National University Asian Center, suggested me some theoretical issues of Asian Capitalisms at a symposium. A correspondence with Professor Ha-Joon Chang at Cambridge University gave me insights to develop my own idea of research on East Asian miracle and crisis. I really appreciate all the excellent scholars I mentioned here for providing me valuable intellectual origins in developing my own theoretical framework.

1 Introduction

The East Asian Model as an economic development model has been studied extensively from the views of development economics and institutional economics. Existing discussions on the East Asian Model have largely focused on the economic miracle and crisis that the major East Asian economies like Japanese, Korean, and Chinese economies have experienced. Indeed, studies such as those from the World Bank (1993), Stiglitz and Yusuf (2001), Chang (2007), and Perkins (2013) have inquired on the causes of the 'East Asian Miracle' in the 1980s and 1990s, whereas, after the 1997 Asian financial crisis and the Japanese 'Lost Decade' in the 1990s, works from the likes of Radelet et al (1998), Goldstein (1998), Hunter et al (1999), Muchhala (2007), and Pempel (1999) paid attention to the causes of the crisis in the East Asian Model.

There was controversy over the causes not only of the miracle but also of the crisis of the East Asian Model. The two contesting economics—neoclassical economics that trust in the functions of the free market and Keynesian economics that believe in functions of the state intervention in the market for correcting the market failures—combated in the battleground of the studies on the causes of the miracle and crisis of the East Asian Model. Works from neoclassical economics argued that the virtuous functions of free market were the base of the miracle of the East Asian Model and the too strong intervention of the state was the causes of its crisis. On the contrary, studies from Keynesian economics insisted that proactive state intervention in the market facilitated the miracle of the East Asian Model, and too weak state intervention brought about the crisis of the East Asian Model. The configuration of controversy was 'market vs. state'. The East Asian Model was actually a true test bed of the theoretical validity of the two different economics. Recently, institutional economics including Regulation Theory entered in the battleground armed with their own theoretical perspectives arguing that institution mattered in the miracle and crisis of the East Asian Model. Especially, Chang (2007) and Boyer et al (2012) approached to the East Asian Model based on institutional economics and Regulation Theory, respectively.

It was also controversial what happened to the East Asian Model itself after the crisis. Some studies such as Fields (2012) argued that the East Asian Model has collapsed after the 1997 Asian financial crisis and it has converged

DOI: 10.4324/9781003332725-1

toward the Anglo-American Model. Other studies such as Henderson (2011) and Walter and Zhang (2012) focused on the changes and continuity in the East Asian Model after the 1997 Asian financial crisis suggested that some elements of the East Asian Model have changed, but others have sustained with continuity. As of now, it would be wrong to assume the end of the East Asian Model as a development model distinctive from the Anglo-American, Rhine, and Nordic Models. According to the prospects of Richter (2000), even though Asian economic crisis was driving governments and corporations alike toward a more market-oriented version of capitalism, this does not mean that the East Asian countries will mindlessly adopt the Anglo-American Model. As we will show in this study, the East Asian Model neither collapsed nor converged toward other models. Instead, we will argue that it has transformed into a hybrid model in which the elements of the East Asian Model have combined with those of other development models.

Rather than presenting a story of success and failure, this study will focus on the transformation and sustainability of the East Asian Model. The transformation and sustainability issues are new research agenda for the study on the East Asian Model[1]. To this end, we will analyze the processes underpinning the transformation of the East Asian Model in Korea, China, and Japan. The sustainability issues are important for pursuing a sustainable New East Asian Model beyond both the existed East Asian Model and the transformed hybrid model. Actually, the ultimate goal of this study is to suggest a New East Asian Model that is economically, socially, and ecologically sustainable. For this purpose, this study tried to widen the theoretical horizon beyond the dichotomy of 'market vs. state'. The factors of institutions and culture, as well as civil society in a country, were included in analyzing the transformation and sustainability of the East Asian Model. The reason why we choose these three countries is that Japan was the creator of the East Asian Model and Korea showed a typical East Asian Model, while China has adopted the East Asian Model with its own version. Moreover, it is not only because Japanese, Korean, and Chinese economies are the three leading economies in the East Asian region in terms of dynamism of economic activities[2] but also because the interactions among the three countries through the international division of labor are so strong that economic cooperation among three countries with choosing their own domestic development model is crucial to the co-prosperity of the East Asian countries including Japan, Korea, and China.

In order to analyze the transformation of the East Asian Model in these countries, we will utilize a framework for analyzing a development model. The Five Sector Model, which focuses on the corporate sector, the financial sector, the labor sector, the state sector, and the foreign sector in a development model, was constructed. In constructing the Five Sector Model, Regulation Theory approach and Varieties of Capitalism approach were referred. This analytical framework will, in turn, help us identify the core of the East Asian Model. This core, which is common to any country in the East Asian Model, will then be used to inform variants specific to Korea, China, and Japan. The different variants of the East Asian Model, that is, Japan Model, Korea Model, and China Model will be specified based on the framework of Five Sector Model. Next we will clarify the transformation processes of the East Asian Model underwent in three countries during the last two or three decades. Four major trends of the institutional changes such as marketization, privatization, liberalization, and flexibilization in the state sector, financial sector, corporate sector, and labor sector were analyzed.

These institutional changes not only significantly transformed the East Asian Model in these three countries; but they also brought about serious socio-economic problems, including major crises and polarization. In addition to highlighting the major problems which emerged from the transformation processes of the East Asian Model in Korea, China, and Japan in terms of sustainability, we will also propose an agenda of institutional and cultural reforms that can promote a sustainable growth regime for the region. Lastly, we will stress the need of a New East Asian Model toward a progressive development model. In this study, some data from international institutions were used to analyze the transformation processes and sustainability in the East Asian Model: OECD Database, World Bank Database, Economic Freedom Index (Fraser Institute), Financial Reform Dataset (IMF), Global Financial Development Database (World Bank), Asian Productivity Database (Asian Productivity Organization), Global Competitiveness Index (World Economic Forum), World Inequality Database (World Bank), Global Gender Gap Index (World Economic Forum), Global Creativity Index (Martin Institute), Main Science and Technology Indicators (OECD), Green Growth Index (Global Green Growth Institute), and World Values Survey (World Values Survey Association).

The structure of this book is as follows. In Chapter 2, the East Asian miracle in the second half of the 20th century and economic crisis in the 1990s are revisited. The different views on the causes of miracle and crisis of the East Asian Model were reviewed. Controversies over the role of the state and market on the miracle and the crisis of the East Asian Model revisited with our own perspective. Moreover, the role of culture on the miracle and crisis of the East Asian Model was discussed. Finally, the need for new research agenda of transformation and sustainability was suggested. Chapter 3 looks at the prototype and variants of the East Asian Model based on the Five Sector Model for analyzing a development model. The core of the East Asian Model was specified in terms of state sector (state type and policy paradigm), corporate sector (corporate system and product market), financial sector (financial system and financial market), labor sector (labor system and labor market), and foreign sector (trade regime and world market). Particular attention will be made in this section to outlining the differences between the East Asian Model and Western development models (Anglo-American, Rhine, and Nordic Model), while also comparing three variants of the East Asian Model (Japan Model, Korea Model, and China Model) to one another.

Chapter 4 analyzes the transformation of the East Asian Model as Japan, Korea, and China underwent marketization, privatization, liberalization, and flexibilization. Marketization and privatization in the state sector, especially in China, were analyzed. The liberalization of financial markets such as financial 'Big Bang' in Japan Model, rapid financial liberalization in the Korea Model, and deliberate financial liberalization in the China Model was highlighted. Transformation of the corporate system in the East Asian Model, especially in Japan, was analyzed. Moreover, the flexibilization of labor markets in terms of employment system and wage system was analyzed. Special attention was paid on the changes in the lifetime employment system in Japan and Korea. In discussing the consequences of the transformation, incremental institutional change hypothesis was adopted. We will argue that the consequence of the transformation was hybridization rather than transition of the development model.

In Chapter 5, we examine growth and crisis in the East Asian Model, with specific reference to the Lost Decades in Japan, the 1997 financial crisis in Korea, and the New Normal Era in China. It is shown that Japan and Korea experienced two to three decades of high growth, which was followed by a long-term crisis. It is argued that Japan abruptly entered into its 'Lost Decade' just after the bubble burst in 1991 and that the stagnation of near zero-growth rates has sustained for two decades thereafter, which was called 'Two Lost Decades'. It will be highlighted that Korea faced the 1997 financial crisis after 'Golden Age of Korean Capitalism' from 1987 to 1996. Moreover, it is argued that after the 1997 financial crisis, Korea experienced two decades of low growth. It is stressed that even though China, which experienced extraordinarily high growth after the reform and opening in 1978, has since not experienced economic downtown to the same degree as Japan or Korea, the factors of a latent crisis have accumulated under the high growth period. Moreover, it is shown that with medium growth, Chinese economy entered into so-called 'New Normal' Era.

Chapter 6 highlights the miracle, crisis, and transformation of a developmental state through a case study of Korea. Here, the dramatic changes in Korea Model (or Park Chung Hee Model) will be analyzed. Korea's model of industrialization is specified. It is argued that Korea's Miracle is called a developmental state miracle. Dramatic changes in the Korean Model throughout the miracle, crisis, and transformation were analyzed. The two great transformations in Korea Model were specified: the first great transformation (from 1987 civil protests and workers' struggles) and the second great transformation (after 1997 financial crisis). Especially transformation of the growth regime from export-led growth to Fordist growth (wage-led growth) was highlighted. It is argued that the consequences of the transformation resulted in unsustainable growth: jobless growth and polarized growth. Moreover, prospects for a New Korea Model were discussed.

Chapter 7 discusses the economic, social, and ecological sustainability of the East Asian Model. The elements of the unsustainable growth regime that appeared in the transformation process were highlighted. In order to analyze the economic sustainability of Japan, Korea, and China, Global Competitiveness Index, which measures national competitiveness through the set of institutions, policies, and factors that determine the level of productivity, was referred. Competitiveness in terms of innovation capability and human resource development as well as goods/labor market efficiency and financial market development were analyzed. For the analysis of social sustainability, jobless growth vs. job-rich growth and polarized growth vs. shared growth were discussed. Especially, productivity and wage differentials between firms, income inequality in terms of Gini coefficient, and top 10% income share were analyzed. Environmental performances in terms of CO_2 emissions and CO_2 intensity trends and renewable energy supply were analyzed for the discussion of ecological sustainability. In addition to this, institutional reforms for a sustainable growth regime were suggested. The data such as reduction in market income inequality by tax-and-transfer system, public social expenditures as % of GDP, and debt-to-GDP ratio were used for discussing the agenda of institutional reforms for a sustainable growth.

Finally, Chapter 8 offers a vision for a New East Asian Model with a new growth regime and a new mode of regulation suggesting an alternative policy paradigm. It is argued that after the Great Recession in 2008, there was a fall of finance-led growth regime that was unsustainable. A new progressive development model in Post-Great Recession era as well as in the Fourth Industrial Revolution age was specified. We will focus on the agenda such as knowledge-led growth regime for a sustainable growth, a symbiotic market economy for sustainable shared growth, and publicness for a new mode of regulation. The macroeconomic circuit of a knowledge-led growth regime was specified in detail. A symbiotic market economy, which comprises of a creative economy, a cooperative economy, and a clean economy, was specified. The publicness of the East Asian Model in comparison to that of Western development models such as Anglo-American Model, Rhine Model, and Nordic Model was highlighted. Moreover, an alternative policy paradigm including a decentralized state for balanced regional development, an economic safety net for the stability of the national economy, bottom-up economics for reducing polarization between large firms and small- and medium-sized enterprises (SMEs), a solidaristic knowledge policy for reducing knowledge differentials between workers, flexicurity of labor market for dynamic stability of employment, and a new welfare regime for sustainable human development.

Notes

1 The diversity of the East Asian Model or Asian capitalisms is another new research agenda. For example, Boyer et al (2012) analyze the diversity of Asian capitalisms focused on the cases of Japan, Korea, and China.

2 Even though Taiwan belongs to the East Asian Model, this study excluded the case of Taiwan (and the other 'Asian Tigers' like Hong Kong and Singapore) in order to concentrate on China that has emerged as a leading country who adopted an East Asian Model. This book intentionally confined the study on the comparative analysis on three major countries of Japan, Korea, and China, whose economies have great impacts on the global economy.

2 The East Asian Miracle and Crisis Revisited

The 'East Asian miracle' was one of the most popular topics in development economics in the 1980s. In response to Japan, Korea, Taiwan, and Singapore's dramatic economic growth in the 1960s–1980s reports trying to explain these success stories, such as the World Bank's 1993 report 'The East Asian Miracle', entered the academic and policy spotlight. The report tried to find out the causes of the East Asian miracle. It introduced different views on what caused East Asia's success in a rapid growth. Since the 1990s, there have been controversies over the very existence of the miracle and the causes of the miracle. Later, in 2000s, as China emerged as a new economic giant with unprecedented high economic growth, the causes of the Chinese miracle were highlighted.

However, the East Asian financial crisis in 1997 and Japanese 'Lost Decades' in the 1990s–2000s inspired another crop of literature to emerge, this time trying to explain the causes of the region's economic crisis. In the 2000s, the hot issue of development economics became the East Asian crisis instead of the East Asian miracle. There have also been controversies over the causes of the crisis. Very ironically, in some cases, the same policies that were put forth as being responsible for the miracle were also presented as being responsible for the crisis. Revisiting the East Asian miracle and crisis is thus key to clarifying and better situating the role entities such as the market, government, and culture played in shaping economic fortunes throughout the region by answering the following questions: what is the essence of the nature of the miracle?, what caused the miracle?, what is the nature of the crisis?, and what brought about the crisis?

According to the World Bank (1993), the essence of East Asian miracle was rapid growth with equity.[1] High rate of growth and reduced inequality are the defining characteristics of East Asian economic miracle (World Bank 1993: 27). Specifically, the bank's comparison of GDP, investment, and total factor productivity (TFP) growth data among high performing Asian countries such as Japan, Korea, Taiwan, Hong Kong, Singapore, Thailand, and Indonesia showed the relatively equal income distribution of these states compared with other Latin American and African countries. The unusual low and declining levels of inequality with rapid growth is contrary to historical

DOI: 10.4324/9781003332725-2

Table 2.1 Decadal Growth Rate of per Capita GDP in Japan, Korea, and China

	(Annual Average Growth Rate: %)				
	1961–1970	*1971–1980*	*1981–1990*	*1991–2000*	*2001–2010*
Japan	9.4	4.5	4.5	1.3	0.7
Korea	9.5	9.3	9.9	7.0	4.4
China	5.0	6.3	9.3	10.5	10.6
World Average	5.5	3.9	3.1	2.8	2.8

Note: GDP in current US dollars.

Source: World Bank, World Development Indicators.

experience and contemporary evidence in other regions. Therefore, the World Bank report argued that this rapid growth with equity deserved to be called a miracle. Though it did not include the case of China, the country's unprecedented rapid economic growth after reform and opening policies in 1978 makes us include China as part of the East Asian miracle. Looking at the growth performance of Japan, Korea, and China in Table 2.1 highlights the remarkable nature of their economic growth rate. Among these countries, Japan was the first mover with growth rates accelerating in 1955, with Korea leading for three decades starting in the 1960s and China taking over from the 1980s onward. In this way, Japan, Korea, and China have led the East Asian miracle successively for a half-century from the 1960s. When we compare the growth performances of Japan, Korea, and China with those of the other regions around the world, the East Asian Miracle is more evident. Maddison (2006) showed that the annual average growth rate of Korea in 1950–1999 was 6.0%, while those of Japan and China were 4.9% and 4.2%, respectively. 'Asian Tigers' like Hong Kong, Singapore, and Taiwan also showed high growths comparable to Japan, Korea, and China. These growth rates are far higher than those of Latin America (1.7%), Africa (1.0%), Eastern Europe and former USSR (1.1%), Western Europe (2.9%), and the United Sates (2.2%). Especially, Japan, Korea, and China each recorded global top growth rates in 1950–1973, 1973–1990, and 1990–1999, respectively.

This miraculous growth is even more impressive when compared with historical data on economic growth. According to Picketty (2013), which estimated the growth rate of per capita output since the Industrial Revolution at the continental level around the world, per capita output growth rates on all continents until 1950 have always been under 2% (see Table 2.2). Even during the 'Golden Age of Capitalism' after WW II (from 1950 to 1970), Europe's growth rate was just 3.8%, which was far lower than Japan's and Korea's growth rates in 1961–1970, 9.4% and 9.5%, respectively. Moreover, if we see the data of the continent level, Asia's annual average growth rate in 1990–2012 was 3.8%, which is comparable to Europe's growth rate in 1950–1970. According to the estimation of Maddison (2006), which shows the growth rate of per capita GDP of the high performed economies in

Table 2.2 Per Capita Output Growth since the Industrial Revolution

	Average Annual Growth Rate				
Year	*World*	*Europe*	*America*	*Africa*	*Asia*
0–1700	0.0	0.0	0.0	0.0	0.0
1700–1820	0.1	0.1	0.4	0.0	0.0
1820–1913	0.9	1.0	1.5	0.4	0.2
1913–1950	0.9	0.9	1.4	0.9	0.2
1950–1970	2.8	3.8	1.9	2.1	3.5
1970–1990	1.3	1.9	1.6	0.3	2.1
1990–2012	2.1	1.9	1.5	1.4	3.8

Source: Piketty (2013, p. 94. Table 2.5).

Western Europe and East Asia after the WW II, Japan achieved the most rapid growth rate in 1950–1973, and Korea achieved the most rapid growth rate in 1973–1999. In the Golden Age of Capitalism, Japan has led the world economic growth while in the neoliberal age, in turn, Korea has led the world economic growth.

The data shown above indicates that Japan, Korea, and China have sequentially achieved unprecedented high rates of economic growth. Despite this, economists such as Paul Krugman argued that East Asia's miracle was a myth. According to him, development in the region was driven by extraordinary growth in inputs like labor and capital rather than by gains in efficiency: 'If there is a secret to Asian growth, it is simply deferred gratification, the willingness to sacrifice current satisfaction for future gain' (Krugman, 1994). Later, Krugman (1997) also argued that East Asia's economic growth has been mainly a matter of perspiration rather than inspiration.[2] This Krugman's argument is called 'the perspiration theory'. If we interpret Krugman's argument in terms of terminology of the economic growth theory, the reason why Krugman argued that 'East Asia's miracle' was a myth is that, in his view, it was based not on intensive growth by the technological progress but on extensive growth by the factor inputs like capital and labor.

The extent to which the East Asian miracle was a reality or a myth depends on the role of TFP in economic growth. The World Bank (1993), Young (1994), Kim and Lau (1994), and Krugman (1994) argued that the contribution of TFP to growth was negligible. In contrast, Howard Pack (2001), Stiglitz and Yusuf (2001) argued that the contribution of TFP to growth was considerable. Many growth accountings of Japan and China show that the contribution of TFP to economic growth was, in fact, considerable from the 1960s and 1990s, respectively. A comprehensive analysis of Korean economic growth between 1970 and 2010 shows that Krugman's perspiration theory is also not true for Korea. The contribution of TFP to GDP growth rate in Korea has increased from 44.6% in 1970–1980 to 76.7% in 2000–2010. Moreover, the proportion of the contribution of technical progress to GDP growth rate has increased from 11.9% in 1970–1980 to 34.5% in 2000–2010

(Kim et al, 2012). Seen this way, the economic growth of Korea has originated not only from factor inputs, resource reallocation, and economies of scale but also from technical progress (Eichengreen et al, 2012; Kim et al, 2012). The growth accountings of Japan, Korea, and even China show that the East Asian miracle was not a myth but a reality. Therefore, so-called 'the perspiration theory' of Paul Krugman was not true for the East Asian Model.

Then, what caused the East Asian miracle? The multiple causes of the miracle can be easily driven from the common factors in the high-performed East Asian countries.[3] High levels of domestic savings and investment, as well as high investments in human capital, were the common factors in the East Asian miracle. Macroeconomic and financial stability and openness to foreign technology were also important factors when compared with other underdeveloped or developing countries in Asia, Latin America, Africa, and Eastern Europe. These robust fundamentals of the national economies have facilitated the high economic growths. There is no difference in the views on the role of these fundamentals to the East Asian miracle.

However, there were controversies over the role of the market and the state in East Asia's economic miracle. The 1993 World Development Report highlighted three competing views on the role played by government: a neoclassical view, a revisionist view, and a market-friendly view.[4] The neoclassical view (Chen, 1979; Wolf, 1988) emphasizes the role of markets in achieving high economic growth. Adherent of the neoclassical view argues that providing a stable macroeconomic environment and a reliable legal framework to promote domestic and international competition was a cause of high growth. They stress the sound fundamentals of the national economy for the high economic growth, which suggests that the policy of 'getting the basics right' is one of the secrets of the miracle. This view argued that there were limited price distortions in the high performing East Asian economies. According to the view, the competitive factor markets, such as the competitive labor market, were one of the driving forces behind East Asia's economic miracle. Therefore, 'getting the prices right' is another secret of the miracle. The view saw the favorable effects of the free market on the East Asian miracle. The free market doctrine of the neoclassical economics is based on this view.

Contra the neoclassical view, the revisionist view (Amsden, 1989; Haggard, 1990; Wade, 1990) presents the role of the state as central to achieving the East Asian miracle. Adherents of the revisionist view think that East Asia does not wholly conform to the neoclassical model. For example, industrial policy and intervention in financial markets are not easily reconciled with the neoclassical framework (World Bank 1993: 9). For proponents of revisionist view, governments in East Asia intervened in factor markets to keep interest rates and wages low, which provided favorable conditions for capital accumulation by industrialists. An example of the role of the state in East Asia is government intervention in the foreign exchange market in order for corporations to increase their competitiveness through the under-evaluation of exchange rates. There were deliberate price distortions for altering incentive structures. Thus, 'getting the prices wrong' was a key of the East Asian miracle. Firms also received various financial and fiscal privileges from the government in the form of policy loans, subsidies, and tax exemptions. According to the revisionist view, state intervention through industrial policy created the East Asian miracle. Wade (1990) argued that industrial policy in East Asia led market rather than following market. This view was backed up by the interventionism of Keynesian economics that thinks the market mechanism is incomplete.

Academic and policy debates have often presented the neoclassical view and revisionist view as two competing paradigms pitting the state against the market. In reality, the market needs the state as much as the state needs the market (Chowdhury and Islam, 1993). In an attempt to reconcile both sides of the argument, the World Development Report 1991 (World bank, 1991) presented a market friendly view of the East Asian miracle. According to this view, government intervention was done in a limited and effective way by providing a competitive climate for private enterprises and keeping the economy open to international trade. Adherents of this view argue that government intervention itself was market friendly. Price distortions were mild. In the market friendly strategy, the appropriate role of government is to ensure adequate investment in people and to provide a competitive climate for private enterprise, keep the economy open to international trade, and maintain a stable macroeconomy. Moreover, the market friendly view argues that government intervention in the market was selective. Selective intervention includes mild financial repression, directed credit, and selective industrial promotion (World Bank, 1993: 9–10). The market friendly view stresses the importance of not only fundamentals but also careful policy interventions. According to the view, 'getting the fundamentals right' was essential to high growth. The view also points out that the East Asian leaders established the principle of shared growth[5] to win the support of the society at large and created a business-friendly environment. In short, the market- friendly view, which is suggested as an eclectic approach, acknowledges the role of both the state and the market in the East Asian miracle.

How can we evaluate these three views on the role of government in the East Asian miracle? Whether the 'getting the prices right' or the 'getting the prices wrong' was coincident with the reality? In Korea, for instance, it is widely known that the government in the 1960s and 1970s deliberately manipulated domestic prices to support import substitution in key heavy industry sectors such as the automobile and machine industries. Moreover, Korea under-evaluated its official exchange rate in order to support export industries. Under a fixed exchange rate regime, the official exchange rates were set above the PPP exchange rates in order for export firms to gain price competitiveness in the world market (Perkins, 2013: 77). This account of government intervention in Korea gives credence to scholars like Stiglitz, who argues that neoclassicals have underestimated the role of strong and effective industrial policy[6] in making the East Asian miracle possible (Stiglitz, 2001).

The key role of government in the East Asian miracle points out that institutions mattered in the miracle. The various institutions reformed or newly created intervened in the market intensively. As World Bank (1993) suggested, the government intervention was selective. Directed credit, selective industrial promotion, protecting domestic import substitutes, and establishing export targets were the example of the selective intervention. Specifically, East Asian countries were characterized by having developmental states in which a set of institutions were tasked with intervening in the market. The industrial policy in the East Asian Model was a symbolic institution through which the state directly intervened in the investment coordination of the private enterprises. Implemented by pilot agencies of industrial policy such as the Ministry of International Trade and Industry (MITI) in Japan, the Economic Planning Board (EPB) in Korea, and the State Development and Planning Commission (SDPC) in China, these interventions in the products market, the labor markets, and financial markets through institutions had a positive and significant impact on economic growth in each country. In this way, institutions mattered in the East Asian miracle.[7] It would be argued that the 'getting the institutions right' was also essential no less than the 'getting the fundamentals right' and the 'getting the prices wrong'.

The role of culture in the East Asian miracle is also controversial. Culture is a way of thinking and a mode of behavior of the people. In short, culture is about values the people have. Generally, culture affects economic growth through its impacts on transaction costs and creativity of the people (Kwon, 2011). Some values can reduce the transaction costs, which may have positive impacts on economic growth. Indeed, Confucian values[8] of the East Asian people, such as accepting hierarchy, valuing perseverance, and attaching great importance to education, thrift, and group orientation, were regarded by some scholars as beneficial to economic growth in the region (Hofstede, 1991). However, such proponents of 'Confucian capitalism' fail to account for the fact that values they deem responsible for the region's relatively recent economic boom have been present long before the East Asian miracle. Contrary to Confucian capitalism, scholars such as Max Weber thought that the Confucian tradition was actually detrimental to modernization and economic development (Weber, 1951).[9] On the other hand, Max Weber argued that Protestant work ethics such as hard work, discipline, and frugality had positive impacts on the development of capitalism. He thought that Protestant ethics, which was the spirit of capitalism, was favorable to the economic growth (Weber, 1930). However, rapid economic growth in Japan, Korea, and China, where the Confucian tradition has been deeply seated in the society shows that Max Weber's view on the negative impacts of the Confucian tradition on the economic growth did not match the facts. There is no reason why the Confucian values in East Asia were harmful to economic growth while the Protestant ethic was beneficial in Europe. These different views on the Confucian values further complicate the use of culture as a strong explanatory variable for Japan, Korea, and China's economic development.

It is essential to revisit the causes of the East Asian financial crisis in seeking a sustainable growth regime of the East Asian countries at the moment of two decades after the financial crisis of the 1990s. The causes of the East Asian crisis in the 1990s are also subject to debate. Neoclassical economists and market fundamentalists argue that too much government regulation of the market brought about the East Asian financial crisis, while the efficient resource allocation through the market brought about the East Asian miracle. In contrast, advocates for government intervention argue that weak regulation on the market, especially on financial market, brought about the crisis in the 1990s, while strong government regulation brought about the miracle in the 1970s–1980s.

Joseph Stiglitz criticizes the neoclassical view, arguing that those who trusted the market underestimated the role of government in the East Asian miracle and overestimated the role of government during the financial crisis (Stiglitz, 2001: 517). He argues that the role of government in resource allocation has diminished in the 1900s. He, for example, points out that the rapid liberalization of capital markets before the 1997 crisis gave stress to the risk absorption mechanism. In consequences, the risk of banking sector has increased to bring an abrupt financial crisis (Stiglitz, 2001). Ha-Joon Chang also argues that Asian countries which have recently experienced problems were either the ones that did not follow the East Asian Model or the ones that moved away from such a model. The economic crisis that affected Japan and Korea in the 1990s was therefore the result of departures from the 'traditional' East Asian Model rather than an adherence to it (Chang, 2007). As we will describe in detail later in this study, the major causes of the 1997 Asian financial crisis were the giving up the policies such as the industrial policy inherent in East Asian Model and rapid financial liberalization rather than strong regulation on the market and the weakness of the economic system in the East Asian countries. When considered from the consensus on the causes of the 2008 global financial crisis that the weak regulation on the financial markets was a major cause of the crisis, the immediate causes of the 1997 Asian financial crisis might be rapid liberalization of the financial market, especially capital account.

Then, what was the role of culture in the 1990s East Asian crisis? Some argue that Asian values,[10] such as nepotism and cronyism,[11] were responsible for the crisis since they were hotbed of corruption (Pye, 2000; Pagano, 2002). Before the outbreak of the crisis, Asian values, such as the Confucian values, were praised as a cause of the East Asian miracle. However, just after the outbreak of the crisis, they were blamed for the crisis. How can be reconciled with these two contradictory arguments? Were the Asian values cause of the miracle or the cause of the crisis in the East Asian Model? Asian values have a wider spectrum in which positive and negative elements for the economic performances are included. Valuing perseverance, attaching great importance to education, and thrift might be the positive elements, while nepotism and cronyism might be the negative elements. Therefore, it can be concluded that the positive elements of Asiatic values might be a cause of the miracle, while their negative elements would be a cause of the crisis. These dual characters of the Asian values should be relevantly considered when one analyzes the relationship between the Asian values and the economic growth/crisis of East Asian countries. Moreover, more empirical studies should be performed with a proper theoretical model about the relation between the values of the people and economic growth and crisis.

New debates in development economics emerged in the aftermath of the 1997 East Asian financial crisis since the crisis was overcome and rapid recovery accompanied aftermath of the crisis in the East Asian economies. The issues of transformation and sustainability of the East Asian Model arose with the retreat of miracle and crisis issues. Led by academics such as Henderson (2011), Walter and Zhang (2012), and Boyer et al (2012), these conversations focus on the transformation of East Asian capitalism after the crisis. Works published by these authors, however, do not deal with the extent to which the East Asian Model is sustainable. To address this gap in the literature, this study will analyze both the transformation and the sustainability of the East Asian Model using a consistent analytical framework. Lastly, seeking a New East Asian Model is a novel research agenda that have not yet systematically approached. This study takes up the task of the new research agenda through suggesting a new sustainable East Asian Model based on the analysis of its transformation and sustainability in Japan, Korea, and China.

Notes

1 This position of World Bank (1993) coincided with the view of Stiglitz (2001). As Stiglitz argued, 'whether one calls it a miracle or not, the increases in income and reductions in poverty in East Asia were real and impressive. They showed that development is possible and that rapid development could be associated with egalitarian policies that greatly reduced poverty' (Stiglitz, 2001).

2 This means that workers in East Asian countries worked harder, not smarter.

3 World Bank (1993) argued that six characteristics of high-performed Asian economies can be pointed out when compared with most other developing economies: (1) more rapid output and productivity growth in agriculture, (2) higher rates of growth of manufactured exports, (3) earlier and steeper declines in fertility, (4) higher growth rates of physical capital, supported by higher rates of domestic savings, (5) higher levels and growth rates of human capital, and (6) generally higher rates of productivity growth (World Bank, 1993: 27).

4 The difference among the three views has connections with the different views on the causes of the East Asian crisis occurred in the 1990s.

5 The shared growth means that all groups would benefit from the economic growth.

6 The role of industrial policy in the East Asian miracle will be discussed in detail in Chapter 3.

7 The attempts to clarify the East Asian miracle and crisis focusing on institutions rather than market and state are emerging from the works based on Regulation theory approach such as Boyer et al (2012). Our study on the East Asian Model is largely based on Regulation theory approach.

8 Perkins argued that in Northeast Asia, the people in each country shared a common culture and saw themselves as part of that culture, adding that Confucian values were as important in Japan as elsewhere in East Asia (Perkins, 2013).

9 Max Weber thought that even though both Protestantism and Confucianism valued self-restraint, frugality, and discipline and did not oppose the accumulation of wealth, the former legitimized profit-seeking activities of individuals, while the latter promoted a man of virtue for whom the pursuit of the wealth was not a proper norm.

10 The word 'Asian values' was initially used by authoritarian political leaders in Asia in order to legitimize their dictatorship regimes. In this case, Asian values were defined as the preference for collectivism and communitarianism, loyalty and respect toward figures of authority, and collective well-being of the community. Here, we use this word to represent Asian culture including the Confucian values.

11 Even though nepotism and cronyism are not unique in East Asia, they tend to be much more severe in the region than in the Western world since relation-based contracts are prevalent in the East Asia.

3 The Core of the East Asian Model and Its Variants

3.1 A Framework for Analyzing a Development Model

The theoretical framework for analyzing an economic development model used in this study is based on insights from Regulation Theory and Varieties of Capitalism approach. Regulation Theory attributes spatial diversity and temporal variability in models of capitalism to institutional differences. Differences in institutions of the different capitalist countries in the same age create spatial diversity of capitalism. Thus, for example, Swedish capitalism is different from American capitalism due to the different sets of institutions between the two types of capitalism. Changes in the institutions in a country give rise to temporal variability of capitalism. For example, the 20th-century capitalism is different from the 19th-century capitalism due to structural changes in capitalism between the two periods. Therefore, Regulation Theory argues that institution matters in analyzing a capitalism.

In Regulation Theory, development model is a key concept for analyzing temporal variability or structural changes and spatial diversity or varieties of capitalism. It is comprised of a growth regime and a mode of regulation.[1] The growth regime is, in turn, comprised of a productivity regime and demand regime. Any growth regime has its own macroeconomic circuit, which is characterized by linkages between a productivity regime on the supply side, and a demand regime on the demand side. Mode of regulation, which is a mechanism that gives regularity to a growth regime, is comprised of a set of institutional forms (Boyer and Saillard, 2002). According to Regulation Theory, any capitalist economy has five institutional forms: a monetary regime, a wage-labor nexus, forms of competition, relations of the state with the economy, and forms of insertion of a nation into the world economy. Coherence of a set of specific five institutional forms creates a specific mode of regulation. The characteristics of a development model can be analyzed in terms of these five institutional forms (Boyer and Saillard, 2002).

Varieties of Capitalism approach has similarity with Regulation Theory approach in analyzing the different model of capitalism. Hall and Soskice (2001), in which Varieties of Capitalism approach was suggested, classified capitalism into liberal market economies (LMEs) and coordinated market

DOI: 10.4324/9781003332725-3

economies (CMEs) in terms of five economic spheres in which firms coordinate with each other: industrial relations, vocational training and education, corporate governance, inter-firm relations, and relations with employees. While Regulation Theory approach focuses on macro-level coordination, Varieties of Capitalism approach focuses on micro-level coordination. While Regulation Theory approach stresses the institutional coherence of a development model, Varieties of Capitalism approach puts an importance on the institutional complementarity of a type of capitalism. Thus, the two approaches have similarities and some differences in terms of analytical framework.

In this study, a framework was built to analyze the structure and transformation of a development model involving these five institutional forms. The Five-Sector Model, which is our own framework for analyzing a development model, was constructed on the basis of these two approaches. Drawing from this framework, we introduce five sectors that comprise a development model: the corporate sector (corporate systems and the products market), the financial sector, (financial system and financial market), the labor sector (labor system and labor market, the state sector (state type and policy paradigm), and the foreign sector (trade regime and world market).

The interconnection and interaction among these five sectors are shown in Figure 3.1, with four interconnected systems in the domestic domain (the corporate system, the financial system, the labor system, and trade regime) and four interacting markets (the products market, financial markets, labor markets, and world market). The corporate system includes corporate governance, managerial style, and interfirm relations. The financial system encompasses the monetary system, banking system, and credit system. The labor system involves the labor process, the employment system, and industrial relations. The trade regime comprises the foreign exchange system, trade agreements, and international capital flows, while the world market more or less interacts with the product market, the financial market, and the labor market to the extent that the trade regime is liberalized. Finally, the type of state is determined by the constitution, the legislative system, and social contracts, with the policy regime representing how and to what extent the state intervenes in the four sectors, especially in the products market, financial market, labor market, and world market. In addition to these sectors, systems, markets, and regime, a societal paradigm, which characterizes a community's worldview (Lipietz, 1992), can also shape development models.

The consistency and coherence of a development model is contingent on all five sectors having institutional complementarity. According to the hypothesis of institutional complementarity, fundamental mismatches between institutions adversely affect the performance of a development model (Hall and Soskice, 2001). The hypothesis of institutional complementarity also suggests that there will be no gradual transition from one development model to another because only marginal changes will happen within a given development model. It acknowledges sudden collapse of a development model due to

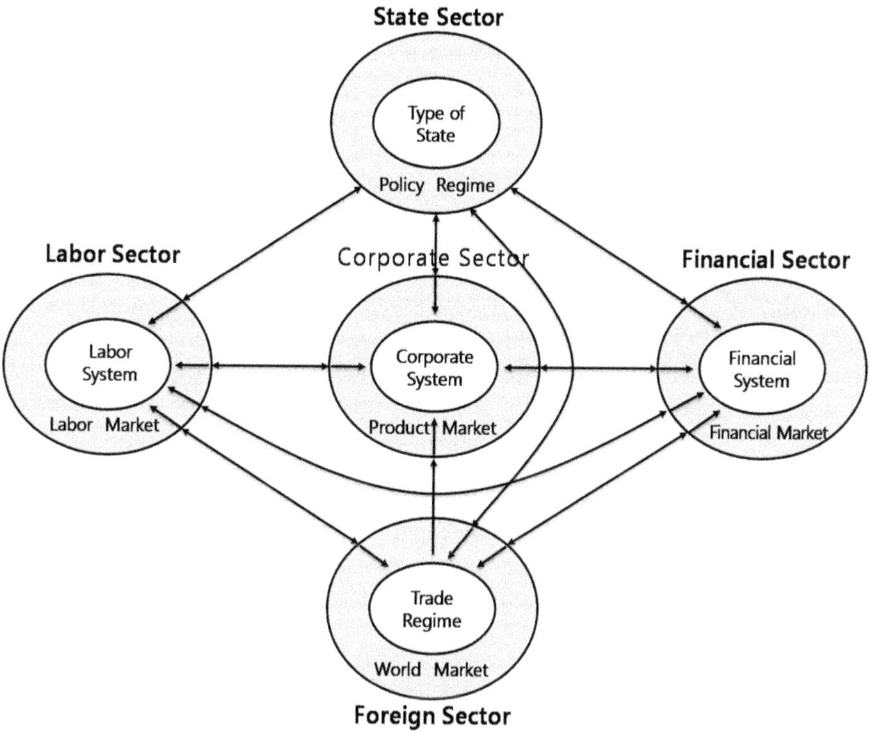

Figure 3.1 A Framework for Analyzing a Development Model: The Five Sector Model

Source: Kim (2018b: 14, Figure 1.1).

the exogenous shocks. Though the hypothesis of institutional complementarity is useful to explain the reproduction of structures within a development model, it cannot explain transformation from one development model to another (Kim, 2018b: 16). On the other hand, the concept of institutional hierarchy, which suggests that some institutions have predominance over others, will be helpful in explaining the variants of a development model. Different forms of institutional hierarchy may make different variants of a development model. For example, as we will discuss later in this chapter, Japan, Korea, and China have different forms of institutional hierarchy, which produced different variants of the East Asian development model.

The transformation of a development model may also be explained by the incremental institutional change (IIC) approach of Mahoney and Thelen (2010),[2] who identify four mechanisms (displacement, layering, drift, and conversion) through which institutional transformation may occur. 'Displacement' occurs when a new model diffuses and displaces the existing model. 'Layering' happens when a new institution coexists with an old institution. 'Drift' occurs when rules may remain unchanged, but existing institutions are neglected by people. Finally, 'conversion' happens when the existing institutions are redeployed to fill new purposes and accomplish new goals. Here, while displacement may mean the transition of a development model, conversion and layering may mean hybridization of a development model. Since the process of transformation includes both transition and hybridization, Mahoney and Thelen's typology will be useful in analyzing the transformation of the East Asian development model in our three case studies.

By the way, the growth and crisis of a development model and long-term transition of a development model can best be analyzed by the methodology of Regulation Theory. According to the theory, a long-term sustained economic growth will appear when a new development model is established. Major crisis[3] will emerge when the existing growth regime has exhausted in realizing productivity and/or when the existing model of regulation no longer works in giving a regularity to the growth regime. Major crisis is a crisis of a development model itself. A long-term stagnation will prevail when a major crisis is lingering. The major crisis will finally be overcome only if a new development model displaces the existing development model (Boyer and Saillard, 2002). This concept of major crisis is very helpful in explaining the 1997 Asian financial crisis and the 'Lost Decades' of Japanese economy. In this study, based on the methodology of Regulation Theory, we adopted, first of all, the hypothesis of institutional complementarity in identifying the core of the East Asian Model. Second, the concept of institutional hierarchy was introduced in specifying the variants of the East Asian Model. Third, the approach of incremental institutional change was used in explaining the transformation of the East Asian Model.

3.2 The Core of the East Asian Model

Despite some well-known stylized facts about the East Asian Model, little is known about the uniqueness of the East Asian Model compared to Western models of capitalism. Here, we highlight the core of the East Asian Model (see Table 3.1) based on applying our theoretical framework for analyzing a development model described above. It will be derived from the common basic institutional forms of Japanese, Korean, and Chinese economies that are different from those of the other development models such as Anglo-American, Rhine, and Nordic Model (Kim, 2018b).

The State Sector: State Type and Policy Paradigm

The major contents of state type with policy paradigm include developmental state, authoritarianism, and industrial policy. The defining feature of the East Asian Model compared to other development models is the role the state played in the economy to achieve industrialization (Johnson, 1982; Woo-Cumings, 2019). In the countries that embraced the East Asian Model,

Table 3.1 The Core of the East Asian Model

Institutional Forms	*Major Contents*
State type	Developmental state
Policy paradigm	Authoritarianism
	Industrial policy
Corporate system	Dominance of conglomerates
Product market	Insider-oriented governance
	Relation-based contracting
Financial system	Bank-based system
Financial market	Financial repression
	Patient capital
Labor system	Long-term employment
Labor market	Seniority wages system
	Enterprise unionism
Trade regime	Strategic opening
World market	Export promotion
	Capital controls

Source: Kim (2018a: 18, Table 1.1).

economic development was the top priority of state activities, which was often referred to as developmental states. Developmental states differed from welfare states and predatory states. Indeed, while the developmental state subordinates social policy to economic policy, the welfare state tends to prioritize social policy over economic policy. A developmental state is also distinctive from a predatory state in that the former supports the activities of corporations, while elites in the latter extract wealth from the corporate sector.[4] Developmental states further distinguish themselves from neoliberal states—which sustain a free market through deregulation—by strongly intervening in the market.

Another feature of developmental states is their relative autonomy from the interest groups in the corporate, financial, and labor sectors. This relative autonomy of the developmental state served to effectively repress the rent-seeking activities of interest groups, allowing bureaucrats who were policy designers and enforcers to implement economic policies that promote broad-based growth without being interfered by the powerful private interest groups (Lipietz, 1987). The existence of stable bureaucratic apparatus that committed to the long-term development contributed the economic growth. However, as democratization proceeded in East Asia, the exigencies of short-term political calculations began to outweigh longer-term strategic concerns. The susceptibility of the bureaucratic apparatus to pressure from powerful interest groups thus increased (Yusuf, 2001).

The policy paradigm of the developmental state in the East Asian countries was industrial policy. The main channel of intervention of the state in the economy was industrial policy. Industrial policy is that the state directly controls and allocates resources in order to foster strategic industries. This was mostly achieved through investment coordination, infant industry protection and export promotion, pro-investment macroeconomic policy, and control over domestic financial flows and foreign exchange. The core of industrial policy may be investment coordination of corporations by the government (Chang, 2007). To implement industrial policy, pilot agencies such as Ministry of International Trade and Industry (MITI) in Japan, Economic Planning Board (EPB) in Korea, and National Development and Planning Commission (NDPC) in China were established. These pilot agencies played a key role in strategic policy design and implementation. As a policy paradigm, industrial policy in the East Asian Model is thus distinguishable from other policy paradigms such as social policy focusing on social welfare in the European Social Model (the Rhine and Nordic models), the neoliberal policy focusing on deregulation in the Anglo-American model, and the Keynesian policy focusing on aggregate demand management in developed countries (Kim, 2018b).

The political regime of developmental states in East Asia was authoritarianism. This was characterized by the concentration of power in the central government, top-down control by the bureaucracy, one-party rule, and even dictatorship. In Japan, the Liberal Democratic Party which ruled for half a century starting in 1955, exercised a de facto one-party dictatorship. Korea's developmental dictatorship regime in which military elites controlled power for 30 years, and China's political monopoly system in which the Chinese Communist Party (CCP) has ruled unilaterally for 60 years also represent different kinds of authoritarianism.[5] The authoritarianism in these East Asian countries contributed to the high economic growth in the countries by implementing the effective industrial policies. Authoritarian regime with enlightened bureaucracies could pursue long-term goals through industrial policy (Yusuf, 2001).

The Corporate Sector: Corporate System and Products Market

In the corporate sector of the East Asian Model, conglomerates' dominance, relation-based contracting, and insider-oriented governance prevailed (Richter, 2000; Walter and Zhang, 2012). Conglomerates such as the Keiretsu in Japan, the Chaebol in Korea, and state-owned enterprises (SOEs) in China dominated the national economy through their monopoly power. Thus, the structure of the products market was highly monopolistic. Conglomerates belonged largely to the main-bank in Japan, Chaebol families in Korea, and the state in China. Main-bank ownership in Keiretsu, family ownership in Chaebol, and state ownership in the SOEs were the different features of the ownership structures of the East Asian Model. The cross-shareholdings or interlocking ownership among the enterprises within the Keiretsu and Chaebol was another important feature of ownership structure. Because Japanese Keiretsu are the descendant of the prewar Zaibatsu within which family ownership dominated, Korean Chaebol has similar characteristics with Japanese Keiretsu except one point that Korean Chaebol is still controlled by the Chaebol family (Kim, 2018b). In China, with the intensive financial and fiscal support from the government, SOEs are also evolving toward conglomerates like those found in Japan (Keiretsu) and Korea (Chaebol) (Richter, 2000: 325).[6]

These ownership structures determined the pattern of corporate governance of conglomerates. In East Asia, insider-control corporate governance where the main-bank (Japan), the Chaebol family (Korea), or the state (China) acted as major shareholders with decision-making rights differed from the corporate governance in shareholder capitalism in which outsider shareholders control management through the board of directors. For example, in the Anglo-American model of corporate governance, in which corporate ownership is separated from the control, the management is pressured by stock markets and outside shareholders, including institutional investors who pursue maximization of stock price earnings ratio (RER) or shareholder value. Firms that adopt this model of corporate governance thus tend to have management practices that pursue short-term profitability and flexibility in order to maximize shareholder value. In contrast to the Anglo-American Model, the firms that have a corporate governance of stakeholder capitalism which characterizes the Rhine and Nordic Models will choose management practices focused on achieving the mutual gains of stakeholders including shareholders and employees. Since the East Asian Model has an insider-control corporate governance, it tends to resemble stakeholder capitalism[7] more than shareholder capitalism. Firms where stakeholder capitalism prevails tend to have stable employment relationships such as long-term employment. However, because the insider-control corporate governance in the East Asian Model is a closed system, it also raises insider–outsider problems, which refers to conflicts of interest between the company's management and the company's shareholders, as well as transparency problems, which prohibits the disclosure of corporate information (Kim, 2018b).

Inter-firm relationships in the East Asian Model are characterized by relation-based contracting (Chang, 2007). Relation-based contracting between firms is premised on trust between economic agents, with transactions between firms being carried not on short-term market conditions but on long-term network relationship. Relation-based contracting is also distinguishable from arm's-length transactions common in the Anglo-American model, in which traders are independent and unrelated to each other. When relation-based contracting prevails between large firms and small and medium-sized enterprises (SMEs), there can be cooperative inter-firm relationships, which—through rent sharing, for example—are mutually beneficial. It can be argued that Confucianism, which stresses behavioral norms such as trust and courtesy in relations between people, also contributed to the prevalence of this model of contracting in Korea, China, and Japan. On the one hand, relation-based contracting had important virtuous functions in the East Asian Model. While relationship-based contracting can make up an immature market system where laws are poorly drafted and contracts are not enforced (Chen, 2009; Lu et al, 2013), it can also correct market failures such as opportunistic behavior and short-termism. On the other hand, relation-based contracts fostered from cronyism significantly distorted market mechanism, which had negative impacts on the efficiency of the economic system.

The Financial Sector: Financial System and Financial Markets

Bank-based, rather than stock market-based financial systems, financial repression rather than financial liberalization, and patient capital rather than speculative capital prevailed in the East Asian Model (Richter, 2000; Stiglitz and Yusuf, 2001; Chang, 2007; Perkins, 2013). Table 3.2 compares two types of financial systems: Anglo-American vs. East Asian Model. Market-based financial system prevails in Anglo-American Model, while bank-based financial system prevails in East Asian Model. In other words, East Asian financial system depends on the role of the banks while Anglo-American financial system depends on the functions of the stock market. Main funding instrument in Anglo-American Model is securities, while loans are main funding instrument in EastAsian Model. Main financial transaction in Anglo-American Model is open market transaction, while bilateral transaction is main financial transaction in East Asian Model. Dependence on banks is low in Anglo-American Model, while that in Anglo-American Model is high. Institutional investors are major shareholders in Anglo-American Model, while banks are major shareholders in East Asian Model. Therefore, stock market controls the corporations in Anglo-American Model, while banks, especially main-banks in Japan, control the corporations in East Asian Model. Main-banks in Japan, main-lending banks in Korea,[8] and state-owned banks in China were pivots of the bank-based financial system in their respective countries by supplying long-term capital to firms to encourage productive investment. Because of the importance of bank lending compared to direct financing from stock markets, the extent of stock market capitalization in countries adopting the East Asian Model was far lower[9] than in countries adopting the Anglo-American Model. Firms' reliance on indirect financing or debt financing from the banking sector also contributed to the development

Table 3.2 Two Types of Financial System: Anglo-American vs. East Asian Model

	Anglo-American Model	*East Asian Model*
	Market-Based Financial System	*Bank-Based Financial System*
Main funding instrument	Securities	Loans
Main financial transaction	Open market transaction	Bilateral transaction
Dependence on banks	Low	High
Major shareholders	Institutional investors	Banks
Corporate control	Stock market	Banks

of long-term relationships between banks and firms, compared to a more open-market-oriented Anglo-American Model.

In the East Asian Model, financial policy was implemented as a complement to industrial policy, while financial capital was subordinated to industrial capital. Government strictly controlled banks and the financial markets. The activities of banks were regulated to play their proper role to supply money to industrial capital. There was a regime of financial repression. Such controls included caps on interest rates, and a strict audit of loans by the government. In Korea and China, for example, banks were owned by the state. Speculative capitals which flow into non-productive activities were effectively banned. This control of banks by the government helped channel patient capital or long-term capitals to firms, allowing for high levels of productive investment. All in all, the bank-based financial system and financial repression, and patient capitals that characterize the East Asian Model contributed to accelerating economic growth (Stiglitz, 2001: 515).

The Labor Sector: Labor System and Labor Markets

The characteristics of the labor sector in the East Asian Model include long-term employment, a seniority-based wage system, and enterprise unionism (Walter and Zhang, 2012). Long-term employment is arguably the most distinctive practice of labor markets in the East Asian Model. Japanese lifetime employment is considered as a best practice of the long-term employment. In a typical system of lifetime employment, new graduates are hired at the bottom rung and rise along the promotion ladder at the same firm, until they retire. Within the firm, the existence of a structured internal labor market in which employees are transferred and promoted according to the administrative rules also limits the hiring of experienced workers from the external labor market. Thus, internal labor market, which is effectively protected from the external labor market, is a closed labor market within the firm. The existence of internal labor market and on-the-job training (OJT) are two important factors facilitating lifetime employment. Firm-specific skills developed through OJT is a core factor facilitating lifetime employment. The co-investment in firm-specific skills by employers and employees[10] discourages the firing of workers by employers, and encourages long-term commitment to the firm by employees. Therefore, job stability is realized. The long-term employment practices, which were based on internal labor market and formation of firm-specific skills, have prevailed in large firms in Japan and Korea (Kim, 2018b).

A seniority-based wage system is also a defining feature of labor markets in the East Asian Model. Table 3.3, for example, shows that the extent of wage increase by the length of service is much stronger in Korea and Japan, and significantly lower in Sweden and the UK. In Korea, the wages of employees with 20–29 years length of service is 2.88 times higher than the wages

Table 3.3 Wage Differentials by Length of Service: 2010

	Less Than 1 Year = 100					
Length of Service	*Less Than 1 Year*	*1–5 Years*	*6–9 Years*	*10–14 Years*	*15–19 Years*	*20–29 Years*
Korea	100	137.7	178.8	212.3	250.0	288.1
Japan*	100	125.9	145.9	165.9	195.5	234.1
UK	100	116.3	130.4	143.7	147.7	156.0
Germany	100	127.6	159.2	172.8	180.5	197.7
Sweden	100	114.8	120.0	122.1	118.4	114.9

Note: Total monthly wages in non-agriculture industries above ten employees.
* For Japan, the length of service are 1–4 years instead of 1–5 year, and 5–9 years instead of 6–9 years.

Source: EUROSTART, Structure of Earnings Survey, 2010. Basic Statistics Survey on Wage Structure, Japan and Korea.

of employees with less than 1 year length of service. Compared to pay-for-performance wage schemes prevalent in Western models, a seniority wage system can be beneficial to employers when the productivity of workers with more tenure is higher than that of workers with less tenure. In other words, when wages curve and productivities curve of workers are parallel and have upward slope, seniority wages system gives a mutual gain to the employer and employees. This increase in productivity of workers is possible when employee skill levels are enhanced with the help of OJT. Long-term employment, seniority wages system, OJT, and firm-specific skills are complements to each other, which highlights the importance of institutional complementarity within the labor system in the East Asian Model (Kim, 2018b).

Enterprise unionism, which is organized at the firm level, constitutes another important element of the labor system in the East Asian Model. Enterprise unionism in the East Asian Model is different from the industrial unionism, which usually prevails in the Anglo-American, Rhine, and Nordic Models (Amable, 2003). Indeed, collective bargaining in countries such as Japan and Kora is concluded between employers and the enterprise union. While under the industrial unionism in the Western model the collective bargaining is largely concluded at the industry level outside the enterprises, industrial relations in the East Asian Model are largely formed at the micro-level (firm level), rather than at the meso-level (industry level), or at the macro-level (national level). Because one of major goals of enterprise unions is to secure longer job tenure, enterprise unionism also supports long-term employment of workers. From the above description, we can identify the complementarity among corporate sector, financial sector, and labor sector in the East Asian Model. Insider-control corporate governance in the corporate sector and bank-based financial system in the financial sector encouraged long-term employment in the labor sector.

The Foreign Sector: Trade Regime and World Market

The East Asian Model made good use of international trade to achieve high economic growth. Through the adoption of export promotion as the major engine of growth, Japan, Korea, and China were able to achieve economies of scale through mass exports and thus total factor productivity (TFP) growth (Chang, 2006). Moreover, since mass exports sustained mass production and thus completed a virtuous circle for economic growth. Here, the export-led growth regime emerged. The success of the export-led growth strategy in the East Asian Model was distinguishable from the failure of import-substitution strategy in most Latin American countries.

Protection of infant industries at the earlier stage of economic development contributed to industrialization. To protect infant industries, Korea, for example, manipulated prices in the 1960s and 1970s to support import substitution in key heavy industries such as machinery, shipping, and automobiles by having an undervalued exchange rate (Perkins, 2013: 77). Laws on foreign exchange control, the regulation of foreign direct investment (FDI), the ban on the inflow of international speculative capital, capital account regulation, and the management of foreign reserves all served to reduce macroeconomic volatility, which encouraged long-term productive investment. Capital control was the most important economic safety net in the East Asian Model since it effectively protected the national economy from the fluctuation of the world market (Stiglitz, 2001; Chang, 2007).[11] Protectionism rather than free trade was the trade regime of the early stage of the East Asian Model. At a later stage in the 1980s, a policy of strategic opening, rather than simple protectionism, was chosen to further strengthen key sectors. Strategic opening was promoted based on industrial policy. The strengthening of strategic industries was a major goal of strategic opening. In this way, trade policy was subordinated by industrial policy. In foreign sector, there were important momentums of economic growth: importing technology (Japan, Korea, and China), using foreign loans (Korea), and allowing FDI (China).

3.3 Variants of the East Asian Model: The Japan Model, the Korea Model, and the China Model

The East Asian Model has three major variants: the Japan Model, the Korea Model, and China Model. Even though these three countries have a common Confucian culture and similar institutions, their different historical trajectories gave each state specific initial conditions for economic development. Specifically, differences in political regime, power relations between social classes, and maturity of civil society in each country led to varying institutional hierarchies. These historical, political, and social differences have created different variants of the East Asian Model in Korea, China, and Japan (Table 3.4). In other words, institutional hierarchy was different among three models.

Table 3.4 Variants of the East Asian Model: Japan Model, Korea Model, and China Model

	Japan Model 1960s–1970s	*Korea Model 1970s–1980s*	*China Model 1980s–1990s*
State type Policy paradigm	Moderate developmental state 'Iron-triangle' growth coalition 'Japan Inc.'	Strong developmental state Developmental dictatorship 'Korea Inc.'	Very strong developmental state Local-state corporatism 'China Inc.'
Industrial policy	Intensive coordination by MITI	Indicative planning by EPB	Imperative planning by SDPC
Corporate system Products market	J–type firm Dominance of Keiretsu Main-bank ownership	K–type firm Dominance of Chaebol Family ownership	C–type firm Dominance of SOEs State ownership
Financial system Financial market	Main-bank system Relational banking	State-owned banks Policy loans	State-owned banks State banking
Labor system Labor market	Anti-Taylorist labor process Lifetime employment Shunto wage bargaining	Taylorist labor process Long-term employment Low wages-long hour	Taylorist labor process Contract labor system Low wages
Trade regime World market	Moderate capital control Import of foreign technology	Strict capital control Introduction of foreign loans & technology	Very strict capital control Introduction of FDI
Mode of regulation	Companyist regulation Coordinated Market economy	Statist regulation Regulated Market economy	Statist regulation Socialist Market economy

Source: Hyungkee Kim (2018: 28, Table 1-2).

The Japan Model

The Japan Model, which emerged in the 1960s, established a standard for the East Asian Model. Japan had an original development state from the 1960s. The Japanese developmental state was characterized by an 'iron-triangle' growth coalition among the ministry officials, politicians, and managers of the Keiretsu. In this aspect, Japan was actually 'Japan Inc.' Along with the close collaboration between government officials and corporate executives, the other feature of 'Japan Inc.' was cooperation between corporations within the Keiretsu. Seen this way, Japan can best be described as a corporate state where government proactively supported the business activities of corporations. Central to the coordination of the Japanese industrial policy was MITI, which played a major role in creating a national consensus on the strategic directions in which the economy should be directed (Richter, 2000: 5–6). Intensive coordination of the economy by MITI was one of defining features of Japan Model. Looking at firms, the Keiretsu, which dominated the Japanese economy, established long-term relationships with main-banks that had a leading role in the corporate governance of Keiretsu. Main-bank system was a distinctive bank-based financial system that supported the growth of the firms and stabilized the economic system in Japan. Main banks supplied corporations with loans for long-term investment and monitored their management as a major shareholder. Relational banking, which was a characteristic of the financial market, was that banks provided financial services on the basis of long-term investment in obtaining firm-specific information through interactions with the customer. Main-bank system encouraged the formation of firm-specific skills and lifetime employment by supplying patient capital.[12]

Keiretsu had a J-type firm in which main-bank ownership, insider-oriented corporate governance, anti-Taylorist labor processes (Toyotism),[13] lifetime employment, seniority wage system (yenko system), and enterprise unionism prevailed (Yamada, 2000; Isogai, 2012). Lifetime employment and seniority wage system were originally two major poles of Japanese-specific industrial relations. Indeed, the Japanese corporate system has traditionally placed greater emphasis on long-term employment relationships. Corporate strategy to promote long-term growth rather than to raise short-term profitability provided employment security to the workers. Long-term relationships have prevailed among economic agents, that is, between labor and management for lifetime employment, between companies and banks for long-term capital procurement, and between large firms and SMEs for long-term material and parts supply (Boyer and Yamada, 2000: 27). The Shunto[14] springtime wage bargaining, which coordinated decentralized firm-level wage negotiations at a national level, had a function of equalizing wage increases. Shunto wage bargaining allowed enterprise unions to negotiate wage hikes on a nationwide basis without interference in firm-level collective bargaining. There was moderate capital control in Japan. At an initial stage of the 1950s–1960s, Japan imported foreign technology rather than introduction of FDI and foreign loans.

These features help paint the image of Japan Model that is characterized by a CME, where relational coordination between economic agents at the firm level plays a major role in resource allocation (Hall and Soskice, 2001). Within this economic system, large companies like Keiretsu had a polar position in the institutional organization of the whole economic system and had strongly promoted social integration in the Japanese society. Yamada (2000) argued that in this respect, Japan had 'companyist' mode of regulation. Companyist regulation rested on a labor-management compromise on employment security and a company-bank compromise on management security (Yamada and Hirano, 2012). Japanese companyist regulation is a long-term trust model emphasizing the pursuit of efficiency through long-term, fixed, and closed relations (Boyer and Yamada, 2000: 28). In short Japan Model can be defined as a micro-corporatism in which employer and labor union conclude collective bargaining and cooperate with each other in the firm (Kim, 2018b).

The Korea Model

Established in the 1970s–1980s, the Korea Model was typical East Asian Model that featured a strong developmental state led by a developmental dictatorship regime.[15] The regime of developmental dictatorship was a politico-economic regime that the state oppressed the political liberty and people's participation in the name of the national interests and development. It was a kind of state-led nationalist industrialization regime. In the regime, the cause of the dictatorship was modernization and industrialization (Lee, 2003: 24). In Korea, the developmental dictatorship was established through the military dictatorship in the early 1960s and strengthened through the 'Restoration dictatorship' in the early 1970s. Developmental dictatorship sustained until 1987 civil protests and workers' struggles, after which democratization proceeded. Through the dictatorship regime, the state strongly intervened in the market. The extensive administrative regulations on the product markets, financial markets, and labor markets were implemented. State control over a financial system, a state-mediated corporate governance system, and a state-intervened labor system were the characteristics of the Korean developmental state. Through the developmental dictatorship, the state could mobilize resources forcibly and promptly into the strategic industries. Thus, it facilitated rapid growth. Viewed from the economic growth at all costs, developmental dictatorship was superior to dictatorship without development as well as democracy without development. In this aspect, developmental dictatorship was a 'necessary evil' for the less developed countries like Korea (Lipietz, 1987).[16]

The state exercised strong influences on corporate investment decisions through industrial policy, the core of which was coordination of corporate investment by the government. Price distortion to protect and promote strategic industries was one of the main practices of the industrial policy. Thus, 'getting the prices wrong' rather than 'getting the prices right' was close to the fact about Korea Model (Amsden, 1989; Perkins, 2013). Industrial policy was promoted through indicative planning designed by Economic Planning Board (EPB). The EPB also controlled the national budget and implemented Five-Year Economic Development Plans. Korea's industrial policy until mid-1980s was regarded as the most comprehensive and systemic around the world (Chang, 2007). The macroeconomic policy in Korea Model focused on investment and export promotion rather than Keynesian aggregate demand management. Korea has been also 'Korea Inc.' Moreover, hyper-centralized political and economic systems and hyper-concentration of resources to the Seoul-metropolitan regions were the major constituents of the Korea Model. In these respects, Korean capitalism was a kind of strong state capitalism (Kim, 2018b).

At the corporate level, the Chaebol, a kind of conglomerate, dominated the national economy. This Chaebol had K-type firms where family ownership, Taylorist labor processes, long-term employment,[17] a low wages-long hours system, seniority wage system, and enterprise unionism prevailed. At the financial level, Korea had a regime of 'financial repression', in which financial policy was subordinated to industrial policy, and the interests of the financial rentier class were subsidiary to the interests of industrial capital. With the state nationalizing banks in the 1960s, a regime of policy loans, through which government implemented various targeted credit programs, was introduced in 1974. The regime of policy loans was the Korean equivalent of the Japanese main-bank system. The financial system of Korea Model can thus be defined by a bank-based financial system plus government-dominated financial system (Chang, 2007: 263–264). Strict capital controls (including foreign exchange rate control) and the introduction of massive foreign loans, were the distinctive features of the country's trade regime. The strategic opening proceeded to the extent that the domestic industries began to have international competitiveness.

All in all, Korea's market economy can thus be classified as a 'regulated market economy' (RME), in which the state intervenes in the market extensively and intensively (Kim, 2006). This RME is distinguishable from a liberal market economy (LME) and a CME, as classified by Hall and Soskice (2001). The RME differs from the LME with Keynesian interventions in that in the former, the state intervenes in the market through industrial policy to coordinate corporate investment while in the latter, the state intervenes in the market through fiscal and financial policies to manage aggregate demand. The RME is also different from the CME in that the former has a state-led hierarchical economy, while the latter has a horizontally coordinated network economy. Korea Model had a statist mode of regulation.

The China Model

The China Model emerged in the 1980s–1990s is officially referred to as 'Chinese Characteristic Socialism'. China Model is regarded as a 21st-century variant of the East Asian Model (Hsu et al, 2011). Because the China Model was established during the gradual transition from a centrally planned economy to a market economy, it had strong legacy of the planned economy. China also had a kind of developmental state. There is a view that the Chinese state is not developmental, since the central government's institutional capacity has been too weak to pursue the East Asian style of industrial policy (Hsu et al, 2011). However, the weakness of industrial policies implemented by the central government does not negate the existence of a developmental state in China, because the central and local governments have intervened in the economy by the imperative planning (strong indicative planning later) and local governments played an active role in promoting economic development.[18]

Carried by the monolithic power of the CCP, the Chinese developmental state intervened extensively and intensively in the economy. However, the existence of economic decentralization amid political centralization (Lu et al, 2013), along with the existence of a coalition between local government and local enterprises, means that China Model can best be identified as 'local-state corporatism'. Local-state corporatism has progressively transformed into a society-wide compromise: the acceptance of the monopoly of the Communist party in the political domain, in exchange for a permanent increase in living standards via rapid and steady growth (Boyer, 2012). Indeed, state backing and state subsidies to local SOEs were significant. In the rural sector, TVEs (township and village enterprises), which were invested in by local governments, individual farmers, and groups constituted another form of local-state corporatism (Henderson, 2011: 34). Thus, China has also become 'China Inc.'

Fiscal decentralization with a tax-sharing system[19] also gave the local economies in the provincial level considerable autonomy. Although industrial policy was implemented through the imperative planning designed by State Development Planning Commission (SDPC) under the leadership of the CCP, it tended to be weak, due to deficiencies in industry-specific strategic development and supply of critical resources that would alter targeted sector's comparative advantage in the market. In the corporate sector, SOEs with many prerogatives in business activities dominated the national economy. These SOEs had C-type firms that were characterized by state ownership, top-down management, weak inter-firm relationships, Taylorist labor process, contract labor system rather than lifetime employment, low wages, and no independent unions. Labor market segmentation between the formal sector and the informal sector or between SOEs and non-SOEs defines the normal pattern in the Chinese wage-labor nexus. In the financial sector, Chinese state-owned banks provided loans to SOEs based on the industrial policy designed by the SDPC under the leadership of the CCP and local states. Thus, state banking was a distinctive feature in China. However, non-SOEs were largely excluded from the loans supplied by the state-owned banks. The financial market segmentation alongside labor market segmentation between SOEs and non-SOEs is one of the most serious problems in China.

Though China (like Japan and Korea) had very strict capital controls, the introduction of large-scale FDI in China was significant when compared to its East Asian counterparts. As Table 3.5 shows, in 2000, the size of FDI inward stock in China was 38 times that of Japan and 44 times that of Korea. In 2017, the size of FDI inward stock in China was 72 times that of Japan and Korea. Moreover, the increasing rate of FDI inward stock in China was greater than in Japan and Korea. The table also shows that FDI outward stock increased much more rapidly than in Japan and Korea. In 2017, the size of FDI outward stock in China became comparable to that of Japan. The accession to WTO (World Trade Organization) in 2001 was decisive momentum

Table 3.5 Foreign Direct Investment in Japan, Korea, and China

	FDI Inward Stock			*FDI Outward Stock*		
	2000	*2010*	*2017*	*2000*	*2010*	*2017*
Japan	50,323 (100)	214,880 (427)	207,488 (412)	278,445 (100)	831,076 (298)	1,519,983 (546)
Korea	43,738 (100)	135,500 (310)	230,597 (517)	21,497 (100)	144,032 (670)	355,758 (1655)
China	193,348 (100)	587,817 (304)	1,490,933 (771)	27,768 (100)	317,211 (1142)	1,482,020 (4672)

Note: The values in parentheses shows the trends of increase in FDI stock.
Source: World Investment Report 2018, UNCTAD.

in Chinese trade regime. From this moment, as China entered deeply into world market, the interaction between Chinese economy and world markets gave significant impacts on both the Chinese economy and the global economy. With adhesion to WTO, China introduced FDI actively, while there was cautious external liberalization from the 2000s with strict capital control.

The type of market economy in China can therefore be defined as a socialist market economy (SME). It is different from the CME of Japan Model in the 1960s–1970s and the RMF of Korea Model in the 1970s–1980s. China Model had statist mode of regulation. Indeed, even though the CCP officially had rigid ideological inclination toward *de jure* state socialism with the primacy of the party over the state, *de facto* economic system in China was basically capitalistic. In this sense, Chinese economic system is defined as a party-state capitalism (Chavance, 2017).

3.4 Comparing Three Models: Difference in Institutional Hierarchy

According to the concept of institutional hierarchy, different prevalent institutions help shape different variants of a development model. The diversity present in the variants of the East Asian Model in Japan, Korea, and China can thus be attributed to differences in each country's institutional hierarchy (Kim, 2018b). First, the relative primacy of the state sectors in each country can be regarded as one where the developmental state was the strongest in China and the weakest in Japan, with Korea in between due to varying levels of authoritarianism in each country. Vis-à-vis industrial policy, indicative planning in Korea was stronger than intensive coordination in Japan, and imperative planning in China was stronger than the indicative planning in Korea due to differences in the relative power of pilot agencies (MITI, EPB, SDPC). Conversely, in terms of the relative autonomy of the corporate sector vis-`a-vis the state, the Keiretsus in Japan enjoyed more freedom than the Chaebols in Korea, while Chinese SOEs enjoyed less autonomy from government than the Chaebols in Korea. This difference in autonomy of corporations between countries can be explained by the more horizontal relationship between Japanese Keiretsus and government through the 'iron-triangle' growth coalition, while Korean Chaebols and Chinese SOEs had a more vertical relationship with their respective states due to the political regimes in place. In terms of the relative autonomy of the financial sector vis-à-vis the state and corporate sectors, main-banks in Japan had higher autonomy than state-owned banks that were under direct government control from the state in Korea and China. Finally, regarding the relative position of the labor sector vis-à-vis the corporate sector, the autonomy of labor unions was the highest in Japan, where micro-corporatism prevailed. While the influence of independent labor unions vis-à-vis corporations was weak in Korea under developmental dictatorship rule, it was the weakest in China, where there were no independent labor unions under the contract labor system. The fact that the mode of regulation in Japan was 'companyism' suggests the predominance of the corporate sector over the other sectors in the country. In contrast, statist mode of regulation in Korea and China suggests the primacy of the state sector over the other sector in the countries.

Notes

1 Here, the word regulation is not English but French. The meaning of regulation in French is quite different from regulation in English. The former means an adjustment mechanism that maintains homeostasis in an organism or regimes, while the latter means state intervention in the market. Therefore, a mode of regulation is a kind of adjustment mechanism, not a form of state intervention.

2 There are two main approaches to institutional change. One is the variety of capitalism (VOC) approach based on the concept of institutional complementarity by Hall and Soskice (2001), which sees change following long periods of institutional stability as the consequence of a radical breakdown primarily caused by exogenous factors. The other is incremental institutional change (IIC) approach by Mahoney and Thelen (2010). It focuses on a slow pace of continual deinstitutionalization and reinstitutionalization, thus emphasizing endogenous changes (Sako and Kotosaka 2012).

3 A major crisis is different from a minor crisis that is a cyclical crisis in the short-term business cycle. Minor crisis will end when a recovery begins sooner or later from stagnation.

4 Acemoglu and Robinson classified political institutions into two contrasting types: extractive institutions in which a small group of power elites exploits the rest of the population, and inclusive institutions, in which the interest of a broad spectrum of people is served in the process of governing (Acemoglu and Robinson, 2012). The extractive state or predatory state has such extractive institutions, while developmental state has such inclusive institutions.

5 Market Socialism has been a Chinese expression of an East Asian authoritarian system (Chen, 2009: 71).

6 The Chinese government has granted the conglomerate status to 120 SOEs in 1997. They were given priority when registering on the stock market and obtaining bank loans. Among them, the top six SOEs-Changhong (TV manufacturing), Haier (white goods maker), Beida Fangzheng (software), Baogang (steel), Jiangnan (shipping), and Huanbei (pharmaceuticals), enjoyed more preferential treatments (Richter, 2000: 325).

7 Actually, Germany and Japan have a similar insider-control model of corporate governance. Japan has a kind of corporate governance of stakeholder capitalism. However, Korea does not have such a corporate governance even though it has inside-control corporate governance.

8 Main-banks in Japan is different from Korea's main-lending banks in that the former are major shareholder of the Keiretsu who borrow from the main-banks while the latter lend to the client enterprises with supplying some business information.

9 See Figure 4.3 in Chapter 4.

10 For the training period, employers invest in firm-specific skills by paying workers (trainees) above their productivity level, while employees invest in firm-specific skills by earning below-market wages. After the training period, employers receive a return on investment in the form of productivity higher than wage levels, while employees receive a return on investment in the form of wages above the market clearing level. Therefore, there will be a win-win game between the employers and employees. This is the raison d'etre of co-investment in firm-specific skills by employers and employees.

11 However, the removal of capital controls in the 1990s in Japan and Korea amplified macroeconomic volatility.

12 Main bank finance may be a sort of 'patient capital' that supports the lifetime employment norms in Japan (Jackson, 2009).

13 Toyotism is a labor process in which conception and execution are united to some extent, with workers developing firm-specific skills. Toyotism thus contrasts with Taylorism, which is defined by the separation of the conception of labor processes from their execution, with workers focusing on simple and repetitive tasks.

14 Shunto means 'a spring struggle', when written in Chinese characters.

15 Because Korea Model is originally designed by President Park Chung Hee, Korea Model is also named Park Chung Hee Model.

16 The positive impacts of developmental dictatorship on the economic growth in Korea raise a complex puzzle to the relationship between political regimes and economic growth discussed by Przeworski and Limongi (1993).

17 Even though Korea had Japanese-type lifetime employment in public sectors and corporate sectors including Chaebol firms and banks, average job tenure in Korea is far shorter than in Japan. For example, in 2000, average job tenure of males in Japan was 13.4 years, while that of Korea was 4.7 years. Therefore, long-term employment rather than lifetime employment is relevant description for the Korean employment system.

18 The Chinese economy ended up with development strategies that in key respects looked much like those pursued by Japan, Korea, and Taiwan: a dependence on foreign trade, the export of manufactured goods, a program of promoting heavy industries, and an active role of government in directing economic activities (Perkins, 2013: 148). Thus, the Chinese state may well be a kind of developmental state.

19 Under the fiscal decentralization with a tax-sharing system, the share of tax revenues of the local governments was 79.8% in 1979. However, this fiscal decentralization has been weakened. Thus, in 1997, the share of local government decreased to 51.2%.

4 The Transformation of the East Asian Model

The East Asian Model has experienced a great transformation during the last thirty years through marketization, privatization, liberalization, and flexibilization of the state sector, the corporate sector, the financial sector, and the labor sector in Japan, Korea, and China. As a consequence, the financial markets were liberalized, and the labor markets were flexibilized in these three East Asian countries. The corporate systems, including the corporate governance, have also changed significantly. The four trends, that is, marketization, privatization, liberalization, and flexibilization created turning points in each national economy. We can highlight the major turning points in Japanese, Korean, and Chinese economies that brought about a great transformation of the East Asian Model in each county.

First, the major turning points in Japanese economy were as follows: start of the high economic growth from 1955, Lewis turning point[1] around 1960,[2] profit-led growth in the 1960s, wage-led growth in the 1970s, export-led growth in the 1980s, appreciation of yen ('yen-daka') and financial liberalization in 1985, bubble economy in the late 1980s, bubble burst and beginning of the Lost Decade in 1991, banking crisis and introduction of shareholder capitalism in 1997, a financial 'Big Bang' in 1998, Koizumi's neoliberalist reform[3] from 2001, failure of democratic reform in 2009,[4] and Abenomics in 2013.[5]

Second, the major turning points in Korean economy were as follows: start of Five-Year Economic Development Plan in 1962, introduction of export-led growth strategy in 1965, Lewis turning point around 1975,[6] introduction of mass production system at the Hyundai motor company in 1976, decrease in economic dependency from 1986,[7] political democratization and collapse of developmental dictatorship with democratization of industrial relations from 1987, financial liberalization and the end of Five-Year Economic Development Plan in 1993, financial crisis and the retreat of developmental state in 1997, democracy combined with neoliberalism in 1998–2007, neoliberalism from 2008.

Third, the major turning points in Chinese economy were as follows: marketization reform and opening policies in 1978, the end of centrally planned economy and introduction of household responsibility system in 1984,

DOI: 10.4324/9781003332725-4

introduction of contract managerial responsibility system to the SOEs in 1987, Deng Xiaoping's tour of the south in 1992[8] which reversed the retreat to a more state-directed economy, official announcement of the socialist market economy (SME) and marketization of public services in 1994, privatization of the SOEs in 1997, globalization of the economy by joining in WTO in 2001, Lewis turning point in early 2000s, transformation of the SDPC (State Development Planning Commission) into the NDRC (National Development and Reform Commission) in 2003,[9] and New Normal era from the 2010s.

4.1 Marketization and Privatization in the State Sector

The greatest transformation of the East Asian Model is its marketization. Indeed, even though the East Asian Model was based on the market economy, the market was more or less strictly regulated by the state. However, this relationship between the state and the market has changed in the last three decades. Marketization was actually a starting point of the transformation of the East Asian Model.

The most dramatic marketization occurred in China. The country's transition from a planned economy to a market economy began with reforms and opening up policies in the late 1970s. From 1979, managers of SOEs could make decisions regarding what to produce, and how to price outputs. Prices of outputs were liberalized. In 1984, there was a reform that heralded an end of the centrally planned economy and replaced it with market forces. Prices of inputs also became liberalized in 1985. The objective of these reforms was to free up prices of inputs with a dual-price system, in which SOEs could continue to receive inputs at state-set prices, while other firms could buy inputs on the market at market prices (Perkins, 2013: 128). Thereafter, there were gradual loosening of price controls and introduction of market mechanism (Lu et al, 2013: 161). Moreover, the household responsibility system, which transferred land use rights to households, was adopted nationwide by 1984. This reform gave peasants the incentive to expand agricultural production, which provided the impetus to develop Town and Village Enterprises (TVEs) (Aglietta and Bai, 2013: 89–90; Perkins, 2013: 127). These TVEs, in which local governments, groups, and individuals invested, became one of the most dynamic sectors of the Chinese economy. In 1987, China introduced a contract managerial responsibility system with profit sharing between SOEs and the government, which separated management from state ownership. The SOEs were given autonomy in management. The autonomy SOEs had in this system allowed them to make decisions on the quantity and variety of outputs, production methods, and sale prices.

After fourteen years of marketization reforms, China decided to officially establish a socialist market economy (SME) in 1994. From 1994, marketization of public services such as education, health care, pensions, and housing was implemented. Financing of public services was marketized. There was a retreat of the state from the provision of health, education, and welfare, that is, a retreat of a public goods regime (Lin, 2008: 7–19; Lu et al, 2013: 125–154). Especially, hospitals have gradually become for-profit institutions. The marketization of public services has generated regional inequalities, especially urban-rural inequalities, in access to the public services. Moreover, fiscal decentralization further increased regional inequality in public social expenditures since local governments had incentives to invest in the fields that brought short-term profits and short-term economic growth. Moreover, as pension and medical care are provided by the corporations, welfare inequality among corporations emerged. In short, since marketization reforms in education, medical care, pensions, and housing were proceeded under the fiscal decentralization, inequalities in public services intensified.

China then decided to introduce a shareholding system and privatize SOEs in 1997 through the policy of 'grasp the large and let go of the small'. Based on this decision, the state privatized many smaller SOEs in non-strategic industries via a variety of means such as equity sales. Large SOEs were then turned into joint-stock companies open to non-state capital investment to encourage market discipline among managers (Chen et al, 2011). In order to transfer the ownership of these SOEs, property rights exchanges were established in the late 1980s. The role of the property rights exchanges was to enable the transfer of state-owned property rights in restructuring local SOEs or injecting private capital into them as a part of the reform of the SOEs (Takeshi, 2009). From the mid-1990s, TVEs were also privatized through the creation of joint stock companies where local governments acted as majority shareholders. The reform of SOEs went further in the 21st century. In order to boost competitiveness and profitability, the Chinese government issued, in 2015, guidelines for SOE reform focusing on mixed ownership, the transition to a modern enterprise system, professional management, better managing state assets with a focus on capital management (OECD, 2017a).

As a result of privatization, the share of private property increased substantially. The share of private property in total national wealth increased from 30% in 1978 to about 70% in 2015. The share of private property in other domestic capital (except housing and domestic corporate equity) and net financial assets increased from 23% in 1978 to 53% in 2015 (Piketty et al, 2017). The corporate ownership also has changed greatly. As Figure 4.1 shows, the share of public ownership in corporations decreased from 100% to about 50% while the share of private ownership increased from 0% in 1978 to 33% in 2015.

Following these privatization reforms, the composition of the number of employed personnel by firm ownership changed dramatically. At the start of China's economic transition in 1978, there were no private sector workers, expect for a negligible number of self-employed. As Table 4.1 shows, all workers were employed by SOEs and collective-owned enterprises until 1978. Cooperative units appeared in 1998, but their share was very small. Workers employed by firms under joint-stock ownership appeared in 1985.

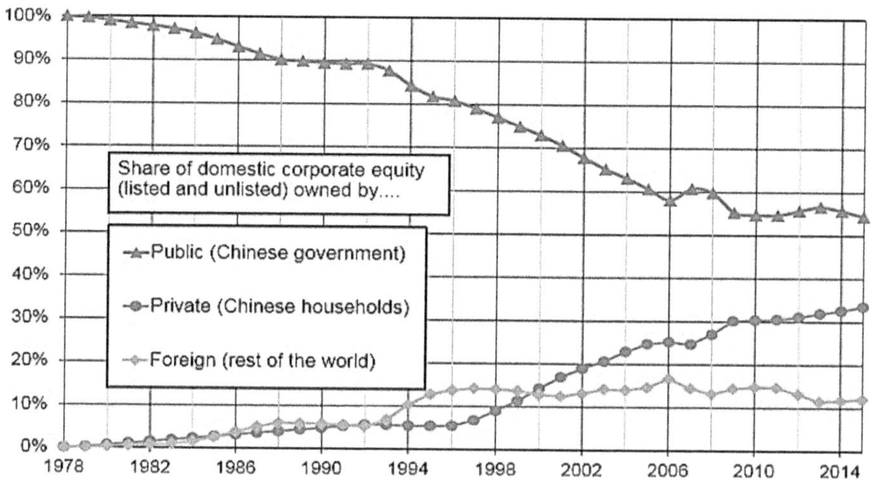

Figure 4.1 Change in Corporate Ownership in China: 1978–2015

Source: Piketty et al (2017).

Table 4.1 Employment Structure by Firm Ownership in Urban China

	1978	*1985*	*1990*	*1995*	*1998*	*2010*	*2016*
State-owned	7451 (78.3)	8990 (70.2)	10346 (60.7)	11261 (59.1)	9048 (41.9)	6516 (18.8)	6170 (14.9)
Collective-owned	2048 (21.5)	2425 (18.9)	3549 (20.8)	3147 (16.5)	1963 (9.1)	597 (1.7)	453 (1.1)
Cooperative					136 (0.6)	156 (0.4)	86 (0.2)
Joint-stock ownership		38 (0.3)	96 (0.6)	53 (0.3)	48 (0.2)	36 (0.1)	18 (0.0)
Limited liability Corporations					484 (2.2)	2613 (7.5)	6381 (15.4)
Share holding corporations				317 (1.7)	410 (1.9)	1024 (3.0)	1824 (4.4)
Private enterprises			57 (0.3)	485 (2.5)	973 (4.5)	6071 (17.5)	12083 (29.2)
Foreign funded		6 (0.0)	66 (0.4)	513 (2.7)	587 (2.7)	1823 (5.3)	2666 (6.4)
Self-employed	15 (0.2)	450 (3.5)	614 (3.6)	1560 (8.2)	2259 (10.5)	4467 (12.9)	8627 (20.8)
Total	9514 (100)	12808 (100)	17041 (100)	19040 (100)	21616 (100)	34687 (100)	41428 (100)

Note: Firms with funds from Hong Kong, Macao, and Taiwan are treated as foreign funded. Unit: 10,000 persons. The values in parentheses represent the share of each unit in employment structure.

Source: Chinese Statistical Yearbook.

However, these numbers were very small, and are now negligible. Limited liability corporations, which appeared in 1998 and rapidly expanded, accounted for 15.4% of urban employment in 2016. Shareholding corporations which appeared in 1995 also employed an increasing share of workers. The sharpest increase in employment came along with private enterprises, which appeared in 1990 and are now the largest employers in China, accounting for 29.2% of total urban employment in 2016. The share of the self-employed also dramatically increased from 0.2% in 1978 to 20.8% in 2016. In sum, as marketization and privatization progressed, the share of state and collective ownership in terms of employment sharply decreased, while the share of private ownership increased rapidly. The scaling back of the public sector and the expansion of the private sector in China were thus the results of marketization and privatization.

A symbol of China's marketization reforms was that planning disappeared as the State Development Planning Commission (SDPC) was transformed into the National Development and Reform Commission (NDRC) in 2003. Planning was replaced by the outline program. However, China promoted marketization gradually with keeping the state while introducing the non-state. New non-state sectors emerged alongside the existing state sector, rather than replacing it. Despite the growth of the private sector, large SOEs still maintained monopolies in key sectors, while smaller locally owned state enterprises were linchpins of local economic activity (Breslin, 2012: 32–44). Still, the number of SOEs in the industrial sector decreased substantially as a result of marketization, with their share decreasing from 10% in 2005 to 5% in 2015. The share of the SOE assets and employment also decreased from 48.1% in 2005 to 38.8% in 2015 and from 27.2% in 2005 to 18.2% in 2015, respectively. Meanwhile, the private sector grew considerably, accounting for about 78% of total employment and about 70% of GDP in 2015.

As a result of privatization, the share of private property also increased substantially, from a 30% share in total national wealth in 1978 to about 70% in 2015. The share of private property in housing increased even more from 52% in 1978 to 98% in 2015, while the share of private property in other domestic capital (except housing and domestic corporate equity) and net financial assets went up from 23% in 1978 to 53% in 2015. At the corporate level, as Figure 4.1 shows, the share of public ownership in corporations decreased from 100% in 1978 to about 50% in 2015, while the share of private ownership increased from 0% to 33% in the same years (Piketty et al, 2017).

In Korea, protests for political and industrial democratization in 1987 led to the collapse of the country's developmental dictatorship. Elected in 1992, the Kim Young Sam administration attempted to dismantle the authoritarian development strategy of the previous regime by establishing a free market system. To achieve this, the Five-Year Economic Development Plans, which were updated for 30 years since 1962,[10] were replaced by a New Economy Five-Year Plan (1992–1996) in 1993. The objective of this plan was to establish competition in order to enhance efficiency of the economy. One of the major agendas of the plan was to increase the competitiveness of Korean industry by strengthening free market mechanisms through deregulation and prompting incentive and participation (Richter 2000: 154). As described above, Korea had an indicative planning from 1962. The Economic Planning Board (EPB) had powers to design economic planning with controlling the national budget and implementing the planning. This EPB was dismantled and absorbed into the Ministry of Finance and Economy (MOFE) in 1994. In addition to this, the MOFE disseminated neoliberal ideas into economic policy. Moreover, the MOFE's status as a monetary policy authority was ceded in 1997 to the Bank of Korea, whose mandate focused on achieving and maintaining price stability. The result was a retreat of the developmental state and the weakening of industrial policy as long-term strategic planning was abandoned (Chang 2007). The 1997 financial crisis decisively dismantled the Korean developmental state, as the restructuring processes imposed by the IMF further promoted liberalization and deregulation (Pirie, 2008). It was the Korean-specific phenomenon that marketization, privatization, and liberalization have proceeded in the process of democratization. Therefore, the transformation process of Korea Model was complex and even contradictory due to the inherent mismatch between political democratization and economic liberalization.[11]

Japan also saw a retreat of its developmental state under the Koizumi administration between 2001 and 2006. The catchword of the neoliberal reform of the Koizumi administration was 'from government to market'. The MITI, which has been a pilot agency of Japanese developmental state, was renamed in 2001 into the Ministry of Economy, Trade and Industry (METI). Contra MITI, this new agency METI was pro-deregulation (Fields, 2012), and helped erode the 'iron triangle' between ministry officials, politicians, and managers of Keiretsu (Walter and Zhang, 2012). Because Japanese developmental state was originally not so strong as those of Korea and China, marketization process was not dramatic but gradual.

In China, the privatization of SOEs was the most salient manifestation of marketization. Unlike the Big Bang approach[12] of Russia and other East European countries, China adopted a gradual approach vis-à-vis privatization. Though the privatization of state assets proceeded in 1997, the process had been closely regulated to ensure the state's continuing control over SOEs assets, while also allowing them to operate as market-oriented companies (Henderson, 2011: 34). China, for example, kept a strong SOE presence in key strategic sectors such as energy and network. Thus, China could avoid chaotic and disruptive results in the process of privatization.

In Japan, the privatization of public enterprises began in the 1980s. The key industries such as The Nippon Telegraph and Telephone, Japan National Railways, and Japan Tobacco and Salt Public Corporation were privatized by Privatization Acts of 1984. But privatization culminated during the Koizumi administration in the early 2000s when Japan Post Agency began to privatize. In 2003-2007, Japan Post transformed from a government agency to

Table 4.2 Economic Freedom Index: Size of Government

	1980	*1985*	*1990*	*1995*	*2000*	*2005*	*2010*	*2015*
Korea	5.97	6.24	6.49	6.42	6.26	6.66	6.85	6.86
China	2.63	3.91	3.65	4.02	3.43	4.54	4.48	5.06
Japan	5.80	5.95	5.83	4.95	5.71	5.72	5.30	4.56
US	5.17	6.05	6.71	6.88	7.03	7.13	6.39	6.40
Germany	5.76	3.74	4.81	5.23	4.95	6.77	6.51	5.51
Sweden	1.63	2.61	2.62	2.60	3.17	3.67	3.72	3.67

Note: Countries with low levels of government spending as a share of total, a smaller government enterprise sector, and lower marginal tax rates earn the highest ratings.

Source: Gwartney et al (2013), Gwartney et al (2018)

a privatized company, which was the most dramatic privatization in Japan (Alexander, 2008; Kim and Huang, 2019). In Korea, four major commercial banks (Chohung Bank, Korea First Bank, Hanil Bank, and Seoul Bank) were privatized by 1983, with foreign investors becoming the largest shareholders in the banking sector (the percentage of total bank assets that were foreign-owned was 77% in 2011) (Barth et al, 2013). However, almost all non-bank financial institutions remained under the control of the Chaebol. Attempts to privatize public enterprises after the 1997 financial crisis also failed due to the resistance of workers. Only POSCO and Korea Telecom were privatized in 2000 and 2002, respectively.

A consequence of marketization and privatization was the reduction in the size of government. Tables 4.2, 4.3, and 4.4 show that the Economic Freedom Index[13] in terms of government size[14] has decreased considerably in China and Korea. Even though it increased between 1995 and 2000 when the 1997 Asian financial crisis broke out, the trends in the tables below indicate a general reduction in the size of government in both countries. In the case of Japan, the size of government temporally increased during the Lost Decade (1991–2000), decreased in the 2000s, and increased again in the 2010s, as

Table 4.3 Economic Freedom Index: Government Enterprise and Investment

	1980	*1985*	*1990*	*1995*	*2000*	*2005*	*2010*	*2015*
Korea	7.0	6.0	8.0	6.0	6.0	8.0	8.0	10.0
China	0.0	0.0	0.0	0.0	0.0	0.0	0.0	2.0
Japan	8.0	8.0	7.0	6.0	6.0	8.0	8.0	7.0
US	8.0	8.0	8.0	8.0	8.0	8.0	7.0	8.0
Germany	6.0	7.0	7.0	6.0	6.0	10.0	10.0	10.0
Sweden	2.0	6.0	7.0	6.0	6.0	8.0	8.0	8.0

Source: Gwartney et al (2013), Gwartney et al (2018)

Table 4.4 Economic Freedom Index: Top Marginal Tax Rate

	1980	*1985*	*1990*	*1995*	*2000*	*2005*	*2010*	*2015*
Korea	0.0	2.0	1.5	5.0	5.0	6.0	6.0	5.5
China	—	6.0	5.0	6.0	6.0	6.0	6.0	6.0
Japan	0.0	1.0	1.5	1.5	5.0	5.0	5.0	3.0
US	0.0	4.0	6.5	7.0	7.0	7.5	7.0	5.0
Germany	2.0	1.0	4.0	3.0	3.0	6.0	5.0	5.0
Sweden	0.0	0.0	0.0	1.5	1.0	1.5	1.0	1.0

Source: Gwartney et al (2013), Gwartney et al (2018)

the stagnation originating from the Lost Decade perdured. Korea is now the most marketized country of the three according to the Economic Freedom Index when it comes to government size, having an even smaller government than the US in 2015. When compared to Sweden, the size of government in Korea is much smaller than that in Sweden, which is the representative social democratic country of the Nordic Model (Table 4.2).

Analyzing the government size index in terms government enterprise and investment reveals that Korea and Japan exhibit trends similar to that of the US and Sweden (Table 4.2). In 2015, Korea's rating (10) highlighted complete economic liberalization like Germany. China, however, earned a zero rating from 1980 to 2010 and a rating of 2.0 in 2015, reflecting the continued importance of the public sector in the country. Looking at the size of the government index in terms of the top marginal tax rate shows that there were drastic changes in Korea's ratings in the first half of the 1990s and in Japan's ratings in the second half of the 1990s as both countries implemented radical tax-cuts (Table 4.4). In Japan, the corporate tax rate was reduced from 37.5% in 1990 to 30.0% in 1999 while in Korea, the top corporate tax rate decreased from 34% in 1991 to 28% in 1996. It is remarkable that China showed the high ratings in terms of the index of the top marginal tax rate comparable to the US. In 2015, Korea and China actually had higher index ratings than the US, indicating that both East Asian countries had lower top marginal tax rates when compared to their North American counterpart. When compared to Sweden that has the highest top marginal tax rate, Korea and China have much smaller government than that in Sweden in terms of top marginal tax rate.

The reduction in the size of government shown above suggests the retreat of the developmental state that was a decisive cause of the 1997 financial crisis in Korea and the Lost Decade in Japan. The demise of industrial policy critically contributed to the crisis by removing the restraints on duplicate investments, by facilitating overinvestment, and by creating and nurturing asset bubbles. In contrast, Taiwan and Singapore remained largely put outside the web of crisis because they continued to have effective developmental states (Henderson, 2011). China's strong developmental state also allowed it to effectively protect itself from contagion during the 1997 Asian financial crisis.

4.2 The Liberalization of Financial Markets

Trends of Financial Liberalization in the East Asian Model

Financial liberalization proceeded in the 1980s in Japan and in the 1990s in Korea. China has been cautious about financial liberalization although there was considerable financial market liberalization after the mid-1990s. While financial liberalization was the most distinctive in the Anglo-American Model, financial repression was a major ingredient of the East Asian Model. Thus, financial liberalization would be a destructive force for the East Asian Model. With the financial liberalization, the elements of shareholder capitalism were introduced into the corporate sector. In shareholder capitalism, maximization of the shareholder value becomes a major goal of the management. Short-term profitability and flexibility are needed for maximization of the shareholder value. Short-termism inherent in the principle of shareholder capitalism has changed the corporate governances and labor markets in the East Asian Model. Trends of financial liberalization can be identified by some indicators or indices. To measure financial liberalization trends, this study first adopts the Economic Freedom Index constructed by Gwartney et al (2012), as well as the Financial Reform Index constructed by Abiad et al. (2008) at the International Monetary Fund. The Financial Reform Index includes sub-indices for directed credit, credit ceilings, credit controls, entry barriers, banking supervision, privatization, international capital, and securities markets.

Looking at Table 4.5 shows the substantial liberalization of credit markets in Japan, Korea, and China starting in the 1980s and 1990s. The credit market in Korea is much more liberalized than in Japan and China. Now, it is even more liberalized than in the US which has used to be the hub of world financial market. China regulated the credit market strictly until the 1980s. But China began to liberalize credit market from the 1990s. Japan liberalized the credit market more in the 2000s. Now, the credit markets in Korea and Japan were liberalized to the level of the Western countries.

Table 4.5 Trends of Credit Market Liberalization in Korea, China, and Japan

	1980	*1985*	*1990*	*1995*	*2000*	*2005*	*2010*	*2015*
Korea	6.13	8.11	8.33	8.33	8.33	9.33	9.33	9.32
China	—	—	—	4.60	6.46	7.23	6.91	7.33
Japan	7.82	7.88	8.22	8.22	8.22	8.50	8.38	8.31
US	9.52	9.47	9.64	9.60	9.81	9.10	6.95	9.34
Germany	7.61	7.58	7.65	6.98	8.33	7.99	7.88	8.33
Sweden	7.59	8.07	9.33	7.81	10.00	9.74	9.97	9.90

Source: Gwartney et al (2013), Gwartney et al (2018)

Table 4.6 Trends of Capital Liberalization in Korea, China, and Japan

	1980	*1985*	*1990*	*1995*	*2000*	*2005*	*2010*	*2015*
Korea	0.00	2.00	5.00	5.00	0.00	1.54	7.69	6.15
China	0.00	2.00	5.00	5.00	0.77	0.77	0.00	0.77
Japan	2.00	5.00	8.00	8.00	7.69	8.46	3.85	0.77
US	8.00	8.00	8.00	8.00	6.92	6.15	3.85	3.85
Germany	8.00	10.00	10.00	10.00	9.23	3.85	3.85	3.08
Sweden	2.00	5.00	10.00	10.00	5.38	3.08	3.08	3.08

Note: Gwartney et al (2013), Gwartney et al (2018)

Source: Kim (2018b: 337, Table 9.1).

Trends of capital liberalization were differentiated clearly in the three countries. As shown in Table 4.6, Korea and China showed the same trend for capital controls until 1995. They had very strict capital controls in the 1980s. However, they liberalized capital controls considerably in the 1990s. After the 1997 Asian financial crisis, China again instituted strict capital controls. By contrast, Korea reinstated capital controls during the 1997 financial crisis but liberalized its capital market abruptly in the 2000s. By 2015, Korea had a much more liberalized capital market than that of the US. Japan liberalized its capital market gradually from the 1980s. In the 1990s, the capital liberalization index of Japan was at the same high level as that of the US and was higher in the 2000s. In 2010, the index showed the same low level of capital liberalization as that of the US. In 2015, Japan showed very low level of capital liberalization.

The overall extent of financial liberalization can be measured by the Financial Reform Index constructed by the International Monetary Fund. Here, a financial reform dataset for 1981–2005 is used for Financial Liberalization Index in Japan, Korea, and China. Figure 4.2 shows that there was almost full financial liberalization after the mid-1990s in Japan and Korea. The figure also shows that China started financial liberalization in the mid-1990s, reaching a 0.5 score in the Financial Liberalization Index in the mid-2000s. With financial liberalization, bank-based financial systems began to shift toward market-based financial systems. This change can be identified from the substantial increase in debt securities. As Figure 4.3 shows, the ratio of domestic private debt securities to GDP, which serves as a measure of financialization, increased significantly in the 1990s (the Lost Decade) in Japan, in the 1990s and 2000s in Korea, and in the 2000s in China. The most drastic change in domestic private debt securities to GDP occurred in Korea just after the 1997 financial crisis, when the ratio increased sharply.

Financial liberalization was one of the major causes of Japan's Lost Decade as it created asset bubble and then bubble burst that brought about the Lost Decade. Rapid financial liberalization after 1993 was an immediate cause

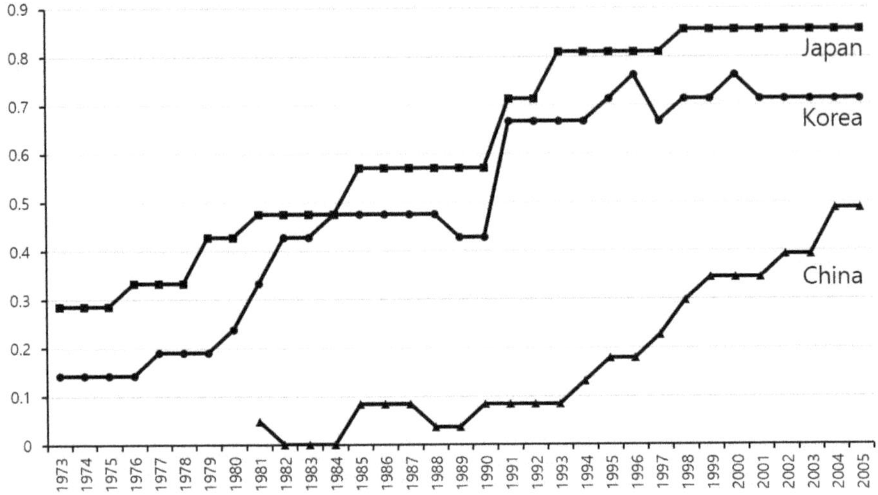

Figure 4.2 Trends of Financial Liberalization Indices in Japan, Korea, and China

Note: Financial Reform Dataset, 2008, IMF.

Kim (2018b), P.338. Figure 9.1

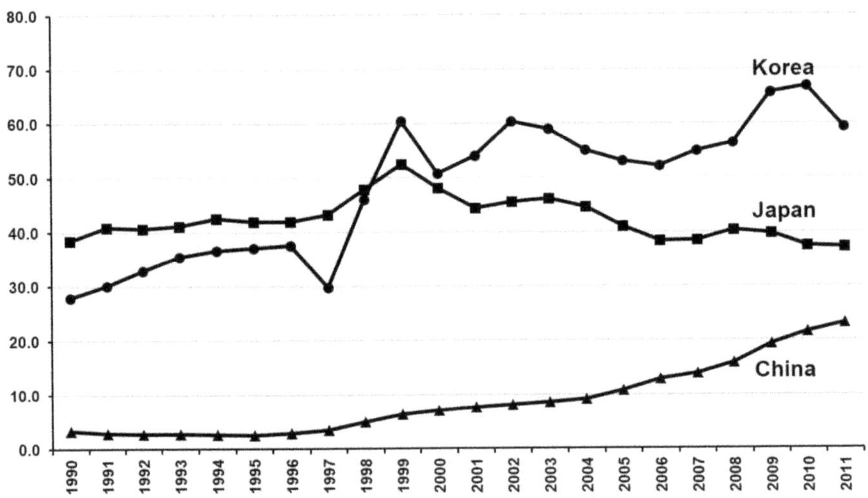

Figure 4.3 Outstanding Domestic Private Debt Securities to GDP

Source: Global Financial Development Database, November 2013 Version, World Bank.

of the 1997 financial crisis in Korea. By contrast, the Chinese economy was not influenced in particular by the Asian financial crisis in 1997 because it had relatively strict financial regulations. It is remarkable that Korea liberalized capital market abruptly while China and Japan strictly controlled capital market after 2005. Korea adopted the policy of excessive capital market liberalization. This has been major factor of volatility of the Korean economy.

Financial 'Big Bang' in Japan Model

Originally, Japan Model had a bank-based financial system where the state viewed the financial system as an instrument of industrial policy designed to transfer the majority of funds from the surplus to deficit units through intermediary markets, especially bank finance (Cargill and Parker, 2001) However, the 1970s, 1980s, and 1990s saw the financial system transition from a bank-based system to a market-based system. These developments started in 1972, when the purchase of foreign securities by banks was liberalized, as was outward FDI. 1973 then saw the introduction of a floating exchange-rate regime and the liberalization of inward FDI. While financial liberalization began in the 1970s, it accelerated in the 1980s, when foreign exchange transactions and interest rates were liberalized in 1980 and 1985, respectively, and banks were allowed to enter the securities business. Finally, the 'Big Bang' in the Japanese capital market was announced in 1996, and the ban on financial holding companies was lifted in 1997, all of which encouraged foreign investors to enter the Japanese stock market (Richter, 2000: 335).

The causes that triggered financial liberalization in Japan were twofold. On the one hand, the development of bond markets was spurred by increasing public sector borrowing. One the other hand, the accumulation of corporate profits as well as corporate savings meant that firms had less of a need to borrow from banks. As household assets accumulated, there was also demand from households for a greater variety of financial products which banks sought to provide, as they pressed for deregulation (Walter and Zhang, 2012). Still, as corporations became more independent from the banking sector, the external portion of bank borrowings drastically declined from 38.9% in the 1960s to 8.9% in the 1980s (Tohyama, 2000). This change in bank financing precipitated the weakening of the main bank system, which supplied stable long-term loans to industry, and monitored the management of the corporations. This financial liberalization, which brought about overinvestment and speculative investment, was a cause of the asset bubble that developed in the 1980s.[15] After the 'Big Bang', cross-border capital transactions were liberalized and the securitization of assets was permitted. The establishment of financial holding companies allowed the Japanese economy to be influenced by international finance as foreign investors entered the Japanese stock market. Even though Japanese financial liberalization did not facilitate foreign capital flight and debt repayment, it generated economic and financial distress that has persisted throughout the 1990s (Cargill and Parker, 2001).

In short, with financial liberalization, the financial system in Japan transformed significantly from a bank-based system to a market-based system. However, the transformation of the Japanese financial system was actually financial hybridization process in which the main-bank system and market-based system were mixed (Kim, 2018b).

Rapid Financial Liberalization in the Korea Model

Korea introduced a rapid financial liberalization program in 1993, just four years before the 1997 financial crisis. In June 1993, 'foreign currency and capital transaction liberalization' program was introduced. This included the deregulation of interest rates, the abolition of policy loans, the granting of more managerial autonomy to banks, the reduction of entry barriers to the financial industry, the liberalization of foreign exchange, and the opening of capital markets (Chang, 2007: 269). As the non-bank financial intermediaries became rapidly deregulated, they moved outside the ambit of the state's supervision, and were put under the control of the Chaebol. This sudden domestic financial liberalization left Korea defenseless in the face of massive financial crisis (Woo-Cumings, 2001). Moreover, Korea aggressively removed capital controls on trade financing and short-term borrowings by financial companies. Because Korea liberalized its capital market too soon, before liberalizing its domestic financial sectors, excessive short-term foreign debt and a high share of foreign portfolio investment in the domestic securities market ensued, which drastically decreased the stability of financial markets. Korea indeed made the mistake of increasing its vulnerability, not only by relying on excessive short-term foreign debt, but also by seeking foreign capital through exchange convertibility, without addressing its fundamental and long-standing financial problems in a timely manner (Cargill and Parker, 2001).

Financial liberalization in 1993, which institutionalized capital market liberalization, was followed by a sharp increase of short-term foreign debt and massive inflows of short-term international capital, or hot money. In addition to the financial liberalization, the abandonment of industrial policy,[16] through which government proactively coordinated enterprise investment, precipitated overinvestment and duplicate investment by the Chaebol firms in 1994–1997. This overinvestment and duplicate investment deteriorated the profitability of the corporations, which gave rise to the sudden reversal of short-term international capital flows. Foreign borrowings of the banking sector also amplified the financial crisis. In short, both financial liberalization and the abandonment of industrial policy in 1993 were the immediate causes of the 1997 financial crisis (Kim, 2018a). Contrary to the argument of IMF Staff (1998), which attributed the 1997 financial crisis in Korea to excessive government intervention in the economy through strong regulations, the actual causes were too rapid financial liberalization, and too weak financial regulation. Contrary to the neoclassical view that too much government interference in the private sector caused the crisis, Korean government's weakening in relation to the Chaebol precipitated the crisis. The fact of the matter was that the Korean government did not take strong enough action, not that it intervened too much. The state deregulated financial sector, when it should have been trying to devise and implement an appropriate set of regulations (Richter, 2000; Stiglitz, 2001; Chang, 2007).

The IMF's restructuring programs, which were implemented just after the 1997 financial crisis, decisively liberalized the Korean financial market and financial system. Banking laws and finance-related legislation were reformed to strengthen the interests of shareholders. Through the amendment of Bank of Korea Act at the end of 1997,[17] the role of the Bank of Korea was also redefined to focus on price stability, rather than enhancing the soundness of bank and financial institutions. As a result, pro-investment and pro-growth monetary policy retreated, in favor of pro-finance monetary policy (Chang, 2006: 273–275). Moreover, capital markets were opened completely. Rapid financial liberalization thus not only increased the instability of the Korean economic system, but also intensified the concentration of economic power in the hands of the Chaebol. Financial liberalization transformed the Korean financial system also from a bank-based system to a market-based system.

Deliberate Financial Liberalization in the China Model

At the end of the Maoist era, China's financial sector was essentially limited to a Soviet-style mono-bank, which primarily managed the deposits of SOEs. This mono-bank was then transformed into a state-owned bank that supplied funds to SOEs for industrialization, much like a Japanese-style main-bank. China's banking reform began in 1984, when the People's Bank of China (PBC) was split into different entities. Following China's announcement of an acceleration of financial sector reforms in 1993, banks were separated into commercial banks and policy banks, with the latter lending to priority areas identified by the state regardless of project profitability (Cargill and Parker, 2001).

After the reform and opening era, the reform of the financial system has proceeded with the SOEs reform. The Chinese financial system was strictly controlled initially by the state. Even though trade liberalization was pursued rapidly and extensively, financial liberalization was not promoted much. In particular, there was strict regulation of foreign portfolio investment. However, China has also seen a gradual shift from a bank-oriented system to a more market-oriented system. This trend can be seen by looking at the share of the banking sector in financial assets, which decreased from 83.5% in 1998 to 73.8% in 2009, while the share of investment (insurance, stocks, bonds, and funds) increased from 8.9% to 19.9%. The share of deposits in individual financial assets also decreased, from 71.8% in 2004 to 64.3% in 2009, while the share of investment in individual financial assets increased from 28.2% to 35.7% (Kang, 2011).

Interest rate liberalization began in 1986, when the terms of lending rates could be determined by mutual agreement between lenders and borrowers. 1996 then saw the liberalization of the inter-bank rate, the reduction of directed credit, and the implementation of general guidelines on loans. Lending rates on foreign currency and deposit rates on large foreign currency accounts were also liberalized in 2000. With foreign financial institutions permitted to do business in some coastal cities like Shanghai, foreign banks were allowed to conduct foreign exchange business in 2001 (Yan et al, 2011). Hot money began to flow in China after 2003, and increased rapidly from 2007. As a result, the volatility of the Chinese economy began to increase. There has, however, been reversals of financial liberalization. For example, after the 1997 Asian financial crisis, China decisively reversed capital liberalization with strict capital controls, as seen in Table 4.6.

China has experienced massive capital flight since 2014. In response, the Chinese government in 2016 once more halted the process of capital account liberalization. China's financial liberalization also slowed down as the country experienced financial turmoil in the mid-2010s, which included a devaluation of the RMB in August 2015, a stock market crash in June 2015, and an interbank cash crunch in April 2016 and December 2016. The Chinese government is now again ready to press ahead with its agenda of financial liberalization by promoting further interest rate liberalization, exchange rate flexibility, capital account convertibility, and domestic financial market opening (Dong and Xia, 2018). To this end, the PBC decided in April 2018 to shelve its window guidance for banks' deposit rates, allowing banks to offer deposit rates to their clients on a business basis.

4.3 Transformation of Corporate System

Marketization, privatization, and especially financial liberalization transformed the corporate system that characterized the East Asian Model. The overall characteristic of transformation of the corporate system in the East Asian Model was introduction of shareholder capitalism in which the main goal of management was the maximization of the shareholder value. As we will see, this change to the corporate system was more profound in Japan when compared to China and Korea.

The Transformation of the Japanese Corporate System

The Japanese corporate system in terms of ownership, corporate governance, human-resource management, and inter-firm relationships changed during the 'Lost Decade', when several reforms designed to enhance shareholder value were legislated and implemented. These reforms, which started from 1997, included the introduction of stock options, the establishment of the executive officer organization, and the legalization of pure holding companies. First of all, change in corporate ownership was a major force that

Table 4.7 Ownership Structure by Type of Shareholder in Japanese Listed Companies

	Govt. & Local Govt.	*City & Regional Banks*	*Trust Banks*	*Business Corporations*	*Foreigners*	*Individuals*
1970	0.6	15.8	—	23.9	4.9	37.7
1975	0.4	19.0	—	27.0	3.6	32.1
1980	0.4	19.9	—	26.2	5.8	27.9
1985	0.3	20.9	—	28.8	7.0	22.3
1990	0.3	15.7	9.8	30.1	4.7	20.4
1995	0.3	15.1	10.3	27.2	10.5	19.5
2000	0.2	10.1	17.4	21.8	18.8	19.4
2005	0.2	4.7	18.0	21.3	26.3	19.9
2010	0.3	4.1	18.2	21.2	26.7	20.3
2015	0.1	3.7	18.8	22.6	29.8	17.5

Note: The number of Trust Banks is included in that of City & Regional Banks in and before 1985 Survey. Unit: %.

Source: 2020 Share Ownership Survey, Tokyo Stock Exchange.

transformed corporate system. As was shown in Table 4.7, the proportion of main-banks (city and regional banks) in share ownership of Japanese listed companies decreased sharply from 15.8% in 1970 to 3.7% in 2015, while the proportion of foreign investors increased rapidly from 4.9% in 1970 to 29.8% in 2015. There was a dramatic change in share ownership structure from the late 1990s in Japanese listed companies: fall of main-banks ownership and rise of foreigner ownership. The Japanese corporate sector also saw an increase in the proportion of institutional investors (such as trust banks) from the late 1980s, as well as the rise in the share of companies listed in the Tokyo Stock Price Index (TOPIX) appointing outside directors, from 29.2% in 2005 to 64.7% in 2013. The ban on the holding company has been lifted by an amendment to the Anti-Monopoly Act in 1997. As the ratio of stock cross-holdings among enterprises has dropped since the 1990s, the share of stable stockholders has dropped from 43% in 1991 to 26% in 2002. The so-called convoy system that is the protective banking policies of the government has also been abandoned. In this way, the system of bank-guaranteed security of firm management was no longer in force (Yamada and Hirano, 2012). The holding companies instead of the main-banks have begun to play a role of monitoring business management. All in all, these changes in corporate ownership forced managers of firms to adopt the principles of shareholder capitalism, which privilege shareholder sovereignty over the managerial sovereignty that prevailed when main-banks were more dominant.

The introduction of stock options, which were effective in aligning the interests of management with those of shareholders, impacted managerial practices. The share of firms that introduced stock options in Japan increased from 6.7% in 2006 to 34.9% in 2013. This expansion of stock options gave management the incentive to increase shareholder value at all costs including cutting jobs and reducing wages. Under the support of institutional reforms of the government, Japanese firms began to combine the traditional managerial sovereignty with the emerging element of shareholder capitalism. The pressure to focus on shareholder value and short-term corporate profitability from outside shareholders also precipitated a shift from the relationship-oriented, stakeholder-oriented model of corporate governance to a market-based, shareholder-oriented model of corporate governance. The rise of foreign ownership also forced managers to introduce shareholder-oriented corporate governance.

Surveys looking at the targets of management in Japanese firms in the 1980s and 1990s show that there was indeed a big change in corporate goals. According to the survey results conducted by Kagono et al. (1983),[18] the top priority goal of management in Japan in 1983 was 'market share', while the 'rise in share price' was the last priority. In contrast, the top priorities of American firms that year were 'return on investment' and 'rise in share price'. However, the survey by Nikkei Newspaper Inc. in 1993[19] showed that the overwhelming top priority of management in Japanese firms became 'rise in profit (67.8% frequency) 'while 'market share' became very low priority (2.9% frequency). This big change in targets of management in a decade tells that the short-term profitability rather than the growth of the firm became the goal of the management in Japan.

As we have seen, shareholders' interests gradually became the center of managerial attention since the 1990s (Colpan et al, 2011). In Japanese corporate governance, the voice of employees and partner banks (main-banks) weakened significantly, while the voice of institutional investors and individual investors strengthened substantially. As shown in Table 4.8, the proportion of listed companies in which employees had a strong voice went down from 44.9% before 2005 to 37.6% after 2005. In contrast, the proportion of listed companies in which institutional investors had a strong voice increased from 26.4% before 2005 to 56.2% after 2005. This survey results of Table 4.8

Table 4.8 Who Has (or Will Have) a Strong Voice toward Management?: The Case of Japan

	Before 2005	*After 2005*
Customer (consumer)	52.7%	54.4%
Employees	44.9%	37.6%
Partner banks	39.8%	27.6%
Institutional investors	36.4%	56.2%
Partner corporations	35.6%	27.8%
Individual investors	18.9%	33.4%
Group corporations	16.7%	16.1%
Other	11.3%	12.4%

Note: This survey was given to listed companies in 2005.

Source: The Report of Survey Research on Corporate Governance, CSR, and Personnel Strategies of Japanese Firms, Labor Policy Research and Training Institute (2007).

suggest that Japanese corporate governance has changed circa 2005 from the stakeholder-oriented to the shareholder-oriented, since the voice of institutional investors toward management was strengthened while that of employees was weakened after 2005. Moreover, as the holding company system was introduced, holding companies instead of the main-banks have begun to play a role of monitoring business management.

Japan also saw its Keiretsu system change. There are two types of Keiretsu: horizontal Keiretsu and vertical Keiretsu. While the former is characterized by cross-shareholding relations between firms, which are led by a main-bank that provides them with financial services, the latter denotes a structure with a complex web of assembler-supplier networks. In the pre-bubble period (1985–1988), strategic alliances between corporations were forged within the boundaries of a given Keiretsu. The rapid rise of asset prices in the 1988–1990 bubble period, however, made affiliated firms exit horizontal Keiretsu, as their financial interdependence decreased. The post-bubble period after 1991 then saw the decline of vertical Keiretsu, which withered due to the standardization of parts, modularization, and cross-border mergers and acquisitions (M&A). Moving away from the closed innovation model to the open innovation model facilitated the disintegration of the Keiretsu. Moreover, Koizumi reform of deregulation and corporate restructuring weakened Keiretsu (Miyoshi and Nakao, 2011). Risk-sharing intervention of Keiretsu to the affiliates firms diminished in the 'Lost Decade' of the 1990s. Foreign investors pressed the managers of the firms to sell off shareholdings in the affiliates. As a modularization in manufacturing, which required less integration of production stages, proceeded, the advantages of Keiretsu-style supply management diminished. Some Keiretsu firms like Nissan became to have arms-length-like transactions with the affiliated firms when Nissan dismissed relational contracting by selling off its affiliates. Because of these changes, Lincoln and Shimotani (2009) argue that the Japanese corporate system in terms of inter-firm relations has begun to resemble that of the Anglo-American Model. However, there is little evidence to suggest that the dense and enduring business networks established by the Keiretsu have completely collapsed. The enduring long-term and reciprocal business relationships that have tied firms into business groups remain distinctive (Walter and Zhang, 2012: 252). Some Keiretsu firms like Toyota transformed into a new Keiretsu in which Toyota, with a radically new purchasing strategy, selected suppliers on the basis of globally competitive target prices, with sustaining its own supply chain networks.

The Transformation of the Korean Corporate System

Korea also showed a pattern of corporate system transformation similar to that of Japan. The ownership structure of corporations changed significantly. The most prominent changes after the 1997 financial crisis were sharp decline of shares of government and public companies and banks and rapid

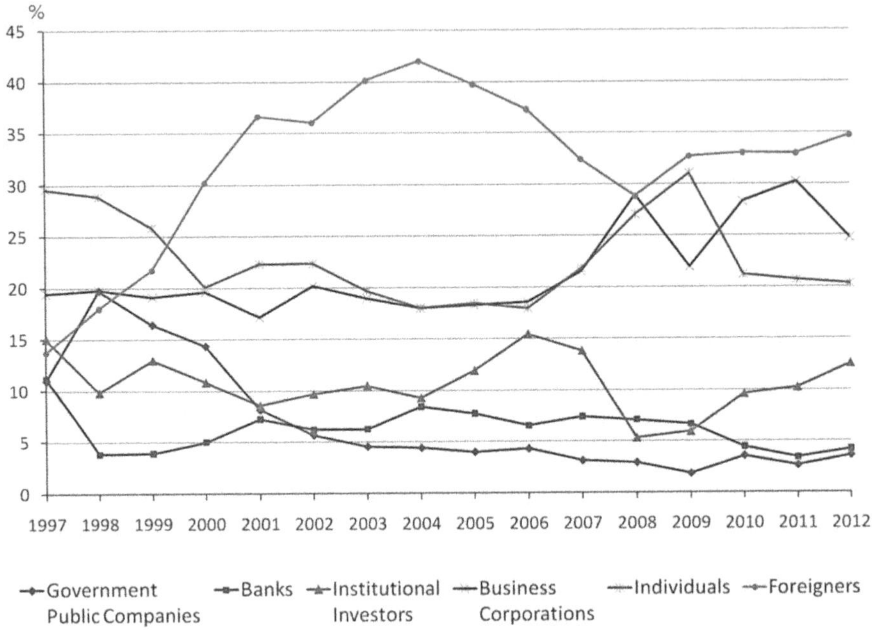

Figure 4.4 Ownership Structure by Shareholder Type in Korean Listed Companies

Note: Data from Korea Exchange.

Source: Kim (2018a), p.346, Figure 9.3

increase of share of foreigners. Figure 4.4, for example, shows that both the share of government and public companies and the share of banks in Korean listed companies decreased from 11% in 1997 to under 5% in 2012, while the share of foreign ownership increased substantially from 14% to 35% in the same period. This change in corporate ownership structure impacted corporate governance, as foreign shareholders and institutional investors pressed management to introduce principles of shareholder capitalism in their corporations.

Changes in Korean corporate governance following the 1997 financial crisis have largely been in line with the Anglo-American Model. For example, the reform of the Chaebol after the 1997 financial crisis included the strengthening of minority shareholder rights, the introduction of outside directorship, and a ban on circular-shareholding. Minority shareholder rights were further strengthened by a lowering of the threshold for various shareholder initiatives, such as the allowance of cumulative voting for directors and class suits. As a result, the voice of minority shareholders in the management was strengthened. Moreover, an amendment to the Commercial Code forced managers and controlling shareholders to be more accountable to minority shareholders. After the 1997 financial crisis, listed companies began to introduce outside directorship. In 2001, companies with assets of at least two trillion won were also required to set up an outside director nominating committee, which would consider candidates recommended by minority shareholders. As a result of these policies, the proportion of listed firms with at least one outside director increased from 34% in 1999 to 62.3% in 2000. In 2007, around 94% of listed firms actually appointed at least one outside director. In 2008, listed companies were finally required to appoint outside directors for at least 25% of board seats. Not only the circular-shareholding among the firms within Chaebol but also unfair intra-group transactions were banned. Debt guarantees between Chaebol subsidiaries were prohibited.

Overall, these regulations attempted to weaken the monopolistic domination of the Chaebol on the national economy. Moreover, the Chaebol reform included the abolition of ceiling on foreign shareholders in individual companies, permission of all forms of M&A including hostile takeovers by foreigners, and restriction on ability of Chaebol to exercise power over the financial affiliates. These changes moved the corporate governance system away from a relationship-based insider model toward an Anglo-American outsider model. In short, there was an attempt to Americanize corporate governance in Korea (Chang, 2007). The governance paradigm of Chaebols has gradually changed from one dominated by family or controlling shareholders to a system in which the power of professional managers and monitoring of markets have increased substantially (Min, 2016). This reform contributed to introducing the elements of shareholder capitalism as well as to reducing the concentration of economic power on the Chaebol. Even though family ownership in Chaebol firms weakened, family ownership structure of the Chaebol itself largely remains. The hierarchical subcontracting relationship between Chaebol firms and suppliers has also not changed. Seen this way, the Korean corporate system after 1997 financial crisis can be described as 'Chaebol system plus shareholder capitalism' with primacy of the former (Kim, 2012).

The Transformation of the Chinese Corporate System

In China, the transformation of the corporate system following marketization and privatization took place in four stages (Kang et al, 2008). The first stage, from 1949 to 1983 saw SOEs dominate, with private enterprise being strictly prohibited. In terms of industrial output, the share of SOEs was 65% in 1985. The share of collective enterprise was 32%. However, the share of private sector was only 3%. SOEs were commanded by the state. In the SOEs, the state was not only the owner but also the manager. There were no modern enterprise structures where separation of ownership from management prevailed. The second stage, from 1984 to 1993, marked the start of the separation between government and enterprise. 1984, for example, saw the state grant autonomy to enterprises by allowing them to retain a certain portion of profit and introducing a stockholding system. A management contract system was also introduced in the mid-1980s, which included profit-sharing rules between enterprises and government agencies. During the latter half of the 1980s, SOEs followed the path of securitization[20]. Separation of ownership from management in SOEs was further enshrined by the State-Owned Industrial Enterprises Law (SOE Law) in 1988 and the Management Mechanism Transformation Act in 1992, which gave independent managerial rights to SOEs (Chen, 2009: 119).

In the third stage, from 1994 to 2005, experimentation in modern enterprise structures began based on the 1993 Company Law, which defined the maximization of owners' interests as the primary goal of corporate practice. Based on the Company Law, the corporatization of the SOEs, which is actually a process of implicit privatization, replaced the previous management contract system in 1994. As of 1996, about 5,800 industrial SOEs had been corporatized. Outside directorship was then introduced in 2004, and the 2005 Company Law made independent directors a legal necessity. In this period, state shareholders still enjoyed overwhelming favoritism over individual investors. Local governments also continued to oversee SOEs to ensure the implementation of the CCP's guiding principles and policies.

The fourth stage, from 2006 onward, saw the continued pursuit of better corporate governance by balancing the power asymmetry between the state shareholder and individual shareholders in companies. Under the 2005 Company law, shareholders were entitled to appeal to the supervisory board to address misconduct by managers and the board of directors. Other developments in Chinese corporate governance included the protection of minority shareholders and the introduction of an employee share ownership plan (ESOP). As a result of such reform, the voices of the individual and minority shareholders were strengthened gradually. The Company Law also introduced employee participation in corporate management. Specifically, the board of directors may include employee representatives, and at least one-third of the members of the supervisory board must comprise of representatives of the company's employees. Even so, the lack of independent unions in China means that employee participation in supervisory boards was basically superficial.

To enhance external monitoring and internal control, the China Association for Public Companies was established in 2012. This self-regulatory body put forward the agenda to improve corporate governance in six areas: independent directors, the boards of directors, external audit and internal control, institutional investors, controlling shareholders, and listed company supervision. Moreover, because the corporate system in the largest SOEs is more centralized, inter-firm relationships remain weak. Indeed, even though inter-firm networks have emerged, such networks have been small in scale, low in density, and limited in institutional trust (Walter and Zhang, 2012: 252).

Chinese corporate governance reform also led to a change in the goal of corporations. After the Company Law was introduced in 1993, the maximization of shareholder interests became the primary goal of corporate practice (Carney, 2012). Though this shift means that an element of shareholder capitalism was introduced among private and foreign-owned enterprises, the fact that SOEs were still under the control of the State Asset Supervision and Administration Commission (SASAC) means the impact of shareholder capitalism in the public sector was negligible.

In sum, the shared characteristic of the transformation of the corporate system in Japan, Korea, and China was the introduction of principles of shareholder capitalism in corporate governance. These elements of shareholder capitalism merged into the Keiretsu system in Japan, the Chaebol system in Korea, and the SOE system in China, producing hybridized corporate systems.

4.4 The Flexibilization of Labor Markets

According to the hypothesis of institutional complementarity (Amable, 2000; Aoki, 2001; Hall and Soskice, 2001), marketization and privatization of the public sector, introduction of shareholder capitalism in the corporate system, and financial liberalization can positively impact economic efficiency when labor markets are flexible. Those reforms in countries adopting the East Asian Model were thus accompanied by the transformation of labor sector from quite rigid to a rather flexible labor market. The most dramatic transformation occurred in the Chinese labor market.

From the 1950s to the late 1980s, the Chinese employment system was characterized by lifetime employment. Under the planned economy, lifetime employment in SOEs was guaranteed. The SOEs had no right to discharge the employees. However, corporate reforms starting in the late 1970s and early 1980s led to a shift from the 'iron rice bowl'—a term symbolizing guaranteed lifetime employment in SOEs before 1978—to contract labor system. In the early 1980s, contract labor system was introduced for newly hired workers, while existing employees were still under lifetime employment. From the late 1980s, the contract labor system was extended to all SOE employees. Chinese labor market was also flexibilized through the introduction of a lay-off program known as *Xia Kang*. *Xia Kang* is a process by which a company notifies employees that their job has been terminated due to adverse financial circumstances. The lay-off from the *Xia Kang* may be temporary or permanent. Marketization and privatization of the SOEs accompanied large-scale SOE downsizing, with about 37 million workers being laid off in the SOE sector from 1998 to 2004 (Aglietta and Bai, 2013: 108–109). The dispatch labor system, in which workers are temporarily employed, has also become popular with Chinese firms. Increase in the share of contractual employees is the best indicator for flexibilization of labor market in China, comparable to increase in the share of non-regular employees in Japan and Korea. As Table 4.9 shows, the share of contractual employees among all formal employees in China increased drastically from 1.8% in 1984 to 40.9% in 1995 (the share was 40.1% in SOEs and 62.8% in other ownership units in 1995).

Table 4.9 Share of Contractual Employees in China

Year	Total Contractual Employees	Proportion (Total Formal Employees = 100)	State-Owned Units	Urban Collective Owned Units	Other Ownership Units
1984	209	1.8	2.0	1.0	8.1
1985	409	3.3	3.7	2.2	11.4
1986	624	4.9	5.6	2.7	14.5
1987	873	6.6	7.6	3.6	18.1
1988	1,234	9.1	10.1	5.8	20.7
1989	1,468	10.7	11.8	7.0	25.1
1990	1,702	12.1	13.3	8.1	26.3
1991	1,972	13.6	14.9	8.9	28.0
1992	2,541	17.2	18.9	11.0	29.8
1993	3,123	21.0	21.9	15.5	37.4
1994	3,839	25.9	26.2	20.1	45.6
1995	6,096	40.9	40.1	37.4	62.8

Note: Other ownership units include cooperative enterprises, joint-stock companies, foreign-owned companies and, Hong Kongese, Macanese, and Taiwanese-owned companies. Data from National Bureau of Statistics of China. Unit: 10,000 persons, %.

Source: Kim (2018a: 348, Table 9.2).

Commodification and casualization further transformed Chinese employment in the past three decades. An alliance of interest between the state and capital, both global and domestic, has rendered labor disorganized and individualized with accompanying commodification of labor (Lee, 2012). To regulate employment relations around the notion of market-oriented, voluntary, and individualist contract labor, China introduced the National Labor Law in 1995, which required all employees to sign labor contracts. However, by 2007, only 50% of enterprises had signed labor contracts with their employees, with the rate among non-state firms being only 20%. Moreover, among those who signed labor contracts, 60–70% were short-term contracts of less than one year (Lee, 2012). Revised in 2006, the New Labor Contract Law introduced contract labor without fixed term. This new law, therefore, made employment more stable, and created a three-tier system where workers with non-fixed-term contracts and fixed-term contracts, exist alongside dispatch laborers. Thus, there is a tiered employment system in which regular contract workers and non-regular dispatch workers coexist. Because there are no independent labor unions that can bargain collectively with employers, the employment status of workers in China is essentially unstable. Thus, the labor market is highly flexible even though labor legislation, such as the National Labor Law, Labor Contract Law, Trade Union Law, and Labor Dispute Mediation and Arbitration Law, formally guarantees job stability to some extent.

Casualization of employment can further be seen by looking at a large amount of migrant workers, *Nongmingong*, in the urban informal sector. In 2013, the number of these migrant workers was about 270 million, which accounted for a third of the total labor force and half of urban employment (Meng, 2012; Lam et al, 2015). The migrant workers from the rural sector constitute a larger part of informal workers in the urban sector. The size of informal workers has increased significantly. If informal worker is defined as worker with no social insurance or no labor contract, the share of informal workers in six large cities (Shanghai, Guangzhou, Fuzhou, Shenyang, Xian, and Wuhan) was 37.2% in 2005 (Park et al, 2012). Informal workers usually have jobs in sectors in which protection of employment by labor law is deficient. If the informal employment is defined as the employment in private business and self-employed (or individual businesses) which lacks the protection of labor laws, the share of the informal employment increased rapidly from 12.9% in 2004 to 36.3% in 2015 (Meng, 2017). Since the dominant employment trend was reorganization of employment away from manufacturing and the increasing prevalence of temporary and dispatch workers in all sectors of the economy, Chinese labor market became highly flexible (Lee, 2012). According to the study of Chi et al (2012), three factors of the enhanced flexibility of the labor market were rapid economic growth, high employee turnover, and the weakness of internal labor market.

The migrant workers are discriminated against urban resident workers in terms of employment conditions and social welfare. First, the share of migrant workers who have labor contracts was 12.9% in 2005, while the share of urban resident workers who have labor contracts was 61.8%. Second, the migrant workers are discriminated against local workers in terms of social protection as seen in Table 4.10. In 2010, the share of migrant workers who have unemployment insurance, health insurance, and pension fund was 10.4%, 32.7%, and 30.0%, respectively. In contrast, for local resident workers, the share was 51.8%, 80.3%, and 80.8%, respectively. There is a huge gap in social protection between local resident workers and migrant workers. There is a broader consensus among the experts that in order to reduce this gap in social protection, it is necessary to connect the social security system across provinces and make the social security benefits portable by reforming the hukou system through, for example, relaxing hukou restrictions.[21]

Table 4.10 Social Protection Coverage in China: Local and Migrant Workers

	Unemployment Insurance		*Health Insurance*		*Pension Fund*	
Year	*Local*	*Migrant*	*Local*	*Migrant*	*Local*	*Migrant*
2005	32.8	6.8	65.3	15.0	73.0	14.0
2010	51.8	10.4	80.3	32.7	80.8	30.0

Note: Unit: %.

Source: China Urban Labor Survey, 2005 and 2010, Institute for Population Studies at the Chinese Academy of Social Sciences.

China's wage structure also changed in the late 1970s. Before 1978, seniority and political loyalty were the main determinants of pay. The traditional stratified wage system based on egalitarianism has been maintained in the planned economy era. The strong egalitarianism prevailed with an 'iron rice bowl' before 1978. This 'bad equality' prevailed in the wage determination system. However, from the reform and opening in 1978, there was a transition from equality principle to competition principle in the wage determination. Wages began to be linked to the efficiency of firms and macroeconomic conditions. This transformation of China's wage system was mainly achieved through pay-for-performance schemes introduced by the government after 1978. The wages reform in the SOEs started in 1985 by the government. In 1986, the government resolution was issued about wages determination within the enterprises. The government gave the SOEs autonomy of wages determination within the limits of the total wage funds regulated by the government. Pay-for-performance wage system was introduced largely to the senior and middle management and sales and marketing jobs (Wei, 2009). Job evaluation system was introduced in the enterprises from 1988. In 1992, pay-for-job and pay-for-task were introduced in the enterprises.

Korea also used to have a system of lifetime employment in large private firms like the Chaebol and in public companies before the 1997 financial crisis. The crisis, however, led to a change in the hiring patterns of major Korean companies. As shown in Table 4.11, the share of new graduates in total job accessions in Chaebol firms, financial and public enterprises decreased from 41.4% in 1995.10–1996.9 to 14.9% in 2000.10–2001.9. In contrast, the share of experienced workers in total job accessions increased from 25.4% in 1995.10–1996.9 to 55.4% in 2000.10–2001.9. This drastic decline in the

Table 4.11 The Change in Hiring Patterns after the 1997 Financial Crisis: Chaebol Firms, Financial and Public Enterprises

	1995.10–1996.9	*1996.10–1997.9*	*1997.10–1998.9*	*1998.10–1999.9*	*1999.10–2000.9*	*2000.10–2001.9*
Total job accessions	268	232	195	362	334	222
Newly graduates	111	88	51	51	51	33
	41.4	38.0	26.2	14.1	15.3	14.9
Experienced workers	68	65	62	139	181	123
	25.4	28.1	31.8	38.4	54.2	55.4
Transfer within company	53	47	59	131	62	41
	19.8	20.3	30.3	36.2	18.6	18.5
Other	36	31	23	41	40	25
	13.4	13.4	11.8	11.3	12.0	11.3

Note: Raw data was from Employment Insurance Database. The data includes 13,081 establishments (1,724 establishments in the top 30 Chaebol firms, 1,502 establishments in public sector, and 9,855 establishments in financial sector). Unit: 1,000 persons, %.

Source: Kim and Cheon (2003: 82, Table 2 (restructured)).

share of new graduate hires, while the share of experienced hires increased rapidly, indicates a collapse of internal labor markets in large firms, which buttressed Korea's system of lifetime employment. This data suggests that lifetime employment system in Korea decisively weakened after the 1997 financial crisis.

The 1998 Act on the Protection of Dispatched Workers further contributed to the flexibilization of Korea's labor sector by opening the path to the widespread non-regularization of employment. Though jobs directly tied to the production process were excluded from the object of the workers dispatching, wide range of jobs such as professional and technical jobs was the object of dispatched workers. The period of the dispatching was on principle one year but can be extended to 2 years. The goal of this act was twofold: first, to allow employers to hire non-regular workers for up to two years and, second, to protect the rights of dispatched workers. Even though the number of dispatched workers is small,[22] the Act served as a catalyst for the rapid non-regularization of employment after the 1997 financial crisis, with the share of non-regular workers increasing from 27.4% in 2002 to 37.0% in 2004. Because labor unions in Korea largely represent and protect the interests of regular workers, non-regular workers are also severely discriminated against in terms of employment, wages, and social insurance.

Similarly to China, a pay-for-performance system has also been grafted onto Korea's traditional seniority wage system. The performance-based annual pay system was introduced after 1997 financial crisis. The adoption rate of performance-based annual pay was 1.6% in 1996. However, after the 1997 financial crisis, it increased sharply to 23.0% in 2000 and to 66.7% in 2012. From 2001, the Korean government also recommended firms to introduce a peak-wage system, where an employee's wage is adjusted downward starting from a certain age in exchange for guaranteed employment until retirement. The adoption rate of this peak-wage system increased from 2.3% in 2005 to 16.3% in 2012.[23] Even though the performance-based annual pay system and the peak wage system did not replace the traditional seniority wage system, they significantly reduced the impact of tenure on the earnings of workers. The data from the Basic Survey on Wage Structure shows that in 1980, the wage of individuals whose job tenure was above 12 years, was 3.26 times that of those with less than one year of job tenure. By 2011, the wage gap between the two groups was reduced to 1.95. This change in job tenure-earnings profile shows that seniority wage system has weakened substantially for the period 1980-2011 (see Table 4.12).

In Japan, flexibilization of the labor market happened during the 'Lost Decade' of the 1990s. The demise of lifetime employment and the seniority wage system which characterized Japanese industrial relations started with the 1985 Labor Dispatching Law, which legalized temporary agency labor for specific occupations such as project-based work and temporary staffing. Revisions of the law in 1996 made it easier to use agency labor by expanding its range of applications. This reform was followed by the revision of

Table 4.12 Change in Job Tenure-Earnings Profile in Korea: Between 1981 and 2011

Job Tenure	*1980*	*2011*
0–1 Year	100.0	100.0
1–3 Year	122.4	110.2
3–6 Year	158.5	128.9
6–9 Year	212.4	143.4
9–12 Year	271.3	157.6
12+ Year	326.1	195.4

Source: Basic Survey on Wage Structure (Raw Data), Ministry of Employment and Labor.

the Labor Standards Law in 1998, which allowed multi-year fixed contracts as an alternative to traditional indefinite contracts. A 2003 revision of the Labor Dispatching Law further flexibilized the Japanese labor market by lifting the prohibition on the use of agency labor in the manufacturing industry, while at the same time extending the maximum employment period of agency workers from one year to three years. The implementation of these various reforms is associated with a decrease in the proportion of regular employees in firms from 82% in 1991 to 63% in 2014. Meanwhile, the share of non-regular employees[24] increased from 18% to 37% in the same year. Non-regularization of employment is now one of the main features of Japan's changing labor market, with large firms relying much more on numerical flexibility, than on functional flexibility.[25]

As corporate governance in Japan moved toward a market-oriented model that pursued the maximization of shareholder value to achieve short-term performance, lifetime employment began to shrink. According to the estimation of Hamaaki et al (2012), the proportion of workers with lifetime employment (for university graduates) in large firms decreased considerably from 65.8% in 1995 to 47.5% in 2008 in 25–29 age group. (see Table 4.13). For 30–34 age group, it decreased from 56.2% in 1995 to 40.3% in 2008.

Table 4.13 Lifetime Employee Share in Large Japanese Firms: For University Graduates

Age	*1995*	*2000*	*2005*	*2008*
25–29	65.8	55.9	50.8	47.5
30–34	56.2	59.7	47.1	40.3
35–39	52.7	53.3	57.9	49.9
40–44	54.0	53.9	50.7	51.0
45–49	55.9	50.7	48.4	52.5
50–54	52.3	55.9	47.0	43.1

Note: Unit: %.

Source: Hamaaki et al (2012), p.838, Table 3.

This shows that the decline of lifetime employment is prominent in the youth. It is remarkable that the share of lifetime employment decreased considerably from 52.3% to 43.1% in the age group 50–54. Kambayashi and Kato (2011) provide more evidence through their cohort analysis that job retention rates for regular employees fell significantly from the late 1990s, particularly among female workers and mid-career hires. Male regular employees who were new graduate hires enjoyed traditional lifetime employment. The biggest losers appeared to be female regular employees aged more than 30 years with relatively short tenures in large firms. Hamaaki et al (2012) also found a decline in the five-year job retention rate for educated young workers. For example, five-year job retention rate for university graduates aged 20–24 declined from 71.9% to 54.0% in 2003–2008. The widely observed drop-out of young workers from the lifetime employment system suggests that it has started to degenerate (Isogai, 2012). In addition to the presence of an inter-generational gap in terms of lifetime employment, younger Japanese job seekers also have more trouble getting their foot in the door, with new graduate hire rates decreasing from 64.1% in 1977 to 52.3% in 2007 (see Table 4.14). Table 4.14 shows the weakening of the internal labor market and lifetime employment system in Japan due to decrease in new graduate hire rates and increase in experienced workers' hire rates.

Japan, like China and Korea, also experienced a transformation from a seniority wage system, to a pay-for-performance system. According to the report on the General Survey on Working Conditions in 2005,[26] 53.2% of Japanese companies have introduced pay-for-performance wage schemes. This trend is especially strong among companies with more than 1,000 employees, with 72.4% of them adopting such systems (Conrad, 2010). The proportion of firms that introduced a pay-for-performance system has indeed increased significantly from 15.0% in 1996 to 23.7% in 2007 (Kambayashi and Kato, 2011: 248). The weakening of the seniority wage system can additionally be observed by looking at changes in Japan's job tenure-earnings profile.

Table 4.14 The Change in Hiring Patterns in Japan

	Job Accessions (A)	*New Graduate Hiring (B)*	*Experienced Workers*	*Job Separations*	*New Graduate Hire Rate (B/A)*
1977	4,305	2,758	1,547	1,977	64.1%
1982	5,285	3,772	1,513	2,530	71.4%
1987	6,068	3,422	2,646	2,752	56.4%
1992	6,836	3,850	2,986	2,620	56.3%
1997	7,391	4,480	2,911	3,379	60.6%
2002	7,718	4,391	3,327	4,051	56.9%
2007	7,727	4,044	3,683	3,281	52.3%

Note: Unit: 1,000 persons, %.

Source: Basic Survey on Employment Structures, Ministry of General Affairs, Bureau of Statistics.

Table 4.15 Change in Job Tenure–Earnings Profile in Japan: Between 1979 and 2012

Job Tenure	*1979*	*2012*
0 Year	100.0	100.0
1–2 Year	116.6	105.6
3–4 Year	131.9	114.3
5–9 Year	163.6	127.9
10–14 Year	200.7	150.8
15–19 Year	235.2	171.6
20–29 Year	272.4	207.5
30+ Year	267.3	224.2

Source: Ministry of Welfare and Labor, Wage Census 2012, Wage Survey 1979.

Table 4.15, for example, shows that in 1979, the wage of individuals whose job tenure was above 30 years, was 2.67 times that of workers in their first year. By 2012, this wage gap was reduced to 2.24 times. Hamaaki et al (2012) also found s gradual flattening of the age-wage profile for lifetime employees in the 1990s followed by a kink in the wage slope at around age 40 in 2007–2008.

The most fundamental change in Japanese and Korean labor markets since the 1990s was the weakening of the bargaining power of unions. Union density in Japan declined from 30.8% in 1980 to 18% in 2012. In Korea, union density went down from 19.8% in 1989 to 9.9% in 2011. Decline of union density, decentralization of collective bargaining within enterprise unionism, and weak bargaining power of the labor unions facilitated the flexibilization of the labor markets in Japan and Korea. The demise of Shunto wage settlements[27] in Japan and national-level wage struggles in Korea also weakened the bargaining power of unions through the decentralization of collective bargaining. Among the three East Asian countries, China has the most decentralized system of collective bargaining; its labor unions also have the weakest bargaining power.[28] In these circumstances, labor market flexibilization in Korea, China, and Japan brought about the polarization of labor markets in each country.

Overall trends of regulation on hiring and firing in the three countries seen in Table 4.16. It shows that liberalization of labor markets in terms of hiring and firing was promoted from the late 1990s in Korea and China. Korea strengthened regulation on hiring and firing in the late 2000s in the midst of the 2008 global financial crisis. China has become closer to the US in terms of hiring and firing regulations. In this sense, it can be said that the Americanization of the Chinese labor market began to occur. In Japan, there were not so many changes in hiring and firing regulations in the 1990s. In fact, Japan strengthened regulations on hiring and firing from the late 2000s in the midst of long stagnation. However, there was a significant decline in lifetime employment and rapid non-regularization of employment in Japan

Table 4.16 Changes in Hiring and Firing Regulations in Korea, China, and Japan

	1990	*1995*	*2000*	*2005*	*2010*	*2015*
Korea	3.53	3.53	4.70	4.71	3.76	3.75
China	4.30	4.30	5.10	5.27	5.45	5.76
Japan	4.82	4.82	4.18	4.62	2.97	3.71
US	7.15	7.15	6.65	7.01	6.81	6.91
Germany	3.94	3.94	1.82	2.42	3.01	5.17
Sweden	3.93	3.93	2.18	1.92	2.52	3.84

Note: Lower ratings mean more regulation. Data from Gwartney, J., Lawson, R., Hall, J, Murphy, R. Economic Freedom of the World, 2018 Annual Report.

Source: Kim (2018b: 355, Table 9.5).

in the Lost Decades. In short, flexibilization of labor markets in the East Asian Model can be summarized as follows: shrinking of lifetime employment, weakening of seniority wage system, and rapid growth of non-regular jobs in Korea and Japan, and a shift from the lifetime employment to the fixed-term contracts in China (Kim, 2018b).

4.5 Results of Transformation: Transition or Hybridization?

What were the impacts of the transformations, which included marketization, privatization, liberalization, and flexibilization, on the existing East Asian Model? As we mentioned, transformation of a development model may be either transition to a new model or hybridization within the existing model. Here, we will discuss whether the transformation of the East Asian Model during last two or three decades can be identified as transition or hybridization based on the incremental institutional change approach of Mahoney and Thelen (2010) described in Chapter 3.

As we have seen, some elements of the liberal market economy (LME) or Anglo-American Model were introduced to the East Asian Model. On the one hand, these elements existed alongside the East Asian Model ('layering'). On the other hand, they pushed the East Asian Model to redeploy new goals such as maximizing shareholder value ('conversion'). In terms of corporate governance, the integration of elements of shareholder capitalism in the Japanese Keiretsu, the Korean Chaebol, and Chinese SOEs, are examples of 'conversion'. In this case, the Keiretsu, the Chaebol, and Chinese SOEs partly pursued the maximization of shareholder value at the expense of stakeholders including employees. The results were flexibilization of labor market that accompanied massive dismissal of employees (SOEs in China) and high level of non-regularization of workers (Chaebol in Korea and Keiretsu in Japan). In some cases, pay-for-performance wages system was combined with the lifetime employment system. In other cases, shareholder-capitalism-type corporate governance was combined with lifetime employment. All these show the cases of hybridization in the process of transformation of the East Asian Model (Kim, 2018b).

Japanese corporate system provides a good example of hybridization in the East Asian Model. The financial and ownership characteristics of Japanese firms have substantially moved in the direction of a market-oriented style in the wake of the 1997 banking crisis. At the time, leading Japanese firms reorganized themselves into hybrid organizational forms by introducing a pay-for-performance wage system and market-oriented corporate governance. However, corporate governance reforms had not radically shifted the Japanese firms to the American style of corporate governance that pursue shareholder values and shareholder-oriented management. The change to the corporate governance of Japanese firms had been more partial and more selective (Isogai, 2014). Here, a new Japanese firm as a hybrid model has emerged. Miyamoto (2019) identifies four types of Japanese firms (J-type firms). About 30% of Japanese firms are 'Traditional J-type firms', which retained lifetime employment and a seniority-wage system. On the other side of the spectrum, 18.2% of Japanese firms are American-type ('A-type firms'), which adopted shareholder-oriented management and abandoned lifetime employment. 39.7% of Japanese firms can be classified as 'New J-type firms', which introduced a pay-for-performance wage system but kept lifetime employment. The remaining 12.2% of Japanese firms are categorized as 'Declining J-type firms', as they axed lifetime employment. Here, 'New J-type firms' are hybrid firms. Jackson (2009) further breaks down Japanese hybrid firms into two types. Type I hybrid firms combine market-oriented finance and corporate governance with lifetime employment, while Type II hybrid firms combine relationship-oriented finance and corporate governance with market-oriented employment and incentives. Jackson argued that Type I hybrid firms have become the predominant pattern among large Japanese firms (Jackson, 2009). According to these studies, hybrid firms became dominant in Japan. Whether New J-type firms as hybrid organizational forms can be sustained over a long period still remains an open question (Isogai, 2012).

Hybridization also occurred in Korean firms, where a pay-for-performance wage system was introduced alongside the existing seniority-wage system. The share of firms using this hybrid wage system was about 22.6% in 2009 (Bae and Kim, 2012). Despite the introduction of pay-for-performance wage schemes, the seniority-wage system still dominates in Korea. This continued importance of seniority wages is one of the distinctive features of hybridization in Korea when compared to Japan. In China, the very concept of a socialist market economy(SME) is a good example of hybridization. China's gradual approach to the transition from a planned economy to a market economy, which showed a contrast to 'Big Bang' radical transformations in the Eastern Europe and the Soviet Union, generated hybrid forms in corporate, financial, and labor sectors (Kim, 2018b). While a seniority-wage system prevailed before reform and opening in 1978, pay-for-task and pay-for-skill schemes became dominant in SOEs from that point on, with a pay-for-performance system that was introduced as a secondary determinant of wages for senior and middle management.

When considering overall trends of marketization, privatization, and liberalization in the East Asian Model, we can conclude that the hybridization between the coordinated market economy (CME) and the liberal market economy LME in Japan, the regulated market economy (RME) and LME in Korea, and the socialist market economy (SME) and LME in China, have in the last two to three decades progressed to different degrees. Table 4.17 and Figure 4.5, for example, show that the public sector was marketized the most in Korea, and the least in Japan by 2015. Among three countries except the US, China, has the most flexibilized labor market, while Japan's labor market is the most rigid by 2015. Finally, capital liberalization index reveals that Korea liberalized capital much more than the US by 2015, not to mention China and Japan where capital liberalization is very low. Of particular note is the gap between Korea and the other East Asian countries when it comes to capital liberalization. This trend was set at the time of the 2008 global financial crisis, during which Korea was the country to implement the least amount of capital controls, making it even more liberalized than the US. Moreover, when we see the changes in labor sector between 1990 and 2015, China liberalized labor market significantly, while Japanese labor market became rigid greatly. In China, there was remarkable mismatch between change in labor market and change in capital market during 1990–2015. In spite of the regulation on capital market was greatly strengthened, labor market was much flexibilized. In contrast, the regulation on both labor market and capital market was strengthened greatly in Japan. When we observe these changes through Figure 4.5 that shows the extent of the mismatch among four sectors, the mismatches in all three countries increased between 1990 and 2015. According to the institutional complementarity hypothesis as described in Chapter 3, these mismatches might pose a serious obstacle to economic efficiency in the East Asian Model.

Table 4.17 Indicators of Transformation in the Japan, Korea, and China Models

	Korea		*China*		*Japan*		*US*	
	1990	*2015*	*1990*	*2015*	*1990*	*2015*	*1990*	*2015*
Size of government	6.49	6.86	3.65	5.06	5.83	4.56	6.71	6.40
Credit market liberalization	8.33	9.32	0.00	7.33	8.22	8.31	9.64	9.34
Labor market flexibilization	3.59	3.75	3.16	5.76	7.20	3.71	7.68	6.91
Capital liberalization	7.42	6.15	2.72	0.77	8.74	0.77	8.74	3.85
Average	6.46	6.52	2.38	4.73	7.50	4.34	8.19	6.63

Source: Gwartney et al. (2012).

<1990>

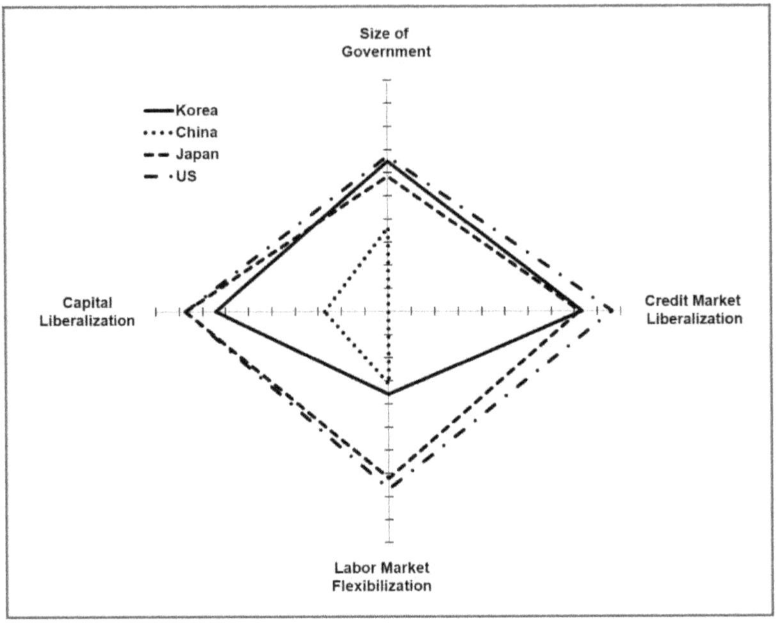

<2015>

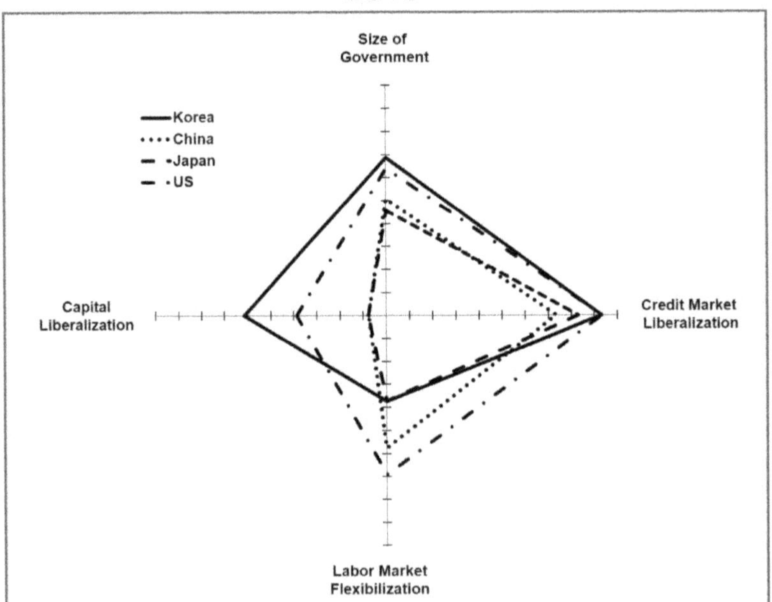

Figure 4.5 Transformation in Korea, China, and Japan Model: 1990 vs. 2015

Notes

1 Lewis turning point is a turning point from which the unlimited supply of labor is shifted to the limited supply of labor. It represents the structural change in the labor market in the course of economic development under the dual structure of national economy (Lewis, 1954).

2 Minami Ryoshin concluded that the turning point in Japanese economy reached by 1960 (Minami, 1968).

3 Prime Minister Koizumi Junichiro (2001–2006) pursued typical neoliberal reform such as deregulation, tax cuts, and privatization.

4 After the Democratic Party of Japan (DPJ) became the ruling party in 2009, it implemented the democratic reforms such as provision of free public schooling through high school, increased child allowance, and fostering green industry and green jobs. However, DPJ's most policy promises were not implemented by the end of 2012 when the party exited from power (Kusida and Lipsey, 2013).

5 Abenomics is an economic policy package introduced by Prime Minister Abe Shinzo. It is based upon so-called three arrows of monetary easing, fiscal stimulus, and structural reforms.

6 Bai Moo-ki concluded that the Korean economy was reached the Lewis turning point by 1975 (Bai, 1982).

7 The decrease in net foreign debts from 1986 definitely showed the signal of the decrease in economic dependency in Korea who suffered from rapidly increasing foreign debts during the industrialization period since 1960s.

8 After Deng Xiaoping's south tour in 1992, China's economic reforms regained momentum that reversed a serious setback from 1989 to 1992. China introduced even more comprehensive economic reforms from 1992 to 2001.

9 There were three stages in the transformation of the Chinese economy: (1) The first wave of economic reforms which included introduction of markets and contracts on the top of the existing institutions and competition by entry and no privatization (1978–1992); (2) The second wave of economic reforms which contained strengthening of market economy institutions, beginning of privatization, downsizing SOEs, and diversification of ownership (1993–2001); and (3) Accession to WTO which included large openness to FDI and trading market access for technology (2001–2010) (Boyer, 2012: 186).

10 It lasted from the First Five-Year Economic Development Plan (1962–1966), to the Sixth Five-Year Economic Development Plan (1987–1991).

11 While political democratization demands the protection of human rights, economic liberalization argues the protection of property rights. There is fundamental conflict between human rights and property rights. Therefore, there is inherent mismatch between political democratization and economic liberalization.

12 The Big Bang approach refers to mass privatization of state enterprises as quickly as possible. For example, in 1992, one year after the dissolution of the USSR, Russia implemented Big Bang privatization reforms. By July 1994, 14,000 state enterprises (70% of Russian industry) had been transformed into joint-stock companies (Blasi et al, 1997).

13 The Economic Freedom of the World (EFW) measure is an effort to identify how closely the institutions and policies of a country correspond with the ideal of a limited government, where the government protects property rights and arranges for the provision of a limited set of 'public goods' such as national defense and access to money of sound value, but little beyond these core functions. The degree of economic freedom is measured in five broad areas: size of government, legal system and property rights, sound money, freedom to trade internationally, and regulation. In order to receive a high EFW rating, a country must provide secure protection of privately owned property, even-handed enforcement of

contracts, and a stable monetary environment. It also must keep taxes low, refrain from creating barriers to both domestic and international trade, and rely more fully on markets rather than government spending and regulation to allocate goods and resources. In many ways, a country's EFW summary rating is a measure of how closely its institutions and policies compare with the idealized structure implied by standard textbook analysis of microeconomics (Gwartney et al, 2013: 2). Therefore, the Economic Freedom Index is just a measure of the liberal market economy or economic liberalization. Even though there are critics that the dataset of Economic Freedom Index has ideological bias toward the neoliberalism, the dataset provides useful information about the extent of government intervention in each country.

14 The index of government size measures the degree to which a country relies on personal choice and markets rather than government budgets and political decision-making. Therefore, countries with low levels of government spending as a share of the total, a smaller government enterprise sector, and lower marginal tax rates, earn the highest ratings in this area.

15 Other causes of the asset bubble were as follows: easier money conditions following the Plaza Agreement in 1985, overconfidence about the outlook for the Japanese economy, poor credit risk management by banks, and weak prudential regulation (Takahashi, 2012).

16 There was the end of Five-Year Economic Development Plan in 1993. Instead, The Five Year Plan of New Economy(1993-1997) was introduced, the core of which was to strengthen free market mechanisms by relaxing or repealing regulation and promoting incentive and participation. This meant the abandonment of industrial policy.

17 The core contents of the amendment of Bank of Korea Act in December 31, 1997 was that top priority goal of the Bank of Korea should be price stability with guaranteeing the independence and neutrality of Bank of Korea.

18 The survey by Kagono et al. (1983) was conducted on top 1,000 corporations in the US and Japan.

19 The survey by Nikkei Newspaper Inc. in 1993 was conducted for the top managers of 450 Japanese listed corporations.

20 The securitization of SOEs facilitated the combination of public ownership and market economy in enterprise system and enhanced the flow of funds between money market and the capital market (Yang, 2020).

21 ILO specialists suggested the policy alternatives to realize the portability of social security benefits in China. The points were enhancing the centralized management of social security funds at the national level and eliminating household registration restrictions to allow migrant workers to register in the social security schemes for urban and rural residents at the place of employment (Research on 'Assessing China's social security coverage of non-standard workers, with focus on platform workers, migrants and women and measures to close gaps and improve portability of social security benefits', EU-China Project 'Improving China's Institutional Capacity towards Universal Social Protection').

22 The number of dispatched workers was 4,302 in 1998, and increased to 77,779 in 2009.

23 Data from the Supplementary Survey to the Labor Force Survey at Establishments by the Ministry of Employment and Labor, 2013.

24 68.7% of non-regular workers were part-time workers in 2014.

25 Numerical flexibility means wage and employment flexibility, while functional flexibility means skill upgrading and transfer. Numerical flexibility usually accompanies wage-cuts and lay-offs, while functional flexibility does not.

26 It covered 5,300 companies with more than 30 employees.

27 Shunto has played the role of collective action for wage settlements. However, company performances, rather than social norms, have grown in importance as determinants of Shunto wage settlements. The rise in wage dispersion, especially from the late 1990s, has been caused by converting the goals of Shunto from coordinated pay bargaining, to acquiescing to wage restraint (Yamada, 2000).

28 China's unions in SOEs are relatively strong, but tightly controlled by the government and the CCP, while unions in private firms are weak and fragmented. Thus, the overall bargaining power of Chinese labor unions is low.

5 Growth and Crisis in the East Asian Model

The transformation process of the East Asian Model saw it go through periods of long-term growth and long-term crisis. As we have seen, Japan, Korea, and China experienced two to three decades of high growth. However, the economic miracle that characterized the East Asian Model was followed by a crisis. Japan abruptly entered into its 'Lost Decade' just after the bubble burst in 1991. The stagnation of near zero-growth rates has sustained for two decades thereafter, which was called 'Two Lost Decades'. Korea faced the 1997 financial crisis after 'Golden Age of Korean Capitalism' from 1987 to 1996. After the 1997 financial crisis, Korea experienced two decades of low growth. China also experienced extraordinarily high growth after the reform and opening in 1978. Even though China has since not experienced economic downturn to the same degree as Japan or Korea, the factors of a latent crisis have accumulated under the high growth period. With medium growth, the Chinese economy entered into the so-called New Normal era.

As was described in Chapter 2, high investment was a major factor in high growth in the East Asian Model. Table 5.1 shows that the investment rates, that is, gross fixed capital formation as % of GDP, in Japan, Korea, and China have been higher all the time since 1970. Japan led a high investment in the 1970s, while Korea led a high investment in the 1990s. China began to lead high investment from the 2000s. It is remarkable that China's investment rate was nearly double that of the United States in 2020 and showed continually increasing trend from 24% in 1970 to 42% in 2020. In contrast, Japan's investment rate showed a decreasing trend since 1970 and now close to US's investment rate. Korea's investment rate was in an increasing trend until the first half of the 1990s, but it decreased after the second half of the 1990s. This data suggests that Japan had investment-led growth in the 1970s, while Korea had investment-led growth in the 1990s.[1] China still has investment-led growth with an extraordinary high investment rate of 40% level.

DOI: 10.4324/9781003332725-5

Table 5.1 Investment Rate: Gross Fixed Capital Formation as % of GDP

Year	*Japan*	*Korea*	*China*	*United States*
1970	38	26	24	21
1975	35	27	29	21
1980	34	33	29	24
1985	30	30	30	24
1990	34	37	24	21
1995	31	37	32	23
2000	28	32	33	23
2005	26	30	39	18
2010	23	30	44	20
2015	25	29	42	20
2020	25	31	43	21

Source: OECD, OECD database.

5.1 Growth and Crisis in Japan Model

Japan acted as a first mover among countries adopting the East Asian Model. The growth and crisis in Japan Model can be summarized as the Japanese Miracle in the 1960s and the Lost Decade in the 1990s. After a high growth era in the 1960s and a period of moderate growth in 1970s–1980s, Japan's growth rates plummeted as it entered its Lost Decades in the 1990s–2000s. There was a dramatic change from Japanese miracle to Japanese Lost Decades. Figure 5.1 shows the trend of annual growth rate of investment in Japan,

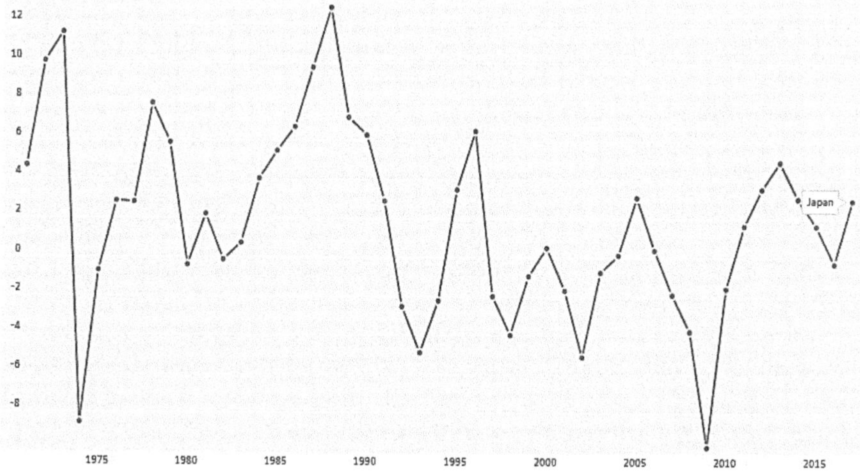

Figure 5.1 Annual Growth Rate of Investment in Japan

Note: Investment growth = growth rate of gross fixed capital formation.

Source: OECD, Economic Outlook (2020).

Table 5.2 Potential Growth Rate Trends in Japan

Fiscal Year	*Potential Growth Rate*	*Total Factor Productivity*	*Capital Stock*	*Hours Worked*	*Number of Employed*
1983–1990	3.98	1.31	2.21	−0.27	0.75
1991–2000	1.79	1.07	1.11	−0.58	0.18
2001–2010	0.77	0.98	0.20	−0.34	−0.09
2011–2017	0.68	0.53	0.09	−0.22	0.28

Note: For example, the 1983 fiscal year is from the second quarter of 1983 to the first quarter of 1984.

Source: Research Data, Bank of Japan, 2018.

which has been severely fluctuated since the 1970s. The figure vividly highlights the Japanese boom-bust cycle, in which the boom begins in the early 1980s and the bust breaks out in the late 1980s. In the bust, the investment rate plunged to −5% level in 1993. The bubble created during the 1980s collapsed abruptly. Thereafter, the long recession of the Lost Decade has emerged. The investment growth rate fell even to −10% in 2009. Even though the growth rate of investment recovered up to 5% in 2013, it fell again to zero level. Due to this long-run decreasing trend of investment growth rate, the long-run economic growth rate in Japan showed a downward slope to zero level.

Table 5.2 indicates that Japan's potential growth rates also declined from 3.98% between 1983 and 1990 to 2% in the 'Lost Decade' of 1991–2000 and to under 1% from 2001 to 2017. Table 5.2 additionally reveals that the contribution of capital stock, employee numbers, and total factor productivity to these potential growth rates decreased over the years, while the contribution of hours worked remained negative. The contribution of total factor productivity was relatively high in the whole period, but the absolute level of TFP decreased. Japan's potential GDP growth rate has fallen sharply since 1991, when the bubble burst occurred.

There are different approaches to explain the causes of the Two Lost Decades in Japan. The neoclassical approach explains that the near zero growth was caused by a decrease in TFP and labor input. The Keynesian approach argues that prolonged recession was caused by overinvestment in the 1980s and insufficient demand in the early 1990s. The Regulation approach emphasizes unfavorable institutional conditions and the instability of a growth regime (Uemura, 2012). Since each approach has some explanatory power to the causes of the Japanese Lost Decades, it will be rational to synthesize the three approaches. In this study, we adopt basically the Regulation approach, which focuses on the growth regime in which institutional factors have significant impacts on the growth and crisis in the national economy.

Let's start with the GDP gap, which shows whether the national economy in the situation of inflation or deflation. Actual GDP growth in Japan was lower than the potential growth rate from the 1990s onward. Therefore, GDP gap (actual GDP–potential GDP)/potential GDP) became negative from the

1990s. The phenomenon of deflation sustained in the Lost Decades. The decrease in GDP gap and negative GDP gap was due to a lack of demand. Japan's large negative GDP gap can be explained by deficient demand caused by chronic excess savings (savings rate minus investment rate). At 30% from the mid-1970s onward, Japan's private saving rate was indeed well over private investment rates. The excessive savings rate was further exacerbated after Japan's asset bubble burst in 1991. Especially after bubble burst in 1991, excessive savings have become much more severe phenomenon. Historically, Japanese people's sense of thrift and precautionary motives due to deficiencies in social welfare were the main reasons behind the country's high savings rate. However, chronic excess savings since the mid-1970s are the result of a large decline in private investment caused by the slowdown of the working age population due to low fertility rates, the decline of TFP growth, and excess investment in preceding periods. Specifically, the decline in the growth rate of the working age population reduced the need to invest in capital equipment for new workers.

Moreover, excess investment accumulated in the high growth period from the mid-1950s to the 1960s lowered the rate of return on capital and TFP and reduced investment rates. The gross rate of return on capital in Japan decreased sharply in the late 1960s; it then recovered in the late 1970s but decreased again after the bubble burst in 1991. It was 0.24 level in the late 1960s. However, it was 0.10 level in the late 2000s. In contrast, the capital coefficient (capital-output ratio) increased from under 2.0 level in the early 1970s to 4.0 level in the late 2000s (Fukao et al, 2010). As excess capital stocks had accumulated in the bubble boom during the 1980s, output-capital ratio fell sharply in 1991. Even though there was the scrapping of capital stock in the second half of the 1990s, potential output-capital ratio has been falling continuously (Uemura, 2012). These trends of gross rate of return on capital and capital coefficient show that the efficiency of investment dropped to a very low level. The decline of Japan's private investment contrasted with the increase in corporate savings and decrease in household savings since the 2000s. This gap between corporate savings and household savings widened rapidly, as shown in Table 5.3. Households are traditionally saving units, while firms are investing units. However, this trend was changed after the Lost Decade, with Japanese firms becoming saving units. Such an abnormal situation indicates that firms did not (or could not) invest much, despite having enough reserves for investment. Meanwhile, corporate assets increased rapidly from the 2000s, while the growth of household assets stagnated and finally became negative in 2013.

All the trends described above changed discontinuously when Japan entered its 'Lost Decade'. The roots of the Lost Decade in the 1990s can be traced to Japan's financial liberalization in the late 1980s following the Plaza Accord in 1985, which depreciated the US dollar vis-à-vis the Japanese yen and German Deutsche mark. The ensuing sharp appreciation of yen[2] induced a massive inflow of foreign capital into Japan, which created massive

Table 5.3 Corporate and Household Saving Trends in Japan

	1980	*1985*	*1990*	*1995*	*2000*	*2005*	*2010*	*2013*
Corporate savings*	10,088	12,685	5,530	3,885	18,067	27,969	32,990	31,451
Household savings**	28,093	33,735	35,970	38,722	26,274	4,184	5,673	−430
Change in corporate assets	12,328	14,593	7,866	8,212	29,953	30,579	36,022	34,788
Change in household assets	27,359	32,461	33,314	35,446	23,915	2,747	4,855	−633

Note Unit: Billion Yen.
* Financial corporations are excluded.
** Private enterprises are included.

Source: Cabinet Office, National Economy Accounting Annual Report.

speculation and asset price bubble through expansionary monetary policies of the government. Japanese economy experienced a large speculative bubble in the second half of the 1980s. To restrain massive speculation and curb strong inflation, the Bank of Japan sharply raised interbank lending rates in 1989, which made the bubble burst. The abrupt fall in asset prices and stock prices that followed saw banks record enormous non-performing loans (NPLs) and made firms to insolvent, leading to a contraction of corporate investment and near zero GDP growth. During the Lost Decades, Japan's per capita income and labor productivity declined. In contrast, government debt increased far above the OECD average, going from 60% of GDP in 1990 to 220% of GDP in 2016. Moreover, deflation prevailed from the late 1990s to the mid-2010s, when Japan's core consumer price index (CPI) inflation was either near zero or negative.

Besides financial liberalization, a chronic lack of demand and a long-term decline in productivity were two other major factors that contributed to Japan's Lost Decades. Lack of demand came from underconsumption and underinvestment, as the sharp fall of stock and land prices following bubble burst led to a drop in corporate investment and household consumption. In short, bubble burst decreased aggregate demand. The fact that the negative GDP gap widened after bubble burst was the evidence of deficient in aggregate demand. A long-term decline in productivity, as shown from the trend of TFP in Table 5.2, caused the decline in potential growth rate. During the Lost Decades, wage growth started to fall behind productivity growth and the real wage growth was near zero level and even negative. The aggregate demand remained stagnant due to low wage growth. These long-term declines in productivity and chronic lack of demand meant that there was a crisis in Japan's growth regime via a vicious circle in which low productivity growth led to low wage growth that, in turn, dampened aggregate demand and GDP growth. This resulted in a long stagnation of 'Two Lost Decades'.

A crisis of mode of regulation also caused the Lost Decades. Japan's mode of regulation before the bubble burst was a companyist mode of regulation (Yamada, 1993), which was a long-term trust model that emphasized the pursuit of efficiency through long-term, fixed, and closed relations resting on two pillars (Boyer and Yamada, 2000: 28). The first pillar was a labor-management compromise around employment security through firm's providing lifetime employment. The other pillar was a company-bank compromise around management security through main-bank system. These two compromises gave the accumulation regime a kind of regularity and the sustainability of Japan Model. However, employment security collapsed due to the non-regularization of employees, while financial deregulation weakened management security. Financial liberalization created management insecurity and employment insecurity. As a result, Japanese companyist regulation eroded (Yamada and Hirano, 2012). This created a crisis of mode of regulation in the Lost Decades. Moreover, the erosion of the existing companyist mode of regulation and the absence of a new mode of regulation created a lack of coordination in the financial system. This destabilized the real economy by encouraging risk-taking behavior of the banks and firms and brought about expansion and burst of asset-price bubbles in the second half of the 1980s and the first half of the 1990s. Seen this way, Japan's crisis in the Lost Decades was not a cyclical crisis but a structural crisis and was not a minor crisis but a major crisis. During the Lost Decades, per capita, income and labor productivity declined, while gross government debt increased from 60% of GDP in 1990 to 220% of GDP in 2016. Gross government debt and net government debt were far higher than those of the OECD average. Moreover, deflation prevailed from the late 1990s to the mid-2010s when core CPI inflation was negative or near to zero in Japan.

There was a shift in growth regime in Japan after the Lost Decade in the 1990s. In the 1980s, there was an export-led growth regime with structural compatibility between the organization of large firms, hierarchical subcontracting, and the segmented labor market in the Japanese economy. However, as the structural compatibility deteriorated and the mode of regulation was eroded in the structural crisis of the 1990s, it transformed in the 2000s into an export-led growth regime with heterogeneous structures and regional integration into Asian economies. This heterogeneity, in part, came from hybridization and polarization in terms of institutional and technical changes occurred during the Lost Decade (Uemura, 2012).

Since the crisis in Japan's Lost Decades was the structural crisis of development model itself, introducing Keynesian policies for aggregate demand management, such as low-interest policy, was not sufficient for the Japanese economy to rebound (Boyer and Yamada, 2000: 115). In fact, the near zero interest rate and even negative interest rates by a quantitative easing of the Bank of Japan, which was one of the three arrows of Abenomics, did not have a significant impact on increasing investment in the Lost Decades.[3] Abenomics refers to the economic policies implemented under Japanese

Prime Minister Shinzo Abe that combined political conservatism with Keynesian expansionist monetary and fiscal policies. For example, massive quantitative easing by the Bank of Japan bringing interest rates at or below zero, along with fiscal stimulus, aimed to increase nominal GDP by 3%, real GDP by 2%, and inflation by 1%. However, Abenomics fell short of achieving its growth rate objectives in 2012–2016, although Japan's 1.2% real per capita GDP growth between 2012 and 2016 was comparable to the United States and OECD average (1.3%) over the same period (OECD, 2017b).

During the 'Lost Decades' in Japan, there were a crisis of growth regime and a crisis of mode of regulation. In short, the crisis of the Japanese economy in the 'Lost Decades' was a crisis of the development model itself. It was a major crisis or a structural crisis. As was described above, marketization and privatization of the public sector, liberalization of financial markets, change in the corporate governance system adopting shareholder capitalism, and flexibilization of labor markets transformed Japan Model significantly into Anglo-American Model. Traditional East Asian Model in Japan, that is Japan Model, was undermined during the Lost Decades. In turn, as Japan Model was undermined, the long stagnation for two decades followed. In this respect, it can be argued that the Lost Decades in Japan was the result of departure from the traditional East Asian Model rather than of adherence to it (Chang, 2007: 53).

5.2 Growth and Crisis in the Korea Model

As Figure 5.2 shows, Korea had a very high growth rate of investment during 1960s and 1970s. The average annual growth rate of investment was 21.5% in 1961–1979. After the slump of 1980–1981, the average annual rate of investment growth was 12.9% in 1982–1996. After 1997 financial crisis investment growth slowed down. Thus, the average annual growth rate of investment was 3.6% in 2000–2019. This trend of investment growth from high investment to low investment created the trend of economic growth from high growth to low growth in Korea. Japanese high growth rate in the 1960s (9.44%) was caught up by Korean high growth rate in the 1960s (9.54%). Following Japan, Korea achieved unprecedented high growth rates from the 1960s until the 1997 financial crisis. This is a symbolic record of the Korean Miracle. High economic growth sustained until the 1997 financial crisis. After the outbreak of the 1997 financial crisis, the trend of low growth appeared. Although growth recovered from –5.47% in 1998 to 11.31% in 1999 and 8.92% in 2000, the average growth rate fell to 4.44% in the 2000s and to 3% in the 2010s. 'From miracle to financial crisis' was the defining feature of growth and crisis in the Korea Model.

The structure of growth in Korea changed significantly between the 1970s and the 2000s. For example, the contribution of labor input and capital input to output growth in manufacturing was relatively high until the 1980s. In contrast, from the 1990s, the contribution of TFP to growth predominate,

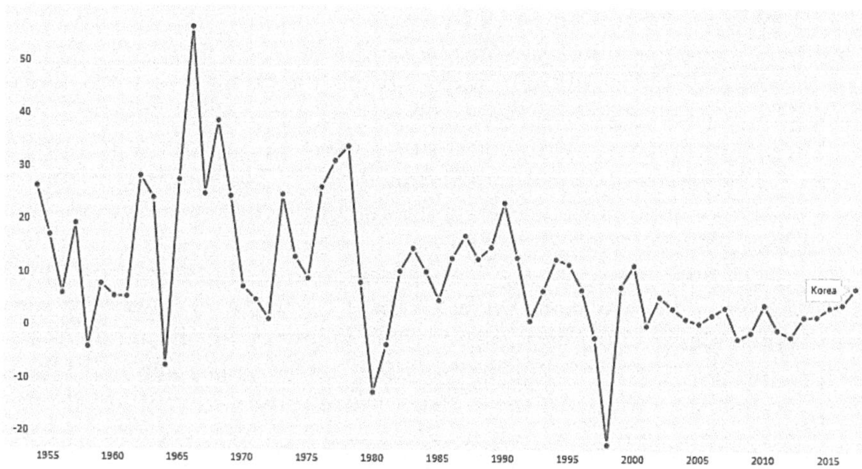

Figure 5.2 Annual Growth Rate of Investment in Korea

Note: Investment growth = growth rate of gross fixed capital formation.

Source: OECD, Economic Outlook (2020).

while that of labor input and capital input became negligible and sometimes even negative. The contribution of TFP to growth was higher than those of capital and labor inputs. Korea's potential growth rate was very high in the 1970s (9.5%), 1980s (9.1%), and 1990s (6.7%), but it decreased significantly after 1997 financial crisis. It was 4.3% in the 2000s. Moreover, as Table 5.4 shows, the potential growth rate declined from 5.0% in 2001–2005 to 3.7% in 2006–2010, 3.4% in 2011-2015, and 2.8% (estimation) in 2016–2020.

Like in Japan, the fall in Korea's potential growth rate was due to the fall of TFP and the growth rate of capital stock. This decline in TFP was partly due to the underdevelopment of service industries, whose productivity relative to the manufacturing sector was 100:46, compared to 100:90 in the OECD. In this context, the movement of workers from manufacturing industries to service industries lowered the TFP of the whole economy. Though Korea's GDP growth has been prominent when compared to the

Table 5.4 Potential Growth Rate Trends in Korea since 2001

	Potential Growth Rate	*Capital Stock*	*Potential Labor*	*TFP*
2001–2005	5.0	2.2	0.9	1.9
2006–2010	3.7	1.8	0.6	1.3
2011–2015	3.4	1.6	0.9	0.9
2016–2020	2.8	1.4	0.7	0.7

Note: Potential labor = (population above 15 years old) × (trend of labor force participation rate) × (1 − natural rate of unemployment).

Source: Kim et al (2017: 24, Figure 8).

OECD average, the slowdown of Korea's economy over the years is clear. This trend is more pronounced when looking at the sharp decrease in Korea's export growth in 2011–2017, which sets it below the OECD average (OECD, 2018a). Investment growth in Korea also slowed after the 1997 financial crisis. The fall of investment growth is partly due to a decrease of returns to capital (Eichengreen et al, 2012). The slowdown of investment growth and deterioration of exports would herald the end of investment-led growth and export-led growth in Korea.

The 1997 financial crisis was the greatest momentum that transformed Korea Model. The two main causes of the 1997 financial crisis were sudden capital market liberalization in 1993 following financial liberalization in the mid-1980s and the retreat of industrial policy through which the government coordinated the investments of private firms. Capital market liberalization and the retreat of industrial policy were promoted by the Korean government's neoliberal policies. In 1993, the Korean government announced the end of the Five-Year Economic Development Plan that has lasted for 30 years. This also meant the end of the industrial policy. Sudden capital market liberalization in 1993 brought about a sharp increase of short-term foreign debts and massive inflows of short-term international capital, or hot money.[4] The retreat of industrial policy facilitated overinvestments and duplicative investments from corporations between 1994 and 1996 (especially in Chaebol firms), which was financed partly by short-term foreign debts. Table 5.5 shows that short-term external debts in Korea increased rapidly just before the outbreak of the 1997 financial crisis. In four years from 1992 to 1996, short-term external debt increased by a factor of 2.5. Financial sector debts also increased by a factor of 2.7. The share of short-term external debts in total external debts was 57.1% in 1996, which was a highly risky position in terms of external debts. This massive inflow of short-term international capital was followed by a sharp reversal of capital flows, which served as the immediate cause of the 1997 financial crisis.

Rodrik and Velasco (1999) define crises as sharp reversals in the direction of capital flows. Specifically, they find that countries where short-term debts owed to foreign banks is greater than foreign reserves have a ten percentage point higher probability of experiencing a crisis than countries

Table 5.5 External Debts before the 1997 Financial Crisis in Korea

	1992	*1993*	*1994*	*1995*	*1996*	*1997*
Total external debts	62.9	67.0	97.4	127.5	163.5	156.2
Short-term external debts	37.0	40.3	53.9	71.9	93.3	63.6
Financial sector debts	43.6	47.5	65.1	89.6	116.5	89.9

Note Unit: billions US $.

Source: Foreign Exchange Regulations and External Debt Division, Ministry of Finance and Economy.

where this ratio (short-term debt/foreign reserves) is below unity. Moreover, Eichengreen et al (2012), which provides the estimates of determinants of capital flow reversals, shows that the share of short-term debt among total debt, short-term debt relative to reserves, and total debt relative to GDP, all is positively and significantly correlated with capital flow reversals. When short-term debt is greater than foreign reserves, foreign banks will be reluctant to roll over short-term loans. And then, there will be a sharp reversal of capital flow. This may cause a financial crisis (Eichengreen et al, 2012: 279). The studies of Rodrik and Velasco (1999) and Eichengreen et al (2012) can well explain one of the main causes of the 1997 financial crisis in Korea.

Another feature of the low growth after the 1997 financial crisis may be partly explained by the slowdown of investment growth. Choi (2006) shows the estimation results of equipment investment function before and after the 1997 financial crisis. From his analysis, two observations stand out. The first interesting observation is that real exports went from being positively correlated with equipment investment before the crisis, to becoming negatively correlated after the crisis. Another noteworthy finding is that the rate of operating profits, which had no statistically significant relationship with equipment investment before the crisis, became positively and significantly correlated after the crisis. These results suggest that corporations no longer had a propensity to invest aggressively without considering profitability after the 1997 financial crisis. The fact that real GDP growth has slowed substantially and that industrial production and exports have stalled in recent years suggest that the Korean economy is entering a period of long-term stagnation like Japan. Figure 5.3 shows that after the 1997 financial crisis, corporate savings begin to be far higher than household savings. The increase in Korean corporate savings caused by low investment while household savings are decreasing further suggests that the Korean economy resembles the Japanese economy since the 1990s. Low investment, increasing corporate savings, and low inflation may be a signal that Korea is falling into a kind of Japanese Lost Decade.

5.3 Growth and Latent Crisis in the China Model

The high economic growth trend appeared in China in the 1980s after 1978 reform and opening. China achieved an unprecedented high growth rate above 10% for two decades in the 1990s and 2000s. The Chinese Miracle emerged in the 1980s following Japanese Miracle in the 1960s and Korean Miracle in the 1970s. However, GDP growth rates slowed to around 7% level in the 2010s and are gradually converging toward that of the OECD average. One of the factors behind China's rapid economic development was an investment, which grew on average at 18.4% between 1980 and 2009, as shown in Table 5.6. Annual average investment growth in 1990–1994 was 32.0%, which is comparable to Korea's high growth rate of investment in the second half of the 1960s. The importance of investment in China is further presented in Table 5.8, where capital input, along with TFP, are the two

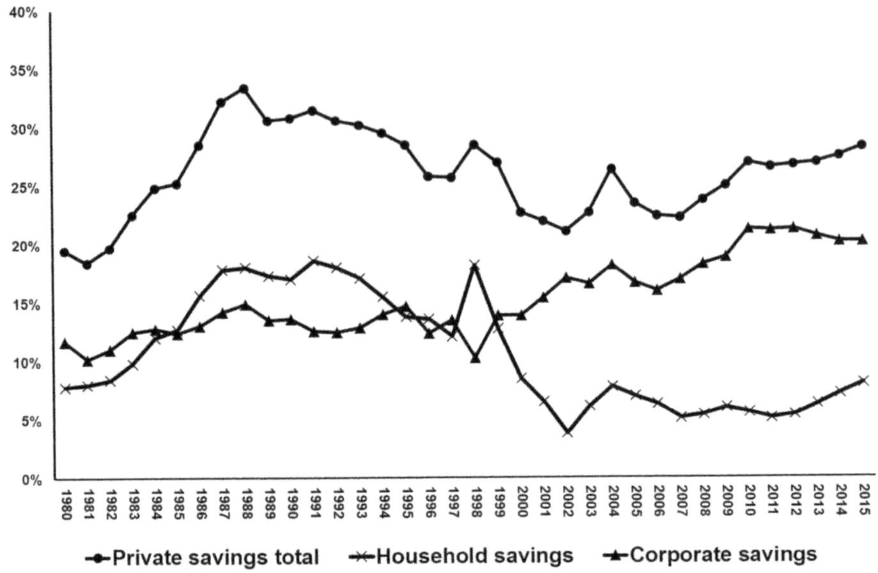

Figure 5.3 Total Private Savings, Household Savings, and Corporate Savings Relative to Nominal GDP in Korea

Source: Bank of Korea, Economic Statistics System.

main sources of economic growth in the country. The contribution of TFP to China's growth rate was negligible in the 1970s. However, it was actually greater than capital and labor input in the first half of the 1980s and became dominant in the first half of the 1990s. This trend reversed from the second half of the 1990s onward, during which the contribution of TFP to growth became secondary to capital input. The contribution of TFP to growth became even smaller in 2010–2015 when the Chinese economy entered into 'New Normal' era (Table 5.7). The recent fall of TFP growth is considered as one of the symptoms of potential crisis of the Chinese economy. Overall, like Korea, China had also an extensive growth regime based on low-wages labor and an intensive growth regime based on technologies.

Table 5.6 Investment Growth Rate in China

Year	*Growth rate*	*Year*	*Growth rate*
1980–1984	13.1	2000–2004	16.9
1985–1989	16.3	2005–2009	19.0
1990–1994	32.0	2010–2014	13.2
1995–1999	13.1	2015–2017	6.1

Note: Unit: Annual Average; %.

Source: China Statistics Yearbook.

With the end of the extraordinary high growth period, Chinese economy had entered 'New Normal' era of slower, more mature, and stable growth as was announced by President Xi Jinping in 2013. China's New Normal is a development model based on the notion of better quality growth with particular emphasis on innovation, services industry, reduced inequality, and environmental sustainability (Green and Stern, 2015). The New Normal of medium growth refers to expectations of a 7% growth rate in the foreseeable future. This slowdown of GDP growth was partly due to a slowdown of investment growth. The average annual growth rate of investment in 2010–2017 was 9.7% and 6.1% in 2015–2017. Under New Normal, priority is on maintaining stable growth with a focus on the quality of growth rather than the speed of growth and ensuring ample employment while pursuing reforms. The policy paradigm of the New Normal was supply-side structural reform. The main goal of the supply-side structural reform was the new growth driver under the New Normal. Reducing excessive production causing deflation and unsustainable rapid growth was another goal of supply-side structural reform. China did not experience the apparent crisis like Japanese Lost Decade and Korean financial crisis. However, it was widely recognized that China has accumulated the factors of crisis latent in corporate and banking sectors.

The causes of China's growth slowdown since the 2010s can be identified from the supply side and from the demand side. Causes from the supply side include excess capacity, the decrease in labor supply due to aging, declining TFP, energy constraints, and environmental concerns. Among these factors, the decrease in TFP from 4.2% in 2005–2010 to 2.0% in 2010–2015 might be the most important element behind China's growth slowdown (see Table 5.7). Causes from the demand side include the slowdown of export growth, the limits of export-led and investment-led growth, and severe income polarization. After the end of the 1990s, maintaining aggregate demand at a level that fully utilizes China's labor force and industrial capacity became an increasing challenge (Perkins, 2013: 163). An atomistic competition or even cut-throat

Table 5.7 Sources of Economic Growth in China

	Capital	*Labor*	*TFP*	*Output*
1970–1975	4.2	1.4	0.1	5.7
1975–1980	4.1	1.4	0.8	6.3
1980–1985	3.4	1.9	4.8	10.1
1985–1990	4.5	1.3	1.8	7.6
1990–1995	3.7	0.7	7.1	11.6
1995–2000	4.4	1.2	2.6	8.3
2000–2005	5.2	0.9	3.2	9.3
2005–2010	6.4	0.1	4.2	10.7
2010–2015	5.4	0.2	2.0	7.6

Source: Asian Productivity Database 2017, Asian Productivity Organization.

competition in most industrial sectors was the engine for the overinvestment accompanying excess capacity (Song, 2001; Boyer, 2012). For example, the capacity utilization rates for five manufacturing industries (steel, cement, aluminum, flat glass, and shipbuilding) in 2012 were 72%, 73.7%, 71.9%, 73.1%, and 75%, respectively, which are much lower than the world normal 81–82% rate.[5] This excess capacity led producers to drive down prices, which decreased profitability, and made the Chinese Producer Price Index for all industrial products drop below 100 from 2012 onward[6] (Fan et al, 2015).

China's excess capacity also led to a decline in investment efficiency. China's capital-output ratio decreased from the mid-1970s to the early 1990s but increased from the mid-1990s (Holz, 2017). Therefore, return on capital was on a decreasing trend from the mid-1990s. According to Bai et al (2006), the return to capital in China reached the peak, 27.9% in 1993 but decreased to the lowest level 17.5% in 2001. It recovered to 21.0% in 2005. Although capital accumulation still drives growth, the efficiency of investment measured by capital-output ratio has been decreased. Especially in the industrial sector, SOEs account for 38% of total industrial assets in 2017, while their return to capital has been below that of private companies. The return on assets (ROA) of industrial SOEs was 4% in 2017, compared with 10% for private firms. Thus, in order to enhance return on assets, SOE reforms including zombie SOE exits and hardening the budget constraints of SOEs are necessary (Zhu et al, 2019). Productivity-enhancing reforms are thus needed as the population is aging rapidly and the labor force is shrinking both in absolute and in relative terms (OECD, 2017a). Informality in labor and financial markets further hinders productivity growth. The lack of labor contracts[7] and social security contributions by employers to migrant workers encourages high turnover rates, which hampers the accumulation of skills. Informality in the financial sector also hampers productivity. Most Chinese private enterprises have financing constraints due to their alienation from state-owned banks. The high interest rates charged by usury lenders impose significant costs on borrowing firms, which pushes them to chase short-term returns instead of long-term productivity improvements (OECD, 2017a).

The factors of latent crisis in China have been accumulated in the financial sector more than the real sector. Corporate debts, for example, is particularly high when compared to OECD countries and other emerging economies. Between 2008 and 2016, corporate debt rose from less than 100% of GDP to 166% GDP.[8] This rapid accumulation of corporate debts, combined with the slowdown in economic activity and the unorthodox practices of financial institutions,[9] have significantly heightened systemic risks (OECD, 2017a). With the accumulation of corporate debts, NPLs have increased since 2013. In 2020, non-financial corporate debt-to-GDP was 160, while that of Japan and the United States was 116 and 85, respectively. Defaults in China's rapidly developing corporate bond market have also become more frequent. This increase in default scale could trigger massive deleveraging as it exposes the banking sector to liquidity risk, which could trigger a financial crisis in the future.

As the Chinese economy entered its 'New Normal' era, the driver of economic growth in the country shifted from investment to consumption and from manufacturing to services. Consumption as a share of GDP decreased until 2006–2010. The slow increase in consumption rendered China's economic growth dependent on investments and exports, which created external imbalances. However, the share of consumption began to increase between 2011 and 2015, while the share of investment to GDP became smaller, and that of net exports became negligible or negative. Consumption's contribution to GDP growth actually became greater than that of investment from 2015 (see Table 5.8), which suggests that China's growth regime is gradually shifting from an investment-led and export-led model to a consumption-led model. Table 5.8 also indicates that China's shift to a more consumption-led growth pattern is driven by the deceleration in investment rather than by a surge in consumption since the contribution of consumption to growth has been relatively stable over the past two decades (OECD, 2017a).

In the New Normal era, China is trying to establish an innovation-led growth. The Chinese government chose innovation as one of five keywords for the current Five-Year plan alongside coordination, sharing, green development, and opening up. The major policy targets emphasize human capital, financing of innovation, and technological innovation. More attention is being paid to quality and greening (OECD 2017a). The green growth is also being emphasized. Now, China adopted the national agenda of innovation-led growth and green growth as the new drivers of growth.

Table 5.8 Share and Contribution of Investment, Consumption, and Net Exports to GDP Growth

	Consumption		*Investment*		*Net Exports*	
Year	*Share*	*Contribution*	*Share*	*Contribution*	*Share*	*Contribution*
1980	77.3	6.1	20.9	1.6	1.8	0.1
1985	71.1	9.5	79.8	10.7	−50.9	−6.8
1990	91.7	3.6	−74.6	−2.9	82.9	3.2
1995	46.2	5.1	46.6	5.1	7.2	0.8
2000	78.1	6.6	22.4	1.9	−0.5	0.0
2005	54.4	6.2	33.1	3.8	12.5	1.4
2010	44.9	4.8	66.3	7.1	−11.2	−1.3
2015	59.7	4.1	41.6	2.9	−1.3	−0.1
2016	66.5	4.5	43.1	2.9	−9.6	−0.7
2017	58.8	4.1	32.1	2.2	9.1	0.6

Note:

(1) Share refers to the proportion of the increment of each component of GDP by expenditure approach to the increment of GDP.

(2) Contribution refers to the growth rate of GDP multiplied by the share of the three components.

Source: China Statistical Yearbook, 2018.

China has been had a structurally unbalanced growth pattern until 2000s due to decreasing wage share and consumption share of GDP (Boyer, 2012). However, from the early 2010s, wage share and consumption share began to increase, which may be a signal of rebalance of growth pattern (Huang and Lardy, 2016). The unbalanced growth issue has been raised most seriously in China. The problems of unbalanced growth were pointed out as inefficient utilization of resources, excess capacities, widening income gap, unfairness and inefficiency in access to public services, labor and financial market segmentations, severe environmental pollution, and increasing social costs of economic growth (Lu et al, 2013). In order to cope with these problems, Chinese government announced the visions of 'harmonious society' in the mid-2000s and New Normal in the mid-2010s. One of the key elements of these visions was balanced growth beyond unbalanced growth.

Notes

1 It is notable that Japan and Korea had in each period also a wage-led growth.
2 The yen-dollar exchange rate nearly doubled from 238.47 to 144.60 between 1985 and 1987.
3 In standard macroeconomic textbooks, this situation is called a liquidity trap. Paul Krugman argued that Japan's lost decade is an example of a liquidity trap. According to the viewpoint of Regulation Theory, a liquidity trap is a symptom of structural crisis or major crisis.
4 Korea's susceptibility to crises has been associated with its use of short-term bank funding to underwrite extensive investment and aggressively pursue growth (Eichengreen et al, 2012: 279).
5 The total capacity utilization rate in the United States was 80.1% in 2013, which is generally seen as a normal level.
6 This fall in producer prices was especially severe in industries such as iron and steel, chemical fibers, and non-ferrous metals. Profitability measured by return on assets of seven manufacturing industries fell from 2011.
7 60% of migrant workers in China had no contract in 2015.
8 The average corporate debt of OECD countries was 85% of GDP in 2016.
9 Chinese banks are known to channel loans through non-bank financial institutions and then reduce capital requirements by holding the loan on their balance sheet as an 'investment receivable' (OECD, 2015b).

6 Miracle, Crisis, and Transformation of a Developmental State

The Case of Korea

The developmental state in Korea has shown the most dramatic changes since the 1970s when Korea Model as a development model has established. Korea model of industrialization was paid attention for its miracle in the 1970s–1980s, catastrophic crisis in the late 1990s, and rapid recovery from the crisis in the 2000s. This chapter aims to clarify the nature and the causes of the miracle, crisis, and transformation. There were two great transformations in the Korean Model since 1962. The first great transformation began in 1987 with worker struggles, and the second transformation started in 1997 with the financial crisis. Dramatic institutional changes followed by the political and labor struggles in 1987 and financial crisis in 1997 have sequentially brought the great transformations of Korea Model. The Golden Age of Korean Capitalism emerged following the first great transformation and it lasted for a decade (1987–1996). The second great transformation brought about an unsustainable growth regime. The old Korea Model, a Korean-type developmental state model, has collapsed decisively just after the 1997 financial crisis and the growth potentials of the existing growth regime have exhausted. After the collapse of the existing Korea Model, a New Korea Model has not yet established in the last two decades.

6.1 A Developmental State Miracle: Korea's Model of Industrialization

The core elements of Korea Model can be identified as follows: developmental state, developmental dictatorship, export-led growth, chaebol-dominated regime, and Seoul Metropolis-centered development regime. The dramatic rapid industrialization of Korea was possible through some of these elements of Korea Model. A developmental state was one of the most important elements of Korea Model. As was described above, a developmental state is a state type in which a state has intervened in the economy extensively in order to achieve industrialization. Even though a developmental state was common in the East Asian Model, Korea Model was regarded as a typical developmental state model. As we described in Chapter 3, industrial policy in the East Asian Model was that the state, through pilot agencies, directly

DOI: 10.4324/9781003332725-6

controlled and allocated resources to support strategic industries with a high growth potential. Because they enjoyed relative autonomy from the corporate, financial, and labor sectors, Korean bureaucrats could effectively repress rent-seeking activities of powerful private interest groups that were harmful to economic growth. (Lipietz, 1987; Chang, 2007). Alongside investment coordination, infant industry protection, export promotion, and control over domestic financial flows and foreign exchange rates were the other core components of Korea's industrial policy. Korean government practiced price distortion as an industrial policy to protect strategic industries. In other words, 'getting the prices wrong', rather than 'getting the prices right', best describes the Korean developmental state (Amsden, 1989; Perkins, 2013). Pilot agencies of the industrial policy in Korea were the EPB (Economic Planning Board). As a policy paradigm, industrial policy in Korea Model was distinguishable from the other policy paradigms, such as social policy in European Social Model (Rhine Model and Nordic Model), neoliberal policy in Anglo-American Model, and Keynesian policy focusing on aggregate demand management in an interventionist model of the developed countries. Industrial policy in Korea effectively channeled the resources into productive sectors and concentrated the resources to the strategic industries that had high growth potentials. Thus, the success of the industrial policy in Korea has played a great role in achieving rapid industrialization and high economic growth in a short period of time.

The economic growth in Korea was unprecedented in the world economic history. Table 6.1 shows changes in per capita GDP in 12 Western European countries (WECs), Japan, Korea, and China since 1820 (the Industrial Revolution in WECs started largely in the 1760s and ended in the 1830s). Korea experienced nearly no economic growth in the 19th century. Per capita GDP in 1911, which was the year just after the colonization of Korea by

Table 6.1 Changes in per Capita GDP in Major Western and East Asian Countries: 1820–2001

	Unit: 1999 International Geary–Khamis Dollars			
Year	*12 WEC*	*Japan*	*Korea*	*China*
1820	1,245	669	600	600
1870	2,088	737	604	530
1920	3,305	1,696	1,009	-
1960	7,607	3,986	1,105	673
1970	10,959	9,714	1,954	783
2001	20,024	20,683	14,673	3,583

Note: The 12 WECs are: Austria, Belgium, Denmark, Finland, France, Germany, Italy, N. etherlands, Norway, Sweden, Switzerland, and United Kingdom. Unit: 1999 International Geary-Khamis Dollars.

Source: Angus Maddison, The World Economy: Historical Statistics, 2006, OECD Development Centre Studies.

Japan, was $777. This increased to $1,330 in 1944, the year before the end of Japanese rule. Growth in this period is sometimes known as 'colonial industrialization', which largely benefited Japan. It can be argued that there was the first industrialization in Korea under Japanese rule. Just after liberation in 1945, per capita GDP decreased to $616. And it increased to $770 in 1950, following mass destruction during the Korean War (1950–1953). In 1960, before the second industrialization, per capita GDP was $1,105.

Dramatic industrialization in Korea only happened after 1962 with the start of the First Five-Year Economic Development Plan. According to the data of Maddison (2006), per capita GDP in Korea increased from $1,105 in 1960 to $14,673 in 2001. In comparison, it took 162 years for similar increases in per capita GDP (from $1,245 in 1820 to $14,728 in 1984) in the 12 WECs and 90 years (from $1,119 in 1894 to $14,773 in 1984) in Japan. Korea's ability to have a 'compressed growth' and achieve similar economic gains in just 41 years thus deserves to be called a 'miracle'.[1]

The growth regimes that made Korea's economic miracle possible were multiple. They can be characterized as an export-led growth regime, an extensive growth and intensive growth regime, and a catching-up growth regime. Export-led growth regime was based on a macroeconomic circuit of 'mass production-high productivity-low wages-mass exports'. Key to this macroeconomic circuit was Korea's high savings and investment rates above 30% level (see Table 6.2), which were mobilized toward mass production. Total savings rate and total investment rate reached peak of 39% level. After 2000, while saving rates sustained at 35% level, investment rate began to decrease. Because consumption was repressed due to low wages, mass production was sustained through mass exports. These mass exports helped Korean firms realize economies of scale, with productivity being further enhanced via imported technology and learning. Together, high productivity and low wages greatly reduced unit labor costs, which allowed Korea's export goods to be priced competitively (Kim, 2012).

Another feature of Korea's growth regime was extensive growth and intensive growth. Extensive growth is achieved by using more inputs of capital and labor without technical progress, while intensive growth is realized through

Table 6.2 Savings Rate and Investment Rate Trends in Korea

Year	*Total Savings Rate*	*Total Investment Rate*
1960	8.1	9.7
1970	21.0	25.7
1980	25.4	34.6
1990	39.3	39.5
2000	34.4	33.2
2010	35.0	32.1
2015	35.4	28.5

Source: Bureau of Statistics, National Statistics Portal.

technical progress. For economists such as Paul Krugman, economic growth in East Asia has mainly been a matter of perspiration rather than inspiration (Krugman, 1997). Indeed, because Krugman thought workers in East Asian countries worked harder, not smarter, he attributed high economic growth in the region to extensive growth rather than intensive growth. However, this is not true of Korea, at least. While there was a 'long hour-high effort' work system in Korea, the production system in Korea realized high productivity through technical progress. Thus, the growth regime of Korea can be identified as 'extensive growth and intensive growth'. The analysis of TFP in Korea indicates that Paul Krugman's 'perspiration theory' is not true. As the growth accounting in Table 6.3 shows, Korea's economic growth originated not only from factor inputs (TF Input) but also from resource reallocation, economies of scale and technical progress[2] (TFP). Specifically, the share of TFP's contribution to GDP growth increased from 35.8% in 1970–1980 to 62.6% in 2000–2010. The share of technical progress' contribution to GDP growth increased as well, going from 9.6% in 1970–1980 to 40.7% in 1990–2000 and 28.2% in 2000–2010. It is evident from the growth accounting that an intensive growth regime dominated from 2000 to 2010 in the Korean economy.

Catching-up growth also characterized the Korea Model. Catching-up growth occurs when economic growth in a following country is achieved by catching-up with the technology of a leading country. Figure 6.1, for example, presents the trajectories of catching-up growth in East Asia, with Japan nearly catching-up with the United States before the Lost Decades, Korea closing the gap with Japan, and China converging slowly toward Korea. As in many states, transfer of technology from the leading country, technological assimilation by learning, and the development of new technologies through R&D investment all contributed to Korea's catching-up growth. Korea's catching-up can further be seen by looking at its very high growth rates, as shown in Table 6.4. Korea's rapid catching-up was indeed possible because per capita GDP growth rate (7.14%) during the country's high growth period

Table 6.3 An Analysis on Factors of Economic Growth in Korea: 1970–2010

	1970–1980	*1980–1990*	*1990–2000*	*2000–2010*
Growth Rate (%)	**7.8**	**9.3**	**5.8**	**4.6**
TF Input (% p)	**5.0 (64.2)**	**5.1 (54.7)**	**3.0 (51.7)**	**1.7 (37.4)**
Labor	3.1 (40.2)	3.4 (36.8)	1.8 (32.0)	1.0 (20.9)
Capital	1.9 (24.0)	1.7 (17.9)	1.1 (19.7)	0.8 (16.4)
TFP (% p)	**2.8 (35.8)**	**4.2 (45.3)**	**2.8 (48.3)**	**2.9 (62.6)**
Resources Reallocation	0.7 (8.7)	0.2 (2.4)	−0.6 (−10.8)	0.8 (16.5)
Economies of Scale	1.4 (17.5)	1.8 (19.6)	1.1 (18.5)	0.8 (18.0)
Technical Progress	0.7 (9.6)	2.2 (23.4)	2.3 (40.7)	1.3 (28.2)

Note: The number in parenthesis is share of each item's contribution to GDP growth.

Source: Kim et al (2012: 147, Table 7.6 (restructured)).

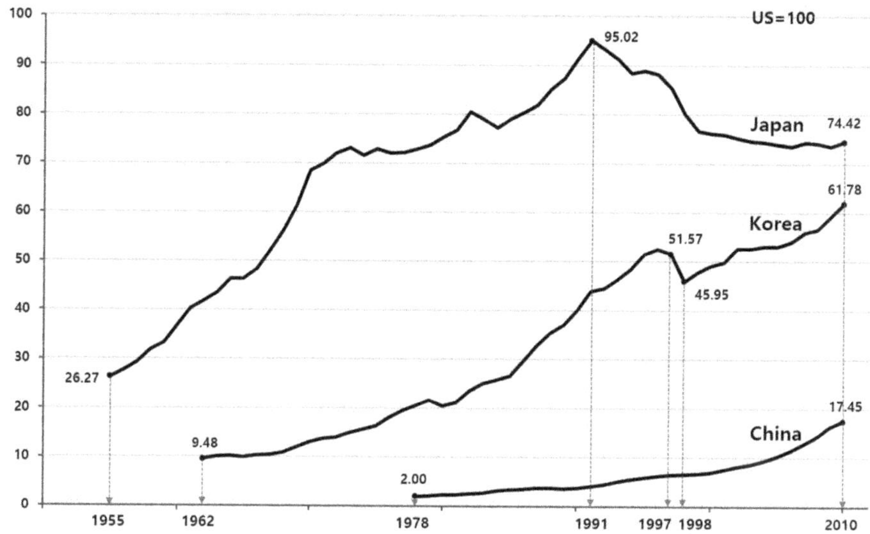

Figure 6.1 Catching-up Growth in Korea, China, and Japan

Source: Heston et al (2012).

(1965–1997) was much higher than that of Japan (5.12%) when it had its economic boom (1961–1990). Generally, catching-up growth slows down as an economy nears the technological frontier set by advanced countries. The recent slowdown of growth in Korea is partly attributable to the exhaustion of catching-up growth.

6.2 Dramatic Changes in the Korean Model: Miracle, Crisis, and Transformation

Seven major turning points in the history of Korean capitalism can be identified since the start of the industrialization process in 1962, the starting year of the First Five Year Economic Development Plan. The first turning point occurred from the late 1960s to the early 1970s, when major Chaebol firms emerged as conglomerates. This advent of Korean monopoly capitalism can

Table 6.4 Per Capita GDP Growth Rates in Japan, Korea, and China

Country	*Period*	*Annual Growth Rate*
Japan	1961–1990	5.12 %
Korea	1965–1997	7.14 %
China	1978–2012	8.83 %

Source: World Bank Database.

Table 6.5 Market Concentration Ratio of Top Five Corporations in Korea

Year	*Beverages*	*Industrial Machinery*	*Primary Metal Products*	*Petroleum and Coal Products*
1960	25.4	30.5	31.5	5.4
1963	36.3	30.9	20.8	13.5
1966	47.2	50.3	43.5	52.6
1968	72.6	45.0	68.4	72.6
1973	81.9	70.1	74.3	77.1
1978	76.5	69.6	62.0	73.8
1983	62.9	61.2	69.1	90.5

Note: Unit: %.

Source: Kim (1988), p.183, Table 25 (reconstructed).

be seen by looking at the market concentration ratio of the top five corporations (CR_5) in four industries (beverages, industrial machine, primary metal products, and petroleum and coal products), which reached about 70% between the late 1960s and early 1970s (see Table 6.5).

The second turning point in the history of Korean capitalism occurred in 1972–1973 with the establishment of a developmental dictatorship[3] and the growth of heavy industry. Korea's strategic export industries at the start of its industrialization process were in labor-intensive sectors such as textiles and garments. The 1970s, however, saw Korea's industrial policy focus toward heavy industry, chemicals, and electronics. To promote these sectors, capital accumulation through high savings and investment by Chaebol firms was actively promoted by Korea's authoritarian government. This push by Chaebol firms and the Korean government to develop more value-added manufacturing contributed to high sustained growth for two decades.

Korea's third turning point came in 1975–1976 with epoch-making changes in its labor market and production systems. Around 1975, Korea reached the Lewis turning point, which marks a shift from an unlimited supply of labor to a limited supply of labor (Bai, 1982). These changes in labor market emerged from the increasing demand for labor by rapid industrialization. After Lewis turning point around 1975, Korea experienced a relative labor shortage and thus saw an increase in real wages. In 1976 Hyundai Motors introduced a mass production system based on a Fordist labor process, where assembly line with a conveyer system speeded up the work of operatives and greatly enhanced labor productivity. This system of mass production enabled the Korean automobile industry to achieve mass export of cars, which fueled high economic growth starting in the late 1970s.

A fourth turning point occurred in 1985–1986 when Korea's economic dependency began to decrease and trade liberalization started to take place. During the initial stages of its industrialization, Korea was dependent on foreign financing, foreign technologies, and international subcontracting to export its goods. This financial, technological, and commercial dependency

Table 6.6 Korea's Current Account and Foreign Debts in the 1980s

Year	*Current Account*	*Total Foreign Debts*	*Net Foreign Debts*	*Debt Service Ratio*
1980	−69	272	196	18.5
1981	−65	324	245	20.1
1982	−56	371	283	20.1
1983	−36	404	309	18.8
1984	−18	431	329	20.1
1985	−22	467	355	21.7
1986	26	445	325	22.6
1987	86	356	224	30.8
1988	128	312	73	14.1
1989	38	294	30	10.9

Note: Debt Service Ratio is the ratio of a country's debt service payments (principle + interest) to its export earnings.

Source: Bank of Korea, Economic Statistics System, Byun (1995: 484, Table 11.8).

led to huge foreign debts and current account deficits. Korea's economic catching-up, however, helped it record a current account surplus for the first time in 1986, as shown in Table 6.6. Korea's total and net foreign debts, as well as its debt service ratio, also decreased in the late 1980s. These data suggest that the risk of debts crisis in Korea reduced significantly. It is under these new economic conditions that the Korean government began to liberalize foreign trade in 1986. The decrease in foreign debts was an epoch-making signal that Korea has escaped from the trap of vicious circle of dependency on the foreign debts. From the dependency theory, there has been a notion that foreign debts bring about the foreign debts, and thus, inflow of the foreign debts ends in the fall of an underdeveloped country. Contrary to the dependency theory's prospects of the eventual debts crisis, such as Frank (1966) and Amin (1976), Korea jumped into a developed country from a poor underdeveloped country once highly dependent on the foreign debts. This deserves to be called a miracle.

Korea's fifth turning point came in 1987 with the collapse of the developmental dictatorship following the June civil protests and the democratization of industrial relations following the July/August workers' struggles. The impact of this turning point was so strong that it accompanied the first great transformation in Korean capitalism in terms of the politics and the economy. The process and consequences of the fifth turning point will be specified in detail when we discuss the first great transformation later.

A sixth turning point, in fact, occurred in 1993, when the government gave up industrial policy and introduced a rapid financial liberalization program. These reforms included the deregulation of interest rates, the abolition of policy loans, the granting of more managerial autonomy to banks, the reduction of entry barriers to the financial industry, the liberalization of foreign exchange, and the opening of capital markets (Chang, 2007). Korea also aggressively removed capital controls on trade financing and short-term borrowing by financial companies. The result of capital market liberalization was a sharp increase in short-term foreign debts and massive inflows of short-term international capital or 'hot money', which eventually led to the 1997 financial crisis (Kim, 2016).

Korea's seventh turning point occurred in 1997 when a financial crisis caused the collapse of the developmental state model and introduced neoliberal policies to the country. The shock of the 1997 financial crisis was so great that it led to substantial changes in the structures of Korean capitalism. This turning point created another great transformation of Korean capitalism.

In sum, Korean economic history since 1962 is characterized by the rise and fall of the developmental state model. There were dramatic structural changes in the Korean economy in less than half a century. Democratization and liberalization were two major engines that have transformed the Korea model of industrialization since the 1960s. Among the seven turning points, two great transformations that had the strongest impact on the Korean economy can be identified. Radical institutional changes followed by political and labor struggles in 1987 and financial crisis in 1997 have sequentially brought the two great transformations. The first great transformation was a shift from a developmental dictatorship to a democratic regime. It is called a period of democratization that started from the 1987 civil protests and workers' struggles. The second great transformation was a shift from a developmental state to a neo-liberal one. It is regarded as a period of liberalization just after the 1997 financial crisis. The decade from 1987 to 1996 can be called as the Golden Age of Korean Capitalism.

The first great transformation saw multiple shifts occur (Kim, 2012). The multiple shifts include a shift from a dictatorship regime to a democratic regime in political arena, a shift from a regulated market economy (RME) to a liberal market economy (LME) in the economic arena, and a shift from an export-led regime to Fordism[4] in the growth regime. From 1962 to 1987, Korea had a RME in which an authoritarian government intervened intensively in the economy. Through the use of instruments such as preferential loans, government intervention facilitated the formation and growth of the Chaebol firms, which became the key players in Korea's export-led growth. Korea's growth regime before 1987 can be described as an export-led growth regime based on mass production, high productivity, low wages, and mass exports. This growth regime was maintained by three pillars: technological dependency through the import of core capital goods and technologies, financial dependency through foreign debts, and commercial dependency through the use of international subcontracting networks dominated by multinational corporations. The labor process model in Korea's export-led growth regime was a kind of Taylorism in that the labor processes were characterized by the separation of conception from execution and hierarchical control over deskilled labor. The labor market was rather flexible. Industrial relations in Korea before 1987 were despotic in that they were militaristic, patriarchal, and paternalistic (Kim, 2003). Labor movements were indeed oppressed by the government, which prohibited rights such as the right to strike and the right to unionize. A flexible labor market, creation of massive labor forces with simple skills, and despotic industrial relations were other important elements that favored the Korean export-led growth regime.

The mode of regulation corresponding to Korea's export-led growth regime is one where developmental dictatorship and market despotism prevailed. Developmental dictatorship implies investment coordination and credit assignment by an authoritarian government as well as statist economic control with extensive administrative regulations on business activities (Lipietz, 1987). Market despotism[5] means disciplinary effects of unemployment on the workers created from eroding of bargaining power of labor unions due to an excess supply of labor, suppression of labor unions, low union density, and lack of a social security system. Both developmental dictatorship and market despotism shaped a mode of regulation that sustained the export-led growth regime. This type of market economy in which developmental dictatorship and market despotism prevail can be defined as a 'regulated market economy'.[6]

Thus, the development model that existed before 1987 can be defined as an export-led growth regime based on a developmental dictatorship and market despotism. The June civil protests and the July/August workers' struggles in 1987 put an end to Korea's dictatorship regime and despotic industrial relations and led to drastic wage increases. The 1987 workers' struggles transformed a low-wage regime into a high-wage regime. On the one hand, high wages gave a shock to the 'mass production-mass export' circuit by lowering price competitiveness. On the other hand, high wages created a new circuit of 'mass production-mass consumption' by shaping a norm of mass consumption. Mass production realized high productivity through economies of scale. High productivity made high wages feasible. The strengthened bargaining power of labor unions with increased union density[7] could transform high productivity into high wages. Here, an institutional factor like the collective bargaining system is exerted. High wages facilitated the shift of the macroeconomic circuit from 'mass production-mass export' to 'mass production-mass consumption'. Thus, the macroeconomic circuit of 'mass production-high productivity-high wages-mass consumption' could be completed. This change suggests that after 1987, the growth regime began to shift from an export-led growth regime to Fordist growth regime.

Korea's shift from an export-led growth regime to a Fordist wage-led growth regime may be an important chapter in the world economic history. Originally, Fordism was a wage-led growth regime found in Western Europe and the United States after the WW II. The virtuous circle of the 'mass production-high productivity-high wages-mass consumption' in the Fordist growth regime sustained a steady high growth from 1945 to 1974. The defining features of Fordism were high investment, high productivity, high growth rates, high profits, and high wages, along with quasi-full employment and a welfare state. Thus, the Fordist era is called the 'Golden

Age of Capitalism'(Boyer and Saillard, 2002). Korea, which had a growth regime akin to Fordist growth regime from 1987 to 1997 was the first country in the periphery of the world system to graduate from an export-led growth model. However, export-led growth did not fully disappear after Fordism emerged. Instead, Korea, spurred by the twin factors of mass exports and mass domestic consumption, combined an export-led growth regime with a Fordist wage-led growth regime.

The decade from 1987 to 1996 can be described as the 'Golden Age of Korean Capitalism' because 'high growth, high productivity, high wages, and quasi-full employment' phenomenon emerged during this period, even though the welfare state was not as mature as it was in Western Europe. As Table 6.7 shows, wage growth during Korea's Golden Age from 1987 to 1996 was higher than labor productivity. The indexation of wages to the labor productivity was one of the main characteristics of the 'Golden Age of Capitalism' (Marglin and Schor, 1990). In contrast, the wage growth was much lower than labor productivity growth both before 1987 and after 1997. Korea was, able to achieve substantial improvements in income distribution during the Golden Age since wage growth has been higher than productivity growth for a decade. High growth with more equity is not only the essence of the Korean Miracle and the East Asian Miracle (World Bank, 1993); but it is also a core feature of the Golden Age of Korean Capitalism. However, after the 1997 financial crisis, the trend of growth rate and income distribution suddenly reversed. Korea experienced low growth and worse income distribution. The Golden Age of Korean Capitalism suddenly ended when the 1997 financial crisis broke out.

Labor market structures in Korea also changed after 1987. The rigidity of the labor market and labor market segmentation by firm size was the most prominent phenomena in the period. The enhanced bargaining power of unions and the formation of an internal labor market after 1987 brought about labor market rigidity. This was especially the case in large firms where unions were strong and where structured internal labor markets existed. Specifically, widening wage and welfare differentials between monopolistic large firms and competitive small and medium-sized enterprises (SMEs) and the blocking of labor mobility from SMEs to large firms led to labor market segmentation by firm size.

Table 6.7 Growth Rate of Real Wages and Real Labor Productivity in Korean Manufacturing Industries

Year	*Growth Rate of Real Wages*	*Growth Rate of Real Labor Productivity*
1980–1986	4.2%	7.4%
1987–1996	9.1%	6.9%
1997–2006	4.1%	8.9%

Source: Korea Labor Institute, KLI Labor Statistics 2007, Ministry of Finance and Planning, Bureau of Statistics.

The second great transformation took place after the 1997 financial crisis, which drastically changed the structure of the Korean capitalism. It was the transition processes from a developmental state to neo-liberal one, from a mass production economy to a knowledge-based economy, and from Fordist growth regime to a hybrid growth regime. The retreat of developmental state and introduction of neoliberal policies such as deregulation and privatization were the most distinctive feature of the second great transformation. This transformation was driven largely by the International Monetary Fund's (IMF) restructuring program such as austerity policies, which struck a decisive blow to Korea's demand-driven Fordist growth regime. The Fordist growth regime, which was based on mass production and mass consumption, was sustainable by Keynesian expansion policies that boosted aggregate demand. However, the Monetarist austerity policy recommended by the IMF undermined the very foundation of the Fordist growth regime. The high interest rates policy especially aggravated the financial and foreign debts crisis of Korean Fordism based on a high-debts model. It also had a destructive impact on the firms and households which were borrowing much from the banks. Numerous bankruptcies occurred because of the high interest rate policy of the IMF (Stiglitz, 2002).

With the decline of the Fordist growth regime, the elements of new growth regimes appeared: a finance-led growth regime and an innovation-led growth regime (Kim, 2012). After the 1997 financial crisis, stock prices began to have a positive correlation with consumption (Choi, 2006). This suggests that the element of finance-led growth regime emerged after the 1997 financial crisis. The information technology that was rapidly introduced to the corporations after the crisis had positive impacts on the productivity growth. And the government actively promoted the start-ups in the venture businesses. The IT industry has risen rapidly under the influences of the New Economy of the United States in the mid-1990s. This helped the emergence of the element of innovation-led growth regime. Thus, the elements of the Fordist growth regime, the finance-led growth regime, and the innovation-led growth regime were mixed to form a hybrid growth regime with neoliberal characteristics.

The economic consequences of the IMF restructuring program during the 1997 financial crisis can be summarized as follows: marketization, liberalization, and monopolization of finance in the financial sector, liquidation of high debts and overinvestment as well as introduction of shareholder capitalism in the corporate sector, flexibilization and polarization of the labor market in the labor sector, and downsizing and privatization of the public enterprises in the public sector (Kim and Kim, 2005). Alexander (2003) shows some economic consequences of the 1997 financial crisis to the corporate sector. The gap between Chaebol firms and non-Chaebol firms in terms of shareholder equity, sales, and profits widened significantly from 1997 to 2001. Meanwhile, the leverage (ratio of liability to assets) of Chaebol firms and non-Chaebol firms decreased sharply from 5.9 to 1.7 and from 5.7 to 0.9, respectively.[8] The ratio of operating income/total assets in Chaebol firms increased from 5.9% in 1997to 6.1% in 2001. The gap in terms of the ratio of operating income/total assets between chaebol firms and non-Chaebol firms significantly widened. Together, these changes suggest the intensification of Chaebol domination and the end of debt-led growth[9] in Korea after the 1997 financial crisis. The 1997 financial crisis also brought about substantial changes to the financial system, investment patterns, and business management. In the financial sector, restructuring is associated with the complete opening of financial markets, the rapid increase in stocks owned by foreign investors,[10] securitization of the financial market, and the introduction of a market-oriented financial system. As for investment patterns and business management, increasing shareholder value became one of the major goals of management. Thus, the tendency of risk-averting management seeking short-term profitability in the investment decisions appeared. The result was a decrease in total investment rate from the 2000s onward, as shown in Table 6.2.

6.3 Transformation of the Growth Regime

The growth regimes that appeared in the process of Korean industrialization over the past 50 years can be summarized as follows: (1) extensive growth, (2) export-led growth, (3) catching-up growth, (4) intensive growth, (5) Fordist growth, (6) finance-led growth, and (7) innovation-led growth. They were major elements of Korean growth regime that appeared sequentially or in parallel since the 1960s. It is very unique in the world economic history that Korea had such a variety of growth regimes within a half-century.

Extensive growth was a growth regime existed at the initial stage of Korean industrialization in the 1960s. It lasted until the mid-1970s. Extensive growth regime, in which economic growth is achieved by inputting more capital and labor without technological process, contributed to achieve high growth in Korea. 'Low wages-long hour' labor regime and low-interest rate regime underpinned the extensive growth regime. Abundant surplus labor forces existed in the rural sector rendered the unlimited supply of labor that sustained low wages-long hour labor regime (Kim, 1988). As rural surplus labor forces depleted after the Lewis turning point around 1975 and real wages started to rise, the extensive growth regime came to an end. Intensive growth regime emerged from the 1980s as total factor productivity became a driver of economic growth. As seen in Table 6.3, the contribution of TFP to GDP growth rate became larger than total factor input from the 1980s. Moreover, from the 1980s, the contribution of technical process to TFP became larger than resources reallocation and economies of scale. Thus, it can be argued that from the 1980s, there was a shift of growth regime from an extensive growth to an intensive growth. However, since the 'long hour-high effort' work system was sustained, extensive growth did not appear completely. In that sense, it can be argued that intensive growth was combined with extensive growth from the 1980s, which was a Korean-specific phenomenon.

Export-led growth has prevailed from the 1970s to the 2000s. The Korean government had pursued import substitution strategies in the early 1960s. However, the government adopted export promotion strategies from the mid-1960s. The government supported the export industries with subsidies and policy loans to the export firms. The strategic export industries in the 1960s were the labor-intensive light industries, in particular textile and garment industries, that had a comparative advantage. From the 1970s, the strategic export industries were heavy and chemical industries such as iron and steel, electronics, shipbuilding, chemical, and automobile industries.[11] Mass export of the products of heavy industries such as automobiles and steel sustained mass production of those products. Thus, export-led growth regime with the nexus of 'mass production-mass exports' was established from the mid-1970s. However, export-led growth regime faced with limitations due to the global depression after the Great Recession in 2008. Depressions in shipbuilding, steel, chemical, and automobile industries in the 2010s due to sharp decrease in exports showed the limitation of the export-led growth regime.

Catching-up growth sustained from 1962 to the 2000s. In the early 1960s, Korea was far from the technological frontier. Thus, Korea could achieve high growth by importing and assimilating foreign technology. The gains from the catching-up growth have been exhausted as Korea was approaching the technological frontier. Almost all the potentials of the catching-up growth were already realized into high growth rate in most Korean industries. The catching-up growth regime cannot become sustainable any longer. This is not only because China is catching-up Korea rapidly and the technological gap between Korea and China is narrowed significantly but also because Korea could not fill the technological gap between Korea and Japan/United States (Lee, 2013). In order to go beyond the catching-up growth, Korea should move 'from imitation to creation'.

Fordist growth, wage-led growth, in other words, appeared after the 1987 workers' struggles. As described above, mass production system introduced in 1976 by Hyundai Motor Company and then spread to other heavy industries. Mass production system, in which a conveyor system was installed and economies of scale were realized, brought about high productivity. Moreover, wage explosion[12] after the 1987 workers' struggles transformed the low-wages regime to the high-wages regime. After the 1987 workers' struggles, the strengthened collective bargaining power of labor unions could index high wages to high productivity. High wages of the working class brought about mass consumption. Finally, mass consumption sustained mass production. The sustained high growth in Fordist growth regime opened the Golden Age of Korean Capitalism in 1987–1996.

Finance-led growth appeared after the 1997 financial crisis when financial liberalization proceeded rapidly. The estimation results of consumption function suggest that the elements of the finance-led growth emerged after the 1997 financial crisis. According to the analysis by Choi (2006), Korea's stock price index went from being negatively correlated with consumption before the crisis to being positively correlated after the crisis. Because a characteristic of finance-led growth is an increase in consumption following a rise in stock prices (Boyer, 2000), this suggests that finance-led growth started to emerge in Korea after the 1997 financial crisis. Moreover, his analysis shows that real wages were positively correlated with consumption before the financial crisis but were negatively correlated after the crisis. This indicates the collapse of Korea's Fordist growth regime, which dominated before 1997.

Innovation-led growth emerged in the early 2000s, just after the recovery from the 1997 financial crisis. The growing importance of IT in Korean corporations can be seen by looking at the increase in the share of the IT industry in equipment investment, which went from 29.6% in 1995–1996 to 37.0% in 1997–2005. The share of the IT industry in Korea's GDP also increased from 3.8% in 1995–1996 to 8.9% in 1997–2005. As information technology spread across the economy, corporations ranging from Chaebol firms to start-ups and venture businesses actively introduced new technologies to improve productivity and gain competitiveness. The corporations including Chaebol firms and venture businesses attempted to achieve technological innovation and organizational innovation. The Kim Dae Jung administration that took office from 1998 to 2002 supported actively the start-ups in venture businesses. Moreover. The Roh Moo-Hyun administration that was in office from 2003 to 2007 promoted the government innovation and a Neo-Schumpeterian regional innovation. In these environments, innovation-led growth emerged in Korea.

6.4 The Consequences of Transformation: Unsustainable Growth

The two great transformations analyzed above had positive and negative aspects. The positive aspects in the first great transformation include the introduction of elements of wage-led growth and intensive growth regime, which are sustainable from the demand side and the supply side, respectively. The negative aspects in the second great transformation include polarization, jobless growth, and poor social investment, which foster unsustainable growth. The old Korea Model, a Korean-type developmental state model, has collapsed decisively just after 1997 financial crisis. However, a new Korea Model has not yet established in the last two decades.

While Korea's per capita income and per capita GDP growth are converging toward the most advanced economies, the country's per capita income is still below the OECD average as of 2020. Korea needs sustained economic growth in order to get the OECD average per capita income. Moreover, the Korean economy has serious sustainability problems characterized by a decrease in growth potential caused by decreasing labor productivity, low fertility rate, jobless growth, polarization, and a deficiency in social investment. Korea's potential GDP growth rate fell rapidly after the 1997 financial crisis, going down from between 7 and 9 percentage points before the crisis to 3 percentage points after the crisis. Since Korea's rapid aging and the lowest fertility rates in the world threatens to shrink the workforce, the potential GDP growth in the future will decrease further.

Increasing TFP as well as the fertility rate is thus essential for sustainable growth. Investment in human resources development and social investment should be substantially increased in order to enhance TFP and fertility rate. Indeed, while the level of R&D investment in Korea is one of the highest in the world, the level of social investment is the lowest among OECD countries.[13] In order to increase public social expenditure as a percentage of GDP, a significant tax increase is indispensable. Especially to increase the top marginal tax rate is needed[14] In addition to taxation, promoting new industries in the age of the Fourth Industrial Revolution through a new industrial policy is also needed. The goal of a new industrial policy should be to enhance the innovation capabilities of firms rather than a direct intervention in resources allocation through subsidies.

Jobless growth is another consequence of Korea's economic transformation. Table 6.8, for instance, shows that employment elasticity[15] in Korea's manufacturing sector became negative in the 1990s. Employment elasticity was also low in other industries, decreasing to near zero between 2006 and 2010. These negative trends in employment elasticity can be explained by Korea's highly capital-intensive or labor-saving production systems. In addition to aggravating unemployment, jobless growth may exacerbate income inequality. Furthermore, the income and consumption losses caused by jobless growth dampen aggregate demand, which jeopardizes the continuing viability of the Korean economy. To stem this threat, job creation has become a top priority in Korea. For a sustainable growth, job-rich growth[16] (International Labor Organization, 2013) is needed. Unlike jobless growth that economic growth doesn't increase or even decrease jobs, job-rich growth increase jobs significantly. For job-rich growth, it is necessary, first of all, to enhance the competitiveness of the SMEs, which account for about 88% of total employment in the country.

Table 6.8 Employment Elasticity Trends in Korea

Year	*All Industry*	*Manufacturing*
1981–1985	0.263	0.398
1986–1990	0.412	0.629
1991–1995	0.308	−0.223
1996–2000	0.449	−0.300
2001–2005	0.316	−0.211
2006–2010	0.009	−0.133

Source: Bureau of Statistics, Survey on Economically Active Population, Bank of Korea, National Income Account.

Alongside jobless growth, polarized growth is one more defining feature of the Korean economy after the 1997 financial crisis. Before 1997, Korea's growth regime had the gains from growth redistributed to the broader people through a trickle-down effect, which resulted in a shared growth. However, the liberalization of financial markets and the flexibilization of the labor market following the crisis have fostered polarization between Chaebol firms and SMEs, between regular workers and non-regular workers, and between Seoul metropolitan areas and the provinces. The dominance of Chaebols in the Korean economy was a major factor that precipitated polarization. Chaebol firms not only enjoyed monopolies in the products markets and factor markets; but they also benefited from fiscal and financial support from the government. The unfair markets and unfair policies contributed to polarization between the Chaebol firms and SMEs. The prevalent rate-cutting practices of Chaebol firms against SMEs, who supply the parts and materials to Chaebol firms, intensified polarization in Korea's corporate sector by transferring surplus from SMEs to Chaebols. According to the OECD (2018a), productivity differentials and wage differentials between firms in Korea are the second largest and largest in the OECD, respectively. These serious productivity and wage differentials between large firms and SMEs contributed to severe polarization among Korean corporations and between members of the country's working class.

Non-regularization of employment amplified polarization within the working class. As shown in Table 6.9, the share of non-regular workers was 35.9% in 2007 and 32.8% in 2016—up from 27.4% in 2002. Non-regular workers are severely discriminated against regular workers in Korea. Hourly wage of non-regular workers was 66.3% of the hourly wage of regular workers in 2016. For dispatched workers, it was just 52.2%. Moreover, Table 6.10, for example, highlights how 43.5% of non-regular workers received social insurance benefits in 2016, compared to 83.8% of regular workers. Table 6.10 also shows how only 41.5% of non-regular workers received a retirement allowance, while 87.8% of regular workers got payments. In social insurance, non-regular workers are discriminated most in terms of National Pension Service, while in corporate welfare, they are discriminated more in terms of bonus payments. The triple discrimination against non-regular workers

Table 6.9 Wage Differentials between Regular and Non-Regular Workers in Korea

Year	*Share of Non-Regular Workers*	*All Non-Regular Workers*	*Fixed-Term Workers*	*Part-Time Workers*	*Dispatched Workers*
2007	35.9%	56.5	64.4	47.1	46.9
2009	34.9%	56.3	65.5	46.8	47.9
2011	34.2%	61.3	69.4	53.9	51.9
2014	32.4%	62.2	64.4	63.0	49.7
2016	32.8%	66.3	66.0	61.9	52.2

Note: Hourly wage of regular workers = 100.

Source: KLI Statistics, Korea Labor Institute.

Table 6.10 Social Insurance and Corporate Welfare Discrimination against Non-Regular Workers in Korea: 2017

	National Pension Service	*National Health Insurance*	*Employment Insurance System*	*Average for Social Insurance**	*Bonus Payments*	*Retirement Allowance*
Total	69.1	74.2	69.6	71.0	70.7	72.6
Regular	85.0	88.4	77.9	83.8	86.2	87.8
Non-regular of which	36.6	45.3	48.7	43.5	39.1	41.5
Part-time	52.4	64.8	69.8	62.3	51.6	59.5
Atypical	20.4	33.3	31.8	28.5	29.5	31.3

*The simple average for the National Pension Service, National Health Insurance, and Employment Insurance System.

Source: KLI Statistics, Korea Labor Institute.

in terms of employment, wages, and social insurance has created a new segmentation in Korea's labor market. In addition to labor market dualism between large firms and SMEs, unequal treatment between regular workers and non-regular workers has contributed to polarization and inequality in Korea. First of all, it is important to reduce non-regular workers. Some of the reasons why employers hire non-regular workers are difficulties for the employers to fire regular employees due to legal strictness as well as persistence of the strong seniority wages system that incurs high wage costs from hiring the regular workers. Therefore, to reduce the overprotection of the regular workers and to reform wage system from the seniority system to pay-for-task or pay-for-performance system are required.

As we have seen, the shift in Korea's policy paradigm from industrial policy through strong government intervention to neo-liberal policy that pursued 'small government' should be ultimately blamed for the polarization. The retreat of the state and the expansion of the market, that is, the reduction of the public and enlargement of the private, was the root cause of the polarization in the country. Besides being economically unsustainable because it shrinks domestic demand, polarized growth may also intensify social conflicts between classes. Realizing shared growth rather than polarized growth has thus become an urgent agenda for Korea. A way Korea can achieve shared growth is to reduce the gap between Chaebols and SMEs. First, the monopolistic domination and unfair privileges which benefit Chaebol firms should be removed. Allowing SMEs to trade with large firms collectively will also prevent considerably surplus transfers from small competitive firms to large monopolistic firms. Because fair competition among economic agents is only effectively realized when the power between traders is equal, Korea's Fair Trade Act should be reformed to legalize the collective bargaining of SMEs with large firms, as is done in Germany.[17] The pursuit of policies to increase the ability of SMEs to innovate is another means to reduce the gap between Chaebol firms and SMEs.

6.5 Prospects for a New Korea Model

The consequences of the great transformations of Korean developmental state were low growth and polarization. Moreover, unsustainable growth regimes have emerged in the transformation processes: jobless growth, finance-led growth, and polarized growth. These growth regimes are economically and socially unsustainable. The old Korea Model collapsed, but a New Korea Model did not emerge as yet. In order to realize a New Morea Model, Korea needs a sustainable growth regime that is job-rich, innovation-led, shared, and low-carbon. A new mode of regulation based on a package of institutional reforms as follows should be set up: welfare state beyond developmental state and neoliberal state, social policy beyond neoliberal policy, new industrial policy for the Fourth Industrial Revolution, stakeholder capitalism beyond shareholder capitalism, combination of bank-based and market-oriented financial systems with prudential financial regulation, flexicurity of labor markets and participatory industrial relations, and strategic opening and capital controls. The establishment of ex-ante economic safety nets (Kaneko, 1998)[18] as well as ex-post social safety net is essential to prevent financial crisis and to realize social cohesion.

Now, Korean economy is confronting a major crisis, that is, a crisis of development model itself. In order to overcome this crisis, Korea needs a new development model or a New Korea Model. Korea needs institutional reforms for a New Korea Model. A new generation of Korean industrialization with a New Korea Model in the age of the Fourth Industrial Revolution will emerge when the country achieves successfully the institutional reforms. The former Park Gun-Hye government had presented an agenda of the creative economy in order to overcome the limit of catching-up growth. Creative economy without economic democracy and welfare state could not solve the problems of low growth and polarization. The former Moon Jae-In government adopted a strategy of 'income-led growth' and 'innovative growth' in order to overcome polarization. The government aimed to achieve 'income-led growth' driven through job creation, especially in the public sector. In addition to expanding public employment, the government attempted to boost household income by sharply raising minimum wages and increasing social spending. The government also aimed to make SMEs a driver of innovation by promoting the Fourth Industrial Revolution and by nurturing innovative start-ups. However, 'income-led growth' could not bring about positive effects on growth and income distribution. It is evident that a sharp increase in the minimum wages brought about decrease in employment. Paradoxically, income-led growth strategy caused job destruction rather than job creation that was a core linkage of the income-led growth. The more data suggests that income-led growth had negative effects on employment, growth, and income distribution. In order to achieve sustainable growth, an 'innovation-led shared growth' should be realized (Kim, 2018b). Like the OECD's message of the Economic Survey on Korea, 'Korea needs to shift from its traditional growth model to a more balanced approach that promotes inclusive growth through reforms to raise productivity in both the large business groups and SMEs' (OECD, 2018a).

Notes

1 The miracle of Korean industrialization is a representative example of the East Asian miracle that was specified by World Bank (1993) and Stiglitz and Yusuf (2001).
2 These three items comprise of total factor productivity (TFP).
3 Developmental dictatorship was a statist modernization system that dictatorship regime mobilized resources with repressing political liberties and participation of the people (Lee, 2003).
4 Fordism had a growth regime in which mass production and mass consumption are combined. It had a wage-led growth regime. High wages made mass consumption possible. And mass production was sustained by mass consumption.
5 This concept of market despotism originated from the work of Burawoy (1985). Burawoy argues that in market despotism, despotic regulation of labor process is constituted by the economic whip of the market (Burawoy, 1985: 123). The disciplinary effect of unemployment is the base of market despotism.
6 Hall and Soskice (2001) classified market economies into liberal market economies (LMEs) and coordinated market economies (CMEs). They included only Western advanced market economies when they analyzed the varieties of capitalism. If we consider the Asian market economies such as the Korean economy before 1987 and the Chinese economy after 1978 in which the state intervened in the market strongly, we can classify market economies into three categories: LMEs, CMEs, and RMEs (regulated market economies).
7 The union density increased substantially after 1987 workers' struggle. For example, the union density increased from 12.3% in 1986 to 18.6% in 1989.
8 The government urged firms to reduce their debt-to-asset ratio to below 200% to comply with the standards set by the Bank for International Settlements (BIS).
9 Debt-led growth means that economic growth was facilitated by high debts.
10 The share of stocks owned by foreign investors increased from 14.6% in 1997 to 36% in 2002.
11 In 1973, the Korean government announced 'The Age of Heavy and Chemical Industries'.
12 The annual average nominal wage growth rate in manufacturing industry was 15.8% from 1987 to 1996. It really deserves to be called wage explosion.
13 This will be discussed in detail in Chapter 8.
14 As mentioned in Chapter 4, Korea has a lower marginal tax rate than the US.
15 Employment elasticity is the employment growth rate divided by the economic growth rate. It, in other words, shows the ability of an economy to create jobs.
16 Unlike the jobless growth that economic growth does not accompany the increase of employment, in the job-rich growth employment increases as the economy grows.
17 The German Competition Act (GWB) has an exemption clause that allows cartels of SMEs to bargain collectively with large firms. Contra the GWB, the Korean Fair Trade Act has a clause that prohibits the collusion of SMEs.
18 Ex-ante economic security net aims to reduce the volatility of the national economy and instability of employment. It includes financial safety net and employment safety net. Financial transaction tax such as Tobin tax is an example of the financial safety net. Flexicurity of labor market would be an example of the employment safety net. This topic will be discussed in greater detail in Chapter 8.

7 The Sustainability of the East Asian Model

The East Asian Model in Japan, Korea, and China allowed all three countries to undergo economic miracles. Japan, Korea, and China have made success of a catching-up growth in sequence. Japan has become at once number two economic power in the world next to the United States. Korea joined OECD countries and became a high-income country. China has become the G2 country with the United States. However, Japan has been experiencing long stagnation of 'Lost Decades'. Korea had a catastrophic 1997 financial crisis followed by subsequent polarization and low growth. China has problems of severe polarization and pollution. Now, the East Asian Model in Japan, Korea, and China is confronting serious problems of sustainability in terms of economic, social, and ecological sustainability. A near-zero growth during Japan's 'Two Lost Decades' and a rapid slowdown of economic growth after the 1997 crisis in Korea suggest that the existing growth regime has collapsed in Japan and is no longer sustainable in Korea. Although China still boasts comparably high levels of growth, the country's present growth regime also raises serious concerns over its sustainability. In the process of the transformation of the East Asian Model for last two or three decades, some forms of unsustainable growth have emerged: a finance-led growth, a jobless growth, and a polarized growth.

The sustainability of a development model has three dimensions: an economic dimension, a social dimension, and an ecological dimension. In order to realize a sustainable development model, Korea, China, and Japan should have a sustainable growth regime. As shown in Table 7.1, extensive growth is economically and ecologically unsustainable because it is not based on technological progress and brings about the depletion of resources. In contrast, intensive growth based on technological progress is economically and ecologically sustainable because it is resources-saving growth. Finance-led growth is also economically and socially unsustainable since it tends to increase macroeconomic volatility and worsen the polarization between the rich and the poor, while innovation-led growth is economically and socially sustainable because it facilitates increases in productivity and encourages social innovation.[1] Jobless growth is economically and socially unsustainable as it brings about a permanent deficiency in aggregate demand and generates

DOI: 10.4324/9781003332725-7

Table 7.1 Elements of a Sustainable and Unsustainable Growth Regime

Growth Regime	*Economic Sustainability*	*Social Sustainability*	*Ecological Sustainability*
Extensive growth	No		No
Intensive growth	Yes		Yes
Finance-led growth	No	No	
Innovation-led growth	Yes	Yes	
Jobless growth	No	No	
Job-rich growth	Yes	Yes	
Polarized growth	No	No	
Shared growth	Yes	Yes	
High carbon-based growth	No		No
Low carbon-based growth	Yes		Yes

social exclusion due to high unemployment. Job-rich growth is economically and socially sustainable since it increases aggregate demand and improves social cohesion. Polarized growth is economically and socially unsustainable because it shrinks domestic demand and may intensify social conflicts between classes. Polarized growth stands in opposition to shared growth, which is economically and socially sustainable because it tends to increase aggregate demand and reduce class conflict. The reason why high-carbon intensity growth is economically and ecologically unsustainable is because the emission of CO_2, besides its negative ecological impact, will incur costs to corporations due to cap-and-trade system and carbon taxes. Moreover, the reduction in CO_2 is required by international agreements such as the Kyoto Protocol. Unlike high carbon-based growth, low carbon-based growth is economically and ecologically sustainable since it reduces environmental costs and increases ecological benefits. In sum, a sustainable growth regime should be intensive growth rather than extensive growth, innovation-led growth rather than finance-led growth, job-rich growth rather than jobless growth, shared growth rather than polarized growth, and low carbon-based growth rather than high carbon-based growth.

7.1 Productivity and Competitiveness in the East Asian Model

The major factors that determine economic sustainability are total factor productivity, return on capital, national competitiveness, the relationship between productivity growth and wage growth, demographic dynamics, and fiscal sustainability. In this section, we will discuss the economic sustainability of the East Asian Model based on these factors focused on productivity and competitiveness. Among the factors, TFP is a core indicator of economic sustainability. The growth regime of the East Asian Model was initially an extensive one. However, extensive growth gradually shifted to intensive growth. Analyses of growth accounting in Japan, Korea, and China (Perkins

Table 7.2 Total Factor Productivity Growth in Japan, Korea, and China

	Japan	*Korea*	*China*
1970–1975	−0.5 (−11)	0.3 (3)	0.1 (2)
1975–1980	1.3 (28)	−2.9 (−38)	0.8 (13)
1980–1985	1.6 (38)	2.1 (23)	4.8 (47)
1985–1990	2.0 (42)	2.4 (24)	1.8 (23)
1990–1995	−0.2 (−15)	1.2 (15)	7.1 (61)
1995–2000	0.4 (39)	0.9 (17)	2.6 (32)
2000–2005	0.9 (77)	1.2 (26)	3.2 (35)
2005–2010	0.3 (274)	2.0 (49)	4.2 (39)
2010–2015	1.2 (31)	0.3 (9)	2.0 (26)

Note: The number (%) in parentheses is share of TFP contribution to economic growth.
Source: Asian Productivity Database, 2017. Asian Productivity Organization.

and Rawski, 2008; Chen et al, 2011; Eichengreen et al, 2012; Kim et al, 2012) highlight how the shift from extensive growth to intensive growth was the result of productivity increases achieved through technological progress. As Table 7.2 shows, TFP growth in Japan and Korea was highest in 1985–1990, while China's TFP was highest in 1990–1995. Table 7.2 also reveals that TFP growth in Japan became negative or near zero in the Lost Decade of the 1990s. Korea showed a sharp decrease in TFP growth in 2010–2015. China also showed slowdown of TFP growth in 2010–2015. TFP contribution to economic growth was negligible in 1970–1975 in all three countries. Afterward, TFP contribution increased. However, it decreased from 2010 to 2015. Recent slowdown of TFP growth and fall of TFP contribution to economic growth raise the problem of economic sustainability in the East Asian Model in Japan, Korea, and China.

Besides TFP factor, return on capital is important, since it is core determinants of investment and main indicators of investment efficiency. Table 7.3 shows that average real return on capital in Korea and China recorded 37.6%

Table 7.3 Average Real Rate of Return on Capital in Japan, Korea, China, and the United States

	Japan	*Korea*	*China*	*United States*
1970–1974	13.5	37.6	21.4	12.0
1975–1979	6.0	29.8	16.4	10.3
1980–1984	5.0	16.5	14.0	8.0
1985–1989	7.4	18.7	13.0	9.4
1990–1994	5.9	14.9	15.0	9.0
1995–1999	4.3	11.0	10.7	11.2
2000–2004	4.9	10.2	13.2	12.0
2005–2009	5.7	9.2	15.0	11.1
2010–2015	4.9	7.2	8.4	10.7

Source: Asian Productivity Database, 2017. Asian Productivity Organization.

and 21.4%, respectively, in 1970–1975. Those real rates of return on capital were triple and double that of the United States. However, the rates of return on capital in Japan, Korea, and China showed the declining trends, compared to the relatively steady trend of 10% level in the United States. It is remarkable that returns on capital in 2010–2015 in three countries were below that of the United States. This means that investment efficiencies in the East Asian Model are lower than those of the United States, the representative country of Anglo-American Model.

Total factor productivity is the result of competitiveness from diverse origins in an economic system. The level of competitiveness can be evaluated by the Global Competitiveness Index (GCI),[2] which measures national competitiveness through the set of institutions, policies, and factors that determine the level of productivity. The GCI is useful to analyze the economic sustainability of a nation, since it can help foster intensive growth and innovation-led growth regime. In this study, we adopted the GCI in order to analyze the determinants of competitiveness in Japan, Korea, and China with reference to those in the United States, Germany, and Sweden.

Looking at the performance of East Asian countries as of 2018, Japan's overall ranking (9th place) is largely driven by high-quality physical and digital infrastructure (4th), a healthy and educated workforce, and a fertile innovation ecosystem. Despite these attributes, Japan's performance is dragged down by its poor macroeconomic environment (93rd), caused mostly by a period of deflation in the 2000s and persistently troubled public finances. Japan has made strides in the technological readiness pillar (15th) because of higher levels of Information and Communication Technology (ICT) usage. A drop in the rankings in the labor market efficiency pillar, however, points to certain difficulties among firms in retaining talent. Ranked 26th overall, Korea's performance is largely driven by its remarkable infrastructure (8th) and a highly favorable macroeconomic environment (2nd). The area in which Korea consistently underperforms is labor market efficiency, in which it ranks 73rd. Korea is also facing deeper challenges regarding labor market flexibility, where it ranks 106th. The country's very low ranking in this category is notably caused by conflictual labor-employer relations and high redundancy costs. All in all, Korea is one of the few advanced economies to have experienced a general decline in performance for most pillars of competitiveness in the 2010s. Contra Korea, China has made progress in all pillars except its macroeconomic environment and infrastructure. The decline in China's macroeconomic environment is explained by a worsening government budget deficit. China's largest gains are observed in technological readiness, owing to higher ICT penetration and the extent to which foreign direct investment has brought new technologies to the country. Other significant advances have been made in the goods market efficiency pillar following a slight reduction in the number of procedures required to start a business (Klaus Schwab and World Economic Forum, 2018).

Competitiveness in terms of innovation capability through the capacity for innovation, company spending on R&D, university-industry collaboration in R&D, availability of scientists and engineers, state of cluster development, availability of the latest technology, and firm-level technology absorption is shown in Table 7.4. Japan excels compared to Korea and China in all seven innovation capability indices. This is especially the case when looking at company spending on R&D, where Japan's 5th place ranking is comparable to the United States, Germany, and Sweden. In availability of scientists and engineers, Japan is comparable to Germany. The most serious problem for Japan in terms of competitiveness is government debt as a percentage of GDP, where the country ranks last (137th) among the ones surveyed. Korea performs relatively well in terms of availability of the latest technology and firm-level technology absorption, but struggles in terms of labor market rigidity, ranking 106th in labor market flexibility and 130th in labor-employer relations. Unlike Korea, China is very weak when it comes to the availability of the latest technology, but performs well in company spending on R&D. China's issues surrounding competitiveness center around the efficacy of corporate boards, where the country ranks 126th.

Outside East Asia, the United States (representing the Anglo-American Model), Germany (representing the Rhine Model), and Sweden (representing the Nordic Model) have very high rankings in capacity for innovation and company spending on R&D. For example, Sweden and the United States rank first in firm-level technology absorption and the state of cluster development, respectively. Sweden and the United States also excel in corporate innovation (company spending on R&D and firm-level technology absorption), while the United States and Germany are among the best-performing countries when it comes to regional innovation (state of cluster development

Table 7.4 Competitiveness in Terms of Innovation Capability: Scores and Rankings

Innovation Capability	*Japan*	*Korea*	*China*	*United States*	*Germany*	*Sweden*
Capacity for innovation	5.1 **21**	4.7 **35**	4.5 **44**	6.0 **2**	5.8 **5**	5.8 **4**
Company spending on R&D	5.6 **5**	4.4 **28**	4.6 **21**	5.9 **2**	5.6 **4**	5.6 **6**
University-industry collaboration in R&D	4.7 **23**	4.4 **27**	4.4 **28**	5.9 **2**	5.4 **7**	5.2 **10**
Availability of scientists and engineers	5.3 **8**	4.5 **38**	4.7 **29**	5.7 **2**	5.2 **11**	4.8 **20**
State of cluster development	5.1 **11**	4.6 **28**	4.6 **27**	5.7 **1**	5.4 **4**	5.0 **16**
Availability of the latest technology	6.3 **11**	5.8 **23**	4.5 **81**	6.5 **6**	6.1 **16**	6.5 **5**
Firm-level technology absorption	5.5 **15**	5.3 **23**	4.6 **58**	6.0 **2**	5.7 **12**	6.0 **1**

Source: Klaus Schwab and World Economic Forum (eds) (2018).

and university-industry collaboration in R&D). The gap between the performances of the United States, Germany, and Sweden and that of China, Korea, and even Japan indicate that the three East Asian countries need to further invest in innovation capability if they want to gain international competitiveness and promote a more sustainable growth regime.

Competitiveness in terms of human resource development is shown in Table 7.5. Here, Japan shines compared to Korea and China when looking at staff training, the quality of primary education, the quality of math and science education, and the local availability of specialized training schools. Korea only beats Japan and China in tertiary education enrollment rate, highlighting Korea's relatively low standing when it comes to the quality of its education system. China does slightly better than Korea by ranking higher than its East Asian counterparts in two categories: the quality of the education system and the quality of management schools. Similarly to innovation capability, the United States, Germany, and Sweden rank significantly higher than Japan, Korea, and China in areas such as the quality of the education system, the extent of staff training, local availability of specialized training schools, and the quality of management schools. Education and training systems reform in Japan, Korea, and China is thus necessary to catch up with the leading countries in human resource development.

Competitiveness in terms of goods market efficiency, labor market efficiency, and financial market development[3] is presented in Table 7.6. Japan, for example, is shown to rank higher than Korea and China in goods market efficiency, labor market efficiency, and financial market development. Korea, on the other hand, has very poor performances in financial market development and labor market efficiency compared to Japan and China. Financial

Table 7.5 Competitiveness in Terms of Human Resource Development: Scores and Rankings

	Japan	*Korea*	*China*	*United States*	*Germany*	*Sweden*
Quality of primary education	5.4 **14**	4.6 **41**	4.7 **38**	5.5 **11**	5.3 **20**	4.7 **35**
Quality of the education system	4.4 **36**	3.5 **81**	4.5 **29**	5.6 **4**	5.4 **9**	4.8 **20**
Quality of math and science education	5.1 **22**	4.6 **36**	4.5 **50**	5.4 **10**	5.3 **15**	4.6 **46**
Quality of management schools	4.3 **59**	4.2 **69**	4.6 **50**	5.9 **6**	5.3 **23**	5.3 **22**
Local availability of specialized training schools	5.3 **25**	4.6 **52**	4.6 **55**	5.8 **10**	5.6 **17**	5.6 **16**
Extent of staff training	5.2 **13**	4.3 **41**	4.5 **36**	5.5 **2**	5.4 **6**	5.4 **8**
Tertiary education enrollment rate (%)	63.4 **39**	93.2 **3**	43.4 **67**	85.8 **9**	68.3 **32**	62.3 **42**

Source: Klaus Schwab and World Economic Forum (eds) (2018).

Table 7.6 Competitiveness in Terms of Goods/Labor Market Efficiency and Financial Market Development: Scores and Rankings

	Japan	*Korea*	*China*	*United States*	*Germany*	*Sweden*
Goods market efficiency	5.2 **13**	5.0 **24**	4.5 **46**	5.5 **7**	5.3 **11**	5.2 **14**
Labor market efficiency	4.8 **22**	4.2 **73**	4.5 **38**	5.6 **3**	5.0 **14**	4.9 **20**
Financial market development	4.9 **20**	3.9 **74**	4.2 **48**	5.0 **2**	5.0 **12**	5.1 **10**

Source: Klaus Schwab and World Economic Forum (eds) (2018).

market development in Korea also falls far behind that of the United States, Sweden, and Germany. As for market efficiency, Korea had relatively good performance in goods market efficiency. These facts mean urgent reforms of labor market and financial market are necessary if Korea wants to improve its international competitiveness.

Looking at Tables 7.7–7.9 brings more factors that determine competitiveness in terms of goods and labor market efficiency and financial market development to the fore. First, analyzing the elements that shape goods market efficiency in Table 7.7 shows that Japan ranks second in the extent of market dominance[4] and the intensity of local competition. Japan is also in excellent standing with respect to the effectiveness of its anti-monopoly policy, placing fifth. However, Japan, as well as China, do poorly in terms of the number of procedures required to start a business. Japan and China's lackluster performance contrasts with that of Korea, which ranks second in the same category. Additionally, Korea is fourth when it comes to the intensity of local competition, but only places 101st in terms of market dominance because of the significant influence of Chaebols in the national economy. Second, the determinants of labor market efficiency presented in Table 7.8 reveal that Japan performs better than Korea and China in terms of cooperation in labor-employer relations and flexibility of wage determination. However,

Table 7.7 Goods Market Efficiency in Japan, Korea, and China: Scores and Rankings

	Japan	*Korea*	*China*
Extent of market dominance	5.9 **2**	3.3 **101**	4.5 **22**
Intensity of local competition	6.2 **2**	6.0 **4**	5.5 **33**
Effectiveness of anti-monopoly policy	5.5 **5**	4.5 **32**	4.5 **30**
No. of procedures to start a business	8 **91**	2 **2**	9 **104**

Source: Klaus Schwab and World Economic Forum (eds) (2018).

Table 7.8 Labor Market Efficiency in Japan, Korea, and China: Scores and Rankings

	Japan	*Korea*	*China*
Cooperation in labor-employer relations	5.7	3.5	4.6
	7	**130**	**50**
Flexibility of wage determination	5.8	5.0	4.6
	15	**62**	**89**
Hiring and firing practices	3.2	3.5	4.5
	113	**88**	**24**
Redundancy costs (weeks of salary)	4.3	27.4	27.4
	9	**112**	**112**

Source: Klaus Schwab and World Economic Forum (eds) (2018).

Japan's standing is very low (it ranks 113th) when it comes to its hiring and firing practices. Contrary to Japan, Korea has a very low score when it comes to labor-employer relations. Korea's labor market is actually the most rigid of the three East Asian countries generally, while China's labor market is the most flexible when looking specifically at hiring and firing practices. Third, looking at aspects of financial market development in Table 7.9 shows that Japan and China perform better than Korea when it comes to the ease of access to loans and the soundness of banks.

Competitiveness is a core agenda of economic sustainability. Sustainability of a development model includes social and ecological sustainability as well as economic sustainability. Since the three dimensions of sustainability should be pursued in parallel, they must be merged into a single sustainable agenda. It is important to note that there are no inherent trade-offs between competitiveness and social cohesion and between competitiveness and ecological sustainability. There can be a win-win policy space in which a productive, inclusive, low-carbon economy is possible even though win-win policies do not depend strictly on competitiveness. Indeed, the perceived trade-offs between economic, social, and ecological factors can be mitigated by adopting a holistic and longer-term approach to growth. For example, Sweden,

Table 7.9 Financial Market Development in Japan, Korea, and China: Scores and Rankings

	Japan	*Korea*	*China*
Ease of access to loans	5.2	3.5	5.2
	8	**90**	**8**
Soundness of banks	5.8	4.3	5.8
	21	**91**	**21**
Availability of financial services	5.2	4.0	5.2
	19	**81**	**19**
Venture capital availability	3.6	2.9	3.6
	28	**64**	**28**

Source: Klaus Schwab and World Economic Forum (eds) (2018).

Table 7.10 Total Fertility Rate Trends in Japan, Korea, and China

	1950–1955	*1970–1975*	*1990–1995*	*2010–2015*	*2025–2030*	*2045–2050*
Japan	3.00	2.13	1.48	1.40	1.07	1.19
Korea	5.05	4.28	1.70	1.26	0.95	1.10
China	6.11	4.85	2.00	1.55	1.16	1.24
More developed regions	2.82	2.15	1.81	1.67	1.25	1.32

Note: Total fertility rates in 2025–2030 and 2045–2050 are based on low variants estimation. More developed regions include Europe, Northern America, Australia/New Zealand, and Japan.

Source: UN Department of Economic and Social Affairs, World Population Prospects: The 2015 Revision.

Denmark, and Finland have not only become the most competitive economies in the world; they are also more cohesive and more ecologically sustainable than other countries (Klaus Schwab and World Economic Forum, 2019).

Some of the most challenging problems in achieving sustainable growth in Korea, China, and Japan are low fertility rates and an aging population. As Table 7.10 shows, total fertility rates in Japan, Korea, and China between 1950 and 1955 were 3.00, 5.05, and 6.11, respectively. However, they decreased to 1.40, 1.26, and 1.67 in 2010–2015 and are predicted to fall further to 1.19, 1.10, and 1.24 in 2045–2050, which is lower than some more developed regions. Population aging is also proceeding rapidly in Japan, Korea, and China. Specifically, the ratio of the population aged 15 to 64 in Korea will decrease from 72.9% in 2015 to 53.4% in 2050. In Japan and China, the ratio will go down from 60.8% to 51.3% and from 73.2% to 58.9%, respectively. Japan and Korea are actually projected to have the fastest aging populations in the OECD countries. This rapid change in age structure can also be observed through the dependency ratio[5] which in Korea, for instance, is predicted to rise sharply from 37.2% in 2015 to 87.2% in 2050.

Changes in age structure in Japan, Korea, and China suggest that all three countries will face serious sustainability problems in terms of demography. Low fertility rates and population aging will, for example, have a negative impact on economic growth and fiscal sustainability by increasing the welfare expenditure burden of government. As Table 7.11 shows, the demographic dividend kicked in during the 1950s and 1960s in Japan and during the 1970s in Korea and China. Estimated impact of demographic change on per capita growth in these periods was positive. However, demographic dividend disappeared by the 1970s in Japan, by the turn of the 21st century in Korea, and by the 2010s in China. Due to low fertility rate and population aging, significant negative impact of demographic change on per capita growth appeared. Korea will have the strongest negative impact in the future (in 2020–2030, 2030–2040, and 2040–2050) among three countries. China may confront with 'aging before becoming affluent' as demographic dividend disappears (Cai and Wen, 2012). It is remarkable that in the future until

Table 7.11 Estimated Impact of Demographic Change on per Capita Growth

	Korea	*China*	*Japan*	*United States*
1950–1960	−0.05	−0.46	0.33	−0.41
1960–1970	−0.01	0.00	0.33	0.12
1970–1980	0.58	0.29	−0.20	0.30
1980–1990	0.50	0.52	0.05	−0.06
1990–2000	0.11	0.09	−0.33	0.00
2000–2010	−0.07	0.24	−0.56	0.06
2010–2020	−0.30	−0.35	−0.62	−0.29
2020–2030	−0.90	−0.41	−0.20	−0.32
2030–2040	−0.78	−0.62	−0.52	−0.07
2040–2050	−0.52	−0.17	−0.26	−0.03

Source: Kohsaka (2013: 18, Table 1.3).

2050, negative impact of demographic change on per capita growth in Japan, Korea, and China will be much greater than that in the United States, where negative impact will be negligible. In order to sustain economic growth and to realize social cohesion, senior and gender development to broaden the labor force participation rate, a reversal of fertility decline through measures such as development of a care economy are needed (Aoki, 2012).

7.2 Unsustainable and Sustainable Growth in the East Asian Model

Economic sustainability is also conditioned by the relationship between productivity and wages. If productivity growth exceeds wage growth, the rate of surplus value will increase.[6] This rise in surplus value will, ceteris paribus, push profit rates, investment, and GDP growth up, yet the ensuing worsening in income distribution will have a negative impact on economic growth from the demand side. In another scenario, wage growth exceeding productivity growth will decrease the rate of surplus value and improve income distribution. However, profit rates and consequently investment will go down, leading to a slowdown in economic growth from the supply side. Therefore, for economic sustainability, productivity growth should match wages growth.

Productivity growth and wage growth trends in Korea, China, and Japan shown in Tables 6.7 (in Chapter 6), 7.12, and 7.13 suggest that changes in

Table 7.12 Growth Rate of Productivity and Real Wages in Japan

	Productivity Growth	*Real Wages Growth*
1971–1980	3.6	3.9
1981–1990	3.5	1.6
1991–2000	1.0	0.3
2001–2010	1.2	−0.5

Source: Japanese Statistics yearbook, Penn World Table.

Table 7.13 Growth Rate of Productivity and Real Wages in China

	Productivity Growth	*Real Wages Growth*
1981–1990	6.3	3.5
1991–2000	9.1	7.5
2001–2010	9.6	12.5

Source: Chinese Statistics Yearbook, Penn World Table.

growth regime were different in each country. In Korea, the growth rate of wages was higher than the growth rate of productivity in 1987–1997, while the growth rate of wages was much lower than that of productivity after the 1997 financial crisis. This suggests that Korea had a wage-led growth before the 1997 financial crisis while it disappeared after the crisis. There was a sort of 'Golden Age of Korean Capitalism' in a decade from 1987 to 1996 where 'high growth-high productivity-high wages-quasi-full employment' has appeared (Kim, 2012). In Japan, the growth rate of real wages was marginally higher than productivity growth in the 1970s. Japan might have had a sort of 'Golden Age of Japanese Capitalism' in the 1970s. This relationship changed in the 1980s, when the growth rate of real wages became far lower than the growth rate of productivity. Japan during its 'Two Lost Decades' in the 1990s and 2000s then experienced anemic productivity growth and wage growth that was near-zero and sometimes negative. In China, the growth rate of wages was much lower than the growth rate of productivity before the 2000s when wages growth exceeded productivity growth. However, this development was geographically uneven, with the Eastern region having much higher levels of per capita GDP than the Western, Central, and Northeastern regions.[7]

As we have seen, wage-led growth emerged in Japan in the 1970s and in Korea in the late 1980s. However, in Japan, a wage-led growth was gradually undermined by an export-led growth from the 1980s (Uemura, 2012; Uni, 2012). Korea had both a wage-led growth alongside an export-led growth for a decade from the 1987 workers' struggles to the 1997 financial crisis. After the 1997 financial crisis, Korea had a finance-led and an export-led growth which achieved much lower growth rates than high growth rates before the 1997 crisis. China had both an investment-led and an export-led growth for last two or three decades before the country moved toward wage-led growth in the 2000s. Financial liberalization in Japan around the mid-1980s created a massive asset bubble, which burst in the early 1990s. In Korea, financial liberalization after 1993 brought about a rapid increase in short-term foreign debt and significant overinvestment that contributed to the 1997 financial crisis. Indeed, Japanese and Korean governments have attempted in vain to raise their national status based on financial development at the expense of industrial policy. The recent economic troubles in Japan and in Korea can thus be seen as the result of a departure from the traditional East Asian Model,

Table 7.14 Employment Elasticity of the Manufacturing Industry in Korea and China

	Korea	*China*
1981–1985	0.40	0.84
1986–1990	0.63	0.34
1991–1995	−0.22	0.16
1996–2000	0.23	−0.45
2001–2005	−0.11	0.26
2006–2010	−0.13	0.15

Source: KLI Labor Statistics, Chinese Labor Statistics Yearbook.

rather than from an adherence to it (Chang, 2007: 53). This liberalization of financial systems in Japan and Korea has been detrimental to the viability of national regulation modes and has propagated macroeconomic instability (Boyer et al, 2012: 335), facilitating the shift to a more fragile and inequitable development model in both countries.

From the 1990s, jobless growth became one of the most distinctive features of the East Asian Model. Employment elasticity of East Asia in 1999–2003, for example, was low compared to Western Europe and North America. Especially, Japan's employment elasticity decreased rapidly from 0.34 in 1991–1995 to −0.24 in 1999–2003, while Western Europe's employment elasticity increased from 0.09 in 1991–1995 to 0.42 in 1999–2003 (Kapsos, 2005). Moreover, as Table 7.14 shows, employment elasticity in the manufacturing industry in Korea and China were rather high in the 1980s, but rapidly reached very low and even negative levels thereafter. One of the reasons why employment elasticity is so low in Korea, China, and Japan is due to the very high capital-intensive or labor-saving production systems in these countries. For instance, China gives firms excessive incentives to develop labor-saving innovations (Stiglitz, 2008). Low employment elasticity may also accompany jobless growth during an economic slowdown. In Korea, China, and Japan, employment growth rates gradually decreased to less than 1% (see Table 7.15). Jobless growth may also enhance income inequality. Because employment

Table 7.15 Growth Rate of Employment: Annual Average Rates (%)

	Korea	*China*	*Japan*
1980–1990	2.4	2	2
1990–2000	1.2	0.8	1.2
2000–2010	0.7	0.5	0.2

Note: The periods for China are 1979–2011, 1991–2011, and 2001–2011.

Source: Kim et al (2012) for Korea data, Japanese Statistics Yearbook, and Chinese Statistics Yearbook.

itself creates income and consumption, it contributes to building up aggregate demand in order to sustain growth. Thus, jobless growth is basically unsustainable.

Alongside jobless growth, polarized growth in China, Korea, and Japan is a serious problem that will make their development models unsustainable. Economic development in these countries started with initial conditions of low levels of inequality following civil wars, revolutions, and land reforms (Aoki, 2012; Perkins, 2013). Even with high growth, Japan until the mid-1980s had one of the most egalitarian societies among developed countries. In China, the planned economy before 1978 generated low incomes, as well as low levels of inequality. Korea also had an economic model that shared growth before the 1997 financial crisis.[8] However, the marketization and privatization in the public sector, liberalization of financial market, and flexibilization of labor market that have occurred in all three countries in the last two decades are fueling polarization.

China's polarized growth regime is characterized by disparities between urban and rural regions, between State-Owned Enterprises (SOEs) and non-state small and medium-sized enterprises (SMEs), and between formal employment and informal employment. In Korea, polarized growth fuels a rift between Chaebol firms and SMEs, between regular workers and non-regular workers, and between the Seoul Metropolitan area and provinces. Rapidly intensifying polarization between regular workers and non-regular workers is being observed in Japan, as well. In China and Korea, the respective dominance of SOEs and Chaebols precipitated polarization, as these firms profited not only from monopoly situations in the products markets and factor markets but also from fiscal and financial support from their governments.[9] The unfair markets and unfair policies are contributing to polarization between the large firms/SOEs and SMEs. For example, in Korea, the prevalent rate-cutting practice of Chaebol firms against SMEs who supply them with parts and materials promoted polarization by transferring surplus from SMEs to Chaebols. As a result, wage differentials between large firms/SOEs and SMEs in Korea and China have widened significantly in the last twenty years as shown in Figure 7.1.

Widening productivity differentials between firms also lead to larger wage differentials. For example, in the OECD countries in 2013, the P90/P50 ratio (the 90th percentiles/50th percentiles) in the firm distribution of labor productivity had a positive correlation with the P90/P50 ratio in the firm distribution of average labor income (OECD, 2018a: 42). Korea held a peculiar position, as it had both the greatest inequality in productivity and the greatest inequality in wages. In Japan, productivity inequality is slightly above the OECD average, but wage inequality is far above it (OECD, 2018a). In order to reduce wage differentials between firms, reduction in productivity differentials between firms is imperative. Korea and Japan thus face the challenge of broadening the productivity base of their economies to generate shared and inclusive growth. To this end, enhancing R&D capabilities and

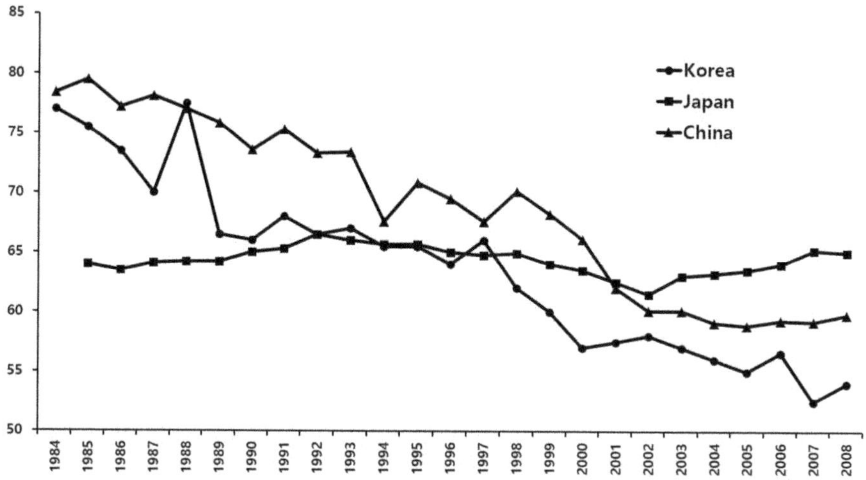

Figure 7.1 Wage Differentials between Large Firms/SOEs and SMEs in Korea, China, and Japan (Large Firms/SOEs = 100)

Source: Bureau of Statistics (Korea), Survey on Mining and Manufacturing Industries (Japan), and Statistics Tables of Manufacturing Industry (China).

bolstering human resource development in SMEs, is essential to break down labor market dualism that helps drive economic polarization (OECD, 2018a).

Non-regularization of employment in Japan and Korea and informalization of employment in China exacerbate polarization. The larger part of non-regular workers is discriminated against the regular workers in terms of employment, wages, and social insurance. These triple discriminations against non-regular workers have created a new segmentation in the labor market. In China, migrant workers (*Nongmingong*) who have temporary work permits to access urban regions are treated as the 'relative surplus population'[10] of the economy outside the urban formal labor markets. Hourly wage of the migrant workers was on average about half that of the urban hukou residents' (Lam et al, 2015). Because of the restrictions imposed by the hukou system[11] in urban regions, migrant workers also lack full access to unemployment insurance, health care, pensions, housing, and education for their children. Migrants' access to unemployment insurance in 2008 and 2010 was, for example, 12.0% and 13.5%, while that of urban hukou residents was 60% and 66%. Additionally, migrants' access to urban health insurance was 20% in 2010, while that of urban hukou residents was 87%. In Japan, the share of non-regular employment, which includes fixed-term, part-time, and dispatched workers rose sharply from 20.3% in 1994 to 37.5% in 2016. The share of non-regular employment in Korea also increased significantly from 27.4% in 2002 to 37.0% in 2004 (it was 32.9% in 2017). Non-regular employment is particularly high among women, who accounted for 68% of non-regular workers in 2015 in Japan and 54.9% in 2016 in Korea.

The fact that non-regular workers receive less training and opportunities for skill development than regular workers do slow productivity growth and widens the wage gap between workers. Hourly wages of non-regular workers relative to regular workers in Korea, for instance, was 66.3% in 2016, as shown in Table 6.9. In Japan, the wage differential between regular workers and non-regular workers increases over time as regular workers gain seniority (OECD, 2017b). Moreover, the fact that most non-regular workers are employed by SMEs means breaking down market labor dualism will also help address the negative effects of precarious employment.

Labor market segmentation not only between large firms and SMEs but also between regular workers and non-regular workers is major factor of polarization and low growth in Japan and Korea. Labor market segmentation between the large firms and SMEs is mainly due to productivity differentials between the two. The productivity differentials come from not only technology gaps between the large firms and SMEs but also the economic structure in which Keiretsu and Chaebol have the monopoly power over the SMEs. Especially in Korea, the Chaebol firms exploit the SMEs by the rate-cutting that reduces profit margins and thus restraints the innovation abilities of the SMEs. Thus, preventing rate-cutting by Chaebol firms through the reform of the Fair Trade Act is necessary to reduce polarization between Chaebol firms and SMEs. To remove the discrimination against the non-regular workers is also necessary to resolve the problems of the non-regular employment. Because employers hire non-regular workers in order to cut labor costs and to enhance employment flexibility, it is essential to break down labor market dualism, where regular workers employed in the primary labor market are overprotected (OECD, 2017b; OECD, 2018a)). Labor market dualism essentially comes from the monopolistic structure of the national economy in which the Chaebol and Keiretsu dominate the SMEs. Moreover, since most non-regular workers are employed in the SMEs, the problem of non-regular employment is ultimately the problem of the SMEs that have the difficulties to improve working conditions including employment security and wages increase. Therefore, the industrial policy, which breaks down dual structure of the Chaebol/Keiretsu dominant national economy, is needed to break down labor market dualism.

Gender inequality is major socio-economic problem in Japan and Korea. According to OECD Earnings Distribution Database, as of 2015, Korea's gender wage gap is the largest and Japan's is third largest in the OECD. Other indicators of gender inequality in both countries are the lowest (Japan) and second lowest (Korea) in terms of share of women in senior management positions in central government in 2015. The data for the 2018 Global Gender Gap Index (Table 7.16) shows that China scored higher than Japan and Korea in 'labor force participation' and 'estimated earned income'. China's performance is especially impressive in the 'professional and technical workers' index, where it stands first alongside the United States, Germany, and Sweden. Gender inequality in terms of 'wage equality for similar work'

Table 7.16 Global Gender Gap Index 2018: Japan, Korea, China, United States, Germany, and Sweden

	Japan	*Korea*	*China*	*United States*	*Germany*	*Sweden*
Labor force participation	0.799 **79**	0.750 **88**	0.831 **64**	0.854 **59**	0.897 **40**	0.956 **13**
Wage equality for similar work	0.696 **45**	0.532 **121**	0.643 **74**	0.796 **8**	0.717 **33**	0.735 **25**
Estimated earned income	0.527 **103**	0.457 **121**	0.621 **73**	0.648 **60**	0.684 **38**	0.785 **14**
Legislators, senior officials, and managers	0.152 **129**	0.141 **133**	0.201 **122**	0.681 **24**	0.413 **87**	0.637 **31**
Professional and technical workers	0.671 **108**	0.927 **86**	1.000 **1**	1.000 **1**	1.000 **1**	1.000 **1**
Economic participation and opportunity	0.595 **117**	0.549 **124**	0.653 **86**	0.782 **19**	0.734 **36**	0.808 **9**

Source: World Economic Forum (2018b).

is, once more, worse in Korea than in China and Japan. However, all three East Asian countries have very low rankings when looking at the index measuring the share of women as legislators, senior officials, and managers. When we look overall in terms of 'economic participation and opportunity' index, Korea's score is lower than China and Japan. This data shows that gender discrimination in Korea is much severe than in Japan and China.

Polarized growth in East Asia contributed to rising income inequality across the region. Specifically, the income shares of the top 10% in Japan, Korea, and China increased significantly, as shown in Table 7.17. In Japan, the income shares of the top 10% went up during the country's Lost Decades, going from 0.335 in 1985 to 0.416 in 2010. In Korea, the income shares of the top 10% rose as well, going from 0.292 in 1985 to 0,371 in 2005 following the 1997 financial crisis, and further increasing thereafter to 0.431 in 2015.

Table 7.17 Top 10% Income Share in Japan, Korea, and China

	Pre-Tax National Income			
	1985	*1995*	*2005*	*2015*
Japan	0.335	0.355	0.424	0.416*
Korea	0.292	0.318	0.371	0.431
China	0.295	0.336	0.419	0.414
United States	0.367	0.401	0.451	0.470**
Germany	0.284	0.293	0.341	0.351
Sweden	0.235	0.265	0.269	0.281

* 2010

** 2014

Source: WID (2017).

The income shares of the top decile in China grew substantially from 0.295 in 1985 to 0.414 in 2015, too.[12] These income share figures for Japan, Korea, and China are higher than in countries such as Sweden and Germany and are now very close to that of the United States, where income inequality is the highest in the OECD.

Gini coefficient trends in Korea, China, and Japan also show that income inequality has increased significantly since the late 1990s. This rise in income inequality is the starkest in China, with the country's Gini coefficient going from below 0.3 in 1981 to above 0.4 in 2012. According to another source, China's Gini coefficient for household disposable income was 0.491 in 2008 and 0.468 in 2018 (Statista, 2019). Additionally, recent analysis using household data reveals that China's Gini coefficient for total wealth went up from 0.45 in 1995 to 0.73 in 2013 (Peking University, 2014). The predictions by Jain-Chandra et al (2018) indicate that China's Gini coefficient with unchanged policies (baseline prediction) will be greater than 0.5 from 2030 onwards. This rise in income inequality can, however, be stemmed with active government policies to address polarized economic growth.

How about wage inequality? Wage inequality in Korea belongs to the highest group in the OECD. Low pay incidence, which is measured by calculating the share of full-time workers making less than two-thirds of median earnings (including bonuses), was around 24% in Korea in 2014. Furthermore, the ratio of wages between workers in the highest income decile and the lowest income decile (D9/D1) is over 5. Unlike Korea, low pay incidence and the D9/D1 ratio in Japan are below the OECD average (OECD Earnings Distribution Database). However, in 2014, relative poverty, which is defined as the share of the population with an income less than half of the median equivalent disposable income, is higher in Japan than it is in Korea (OECD Income Distribution database). All in all, the data presented there suggests that Korea resembles the United States in terms of wage inequality more than Japan does, while Japan's relative poverty statistics are closer to those of the United States.

The regional inequality is another important problem to be addressed in the East Asian Model. In Korea and Japan, the gap between capital city and provinces has been widening. Especially in Korea, half the population, 52.5% of GDP, and 74% of large firms are the shares of Seoul metropolitan region. In Japan, 35% of population and 44.7% of GDP are the shares of Tokyo metropolitan region. For China, in terms of population, the concentration upon capital city Beijing is not so serious as Korea and Japan. However, in terms of per capita GDP, the gap between Beijing/Shanghai and the other provinces is huge. Moreover, the ratio of urban income/rural income in terms of per capita disposable GDP in 2017 was 2.7. The regional inequality in terms of Gini coefficient increased from 0.245 in 1952 to 0.383 in 2013. While per capita GDP of Eastern region in 2020 was 41,240 yuan, that of Western region was 25,416. These data in three countries tell that regional inequality in the East Asian Model should be reduced for inclusive and sustainable growth.

Table 7.18 CO_2 Intensity Trends in Korea, China, and Japan

	kg of CO_2/US Dollar Using 2005 Prices						
	1980	*1985*	*1990*	*1995*	*2000*	*2005*	*2010*
Korea	0.67	0.54	0.49	0.52	0.50	0.43	0.43
China	2.46	1.84	1.64	1.27	0.94	0.97	0.77
Japan	0.42	0.34	0.32	0.32	0.32	0.31	0.29
United States	0.80	0.67	0.61	0.57	0.51	0.46	0.42
Germany	0.65	0.58	0.46	0.38	0.33	0.31	0.28
Sweden	0.43	0.32	0.25	0.26	0.20	0.17	0.15
World	0.67	0.61	0.58	0.54	0.49	0.48	0.45

Source: IEA (2013).

Lastly, let's move to ecological sustainability issues. The shift from high carbon-based growth to low carbon-based growth is imperative to stop global warming and avert environmental crisis. In East Asia, according to the Green Growth Indicators (OECD, 2017e) on CO_2 trends data reveal that production-based CO_2 emissions in Korea and China have increased greatly from 1990 to 2015, while emissions in Japan have remained relatively stable. This general rise in East Asia's production-based CO_2 emissions contrasts with the decrease in emissions observed in Sweden, Germany, and the United States. CO_2 intensity (kg of CO_2/US$) and CO_2 productivity (US$/kg of CO_2) are two other metrics to examine when assessing the ability of East Asian states to decouple greenhouse gas emissions from economic growth. As Table 7.18 shows, CO_2 intensity in Japan, Korea, and China decreased substantially in the last 30 years. Of note is the remarkable reduction in China's CO_2 intensity, although it is still much higher than the world average. The data on CO_2 productivity highlights how both production-based and demand-based CO_2 productivity in Japan are close to the OECD average. However, Korea, and especially China, have CO_2 productivity values that are below that mean.

Compared to China, the overall environmental performance of Korea and Japan has significantly improved since the 2000s (see Table 7.19). One of the most serious challenges to sustainable growth in China is the ecological debts[13] that has been accumulated during the country's extraordinary high growth period. Another reason why China is lagging behind Japan and Korea

Table 7.19 Changes in Environmental Performances Index & Ranking of Korea, China, and Japan

	2002	*2008*	*2014*
Korea	35.9 (135)	79.4 (51)	63.8 (43)
China	38.5 (129)	65.1 (105)	43.0 (118)
Japan	48.6 (77)	84.5 (21)	72.4 (26)

Source: IEA, World Energy Statistics and Balances. https://doi.org/10.1787/enestats-data-en.

Table 7.20 Renewable Electricity: % of Total Electricity Generation

	1990	*1995*	*2000*	*2005*	*2010*	*2015*
Japan	11.48	9.53	9.30	8.58	9.72	14.26
Korea	6.04	1.66	1.42	1.04	1.25	1.94
China	20.41	19.21	16.64	16.18	18.62	23.92
United States	11.53	10.80	8.21	8.58	10.12	13.23
Germany	3.49	4.87	6.20	10.15	16.73	29.23
Sweden	51.00	47.58	57.25	51.29	55.30	63.26*

* Value for 2014.

Source: OECD, Green Growth Indicators.

in curbing carbon emissions is due to the lack of incentives firms operating in the country have to invest in resource-saving innovations. Achieving sustainable development in China therefore requires the implementation of measures to enhance incentives for reducing CO_2 by making firms internalize full social costs of carbon emissions. For example, a carbon tax which will be levied on carbon emissions may be a promising solution (Stiglitz, 2008).

An energy conversion to renewable energy systems is needed for sustainable growth as well. In Korea, renewable energy supply as a share of total energy supply was only 1.48% in 2015, compared to 6.88% in the United States, 12.45% in Germany, and 41.99% in Sweden. In China, the share of renewable energy supply decreased sharply from 24.19% in 1990 to 8.50% in 2015. The share of renewable energy supply in Japan is also small relative to the United States, without mentioning the cases of Germany and Sweden, where the shares of renewable energy supply are much larger. However, elevated political and public awareness on renewable energy after the 2011 Fukushima power plant disaster means Japan's efforts to promote renewable energy are likely to accelerate in the coming years. Table 7.20, which shows that Japan's renewable electricity as a share of total electricity generation went up from 8.58% in 2005 to 14.26% in 2015, indicates that Japan's shift to renewable energy is indeed going apace. At the other end of the spectrum, Korea, with a 1.94% share of electricity generated that was renewable in 2015 (down from 6.04% in 1990), performs far worse than its counterparts in the sample. Korea thus needs to greatly increase renewable energy supply and renewable electricity generation by moving from fossil energy and nuclear energy[14] if it wants to develop a sustainable growth regime.

7.3 Institutional Reforms for a Sustainable Growth Regime

Two Lost Decades with the collapse of the existing growth regime in Japan, symptom of long stagnation of like Japanese Lost Decades in Korea, along with rising social tensions amidst a rapidly widening income gap and increasing pollution in China indicate the presence of unsustainable growth regimes in East Asia Model. As we have seen, jobless growth, finance-led growth, and polarized growth are not sustainable because they will not only decrease growth potential but also destroy social cohesion. Specifically, jobless growth is economically and socially unsustainable because it brings about a permanent deficiency in aggregate demand and heightens social exclusion due to high levels of unemployment. Instead of jobless growth, job-rich growth that creates more decent jobs should therefore be pursued (ILO, 2013). This policy agenda should be realized not only through R&D investment but also through Human Resource Development (HRD) investment. Indeed, R&D investment tends to create jobs for a comparably small number of highly talented workers, while HRD investment is more likely to create jobs for a relatively larger number of skilled workers. R&D-HRD balanced firms with skilled labor-using technology rather than R&D-biased firms with skilled labor-saving technology can contribute to job-rich growth (Kim, 2007).

For job-rich growth, employment-intensive growth regime should be established. One way for East Asian countries to move toward an employment-intensive growth regime is to promote jobs in productive services and social services. There exists, for example, ample room to create public sector jobs in Japan and Korea, where public sector employment as a percentage of total employment is low compared with other OECD member states. Government expenditures as a percentage of GDP in Japan and Korea is also very low by OECD standards (see Figure 7.2). Both countries can thus increase employment by expanding government expenditure, which can be financed by raising taxes.

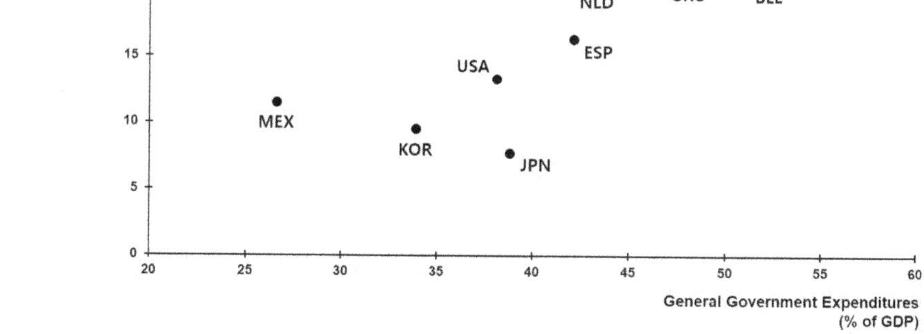

Figure 7.2 Government Expenditures and Public Sector Employment in OECD Countries

Source: OECD Database.

Alongside jobless growth, finance-led growth is economically and socially unsustainable because it gives rise to severe income inequality and macroeconomic volatility, as was evidenced during the Great Recession following the 2008 financial crisis in the United States. Finance-led growth is based on shareholder-oriented corporate governance, liberalization of financial market, and flexibilization of labor market. Speculation and bubble without creating values and consumption based on unearned financial income (interests, dividend, stock price) are unsustainable driving forces of economic growth in the finance-led growth. Japan has been experienced bitterly the results of the tremendous bubble and subsequent bubble burst originated from the finance-led growth that emerged admist the process of liberalization of Japan's financial markets in the bubble economy in the late 1980s (Takeda and Turner, 1992).

Because it generates value through 'creative destruction' (Schumpeter, 2008: 83), innovation-led growth is an economically sustainable alternative to finance-led growth. On the one hand, innovation-led growth is socially sustainable because the profits or rents reaped from innovation can easily be legitimized, unlike unearned financial income from speculative asset bubbles. On the other hand, the fact that innovation processes are inherently dynamic and create few winners and many losers mean innovation-led growth should be carefully managed to avoid social conflict. Japan already had an innovation-led growth and Korea also had an innovation-led growth alongside export-led growth and finance-led growth. China is trying to introduce innovation-led growth. It is necessary to reinvigorate (Japan), intensify (Korea), and set up (China) the innovation-led growth for sustainable growth. Table 7.21 shows R&D intensity (R&D expenditures as a percentage of GDP) trends in Japan, Korea, and China. Specifically, R&D intensity in Korea, which increased sharply from 2.20% in 1995 to 4.22% in 2015, is the highest in the OECD. It is much higher than those in Sweden, Germany, and the United States. R&D intensity in China also rose considerably since the 1990s, though it remains lowest among the three East Asian countries. In Japan, R&D expenditures, which accounts for about 3% of GDP, is concentrated in major corporations.

Table 7.21 R&D Expenditures as a % of GDP: R&D Intensity

	1995	*2000*	*2005*	*2010*	*2015*
Japan	2.61	2.91	3.18	3.14	3.28
Korea	2.20	2.18	2.63	3.47	4.22
China	0.57	0.89	1.31	1.71	2.06
United States	2.41	2.63	2.52	2.74	2.72
Germany	2,13	2.39	2.42	2.71	2.91
Sweden	3.13	3.91*	3.38	3.12	3.26

* Value for 2001 for 2001.

Source: OECD (2018b), Main Science and Technology Indicators (MSTI database).

Meanwhile, the share of R&D expenditures in SMEs is only 6%, compared with 40% on average in the OECD. Additionally, the share of SMEs in Japan that introduced some form of innovation between 2010 and 2012 (47%) was significantly less than in other advanced economies such as Switzerland (76%) and Germany (67%) (OECD, 2017b). Moreover, the type of R&D spending in Japan that is well above the OECD average is focused on manufacturing, while R&D spending in both high-knowledge services and low-knowledge services is substantially below the OECD average. Innovation in Japan thus tends to widen productivity and wage gaps between the manufacturing sector and service sector, and between large firms and small firms.

Polarized growth is also economically and socially unsustainable because it shrinks domestic demand and may intensify social conflict between classes. We previously discussed how shared growth could be achieved by decreasing the gap between large monopolistic firms and SMEs and between regular and non-regular workers by passing laws ensuring fair competition and promoting equal work for equal pay. Moreover, in order to reduce the gap between regular workers and non-regular workers, at least two among the triple discriminations against non-regular workers should be banned. In other words, when the fixed-term contract is effective and there is no opportunity of promotion for the non-regular workers, wages and social welfare should not be discriminated. When de facto long-term employment is guaranteed to the non-regular workers, some wages discrimination should be allowed.

Another way government in Japan, Korea, and China can reduce income inequality and polarization is through income redistribution by taxing the rich and transferring to the poor. The extent to which governments reduce income inequality through redistributive policies can be clarified by comparing the Gini coefficient at market income to the Gini coefficient at disposable income. The role of the state in redistributing income is indicated by the gap (A − B) between Gini coefficient at market income (A) and disposable income (B) shown in Table 7.22. The data in Table 7.22 reveals that the difference between the Gini coefficient at market income and the Gini coefficient at disposable income in Korea is negligible. In other words, the Korean state plays no significant role in income redistribution, especially when compared to Japan, the United States, and Sweden. According to Standardized World Income Inequality Database Version 5.1, the redistributive impact of taxes and transfers in China is also very low, with the reduction in market income inequality due to social spending being almost null in 2013. Moreover, according to the estimation of social spending's impact on income inequality and poverty rates in OECD countries, East Asian states redistribute little. For example, social spending in 2015 reduced the Gini coefficient by around 3% in Korea and approximately 5% in Japan, which is far below the OECD average of 10%. Similarly, social spending in 2015 only reduced poverty rates in Korea and Japan by about 2% points and 6% points, respectively, compared to the OECD's 9% point average (OECD, 2017c).

Table 7.22 Gini Coefficient at Market Income and at Disposable Income: Korea, Japan, United States, and Sweden

Year	Market Income (A)	Disposable Income (B)	A − B	Year	Market Income (A)	Disposable Income (B)	A − B
		Korea				*Japan*	
2006	0.330	0.306	0.024	1985	0.345	0.304	0.041
2007	0.340	0.312	0.028	1995	0.403	0.323	0.080
2008	0.344	0.314	0.030	2000	0.432	0.337	0.095
2009	0.345	0.314	0.031	2003	0.443	0.321	0.122
2010	0.341	0.310	0.031	2006	0.462	0.329	0.133
2011	0.342	0.311	0.031	2009	0.488	0.336	0.152
		United States				*Sweden*	
1984	0.436	0.337	0.099	1983	0.404	0.198	0.206
1989	0.450	0.348	0.102	1991	0.408	0.209	0.199
1995	0.477	0.361	0.116	1995	0.438	0.211	0.227
2000	0.476	0.357	0.119	2000	0.446	0.243	0.203
2005	0.486	0.380	0.106	2004	0.432	0.234	0.198
2010	0.499	0.380	0.119	2010	0.441	0.269	0.172

Source: OECD Database.

The changes in the role of governments in income redistribution over time are highlighted in Table 7.23, which show the trends of government transfers and subsidies index as well as top marginal tax rates index. In Japan, the government transfers and subsidies index, in which a higher score means less income redistribution by government, highlights how the state was prompted to increase transfers and subsidies to lower poverty and income inequality during the Lost Decades. Korea, too, expanded government transfer and

Table 7.23 Government Transfers and Subsidies and Top Marginal Tax Rate Index

		1980	1985	1990	1995	2000	2005	2010	2015
Korea	(1)	9.6	9.5	9.4	7.7	7.7	7.1	8.3	7.0
	(2)	0.0	2.0	1.5	5.0	5.0	6.0	6.0	6.0
China	(1)						8.3	8.3	8.3
	(2)		6.0	5.0	6.0	6.0	6.0	6.0	6.0
Japan	(1)	7.6	7.2	7.0	6.8	6.8	5.1	4.0	4.1
	(2)	0.0	1.0	1.5	1.5	5.0	5.0	5.0	3.0
United States	(1)	7.2	6.7	6.7	6.3	6.5	6.7	5.7	6.0
	(2)	0.0	4.0	6.5	7.0	7.0	7.5	7.0	5.0
Germany	(1)	5.3	5.0	5.3	4.3	2.3	2.3	2.6	3.1
	(2)	2.0	1.0	4.0	3.0	3.0	6.0	5.0	5.0
Sweden	(1)	3.4	3.1	2.0	0.8	4.0	4.0	4.6	4.6
	(2)	0.0	0.0	0.0	1.5	1.0	1.5	1.0	2.0

Note: A higher score means less income redistribution. (1) Transfers and subsidies, (2) top marginal tax rate.

Source: Gwartney et al (2015).

subsidies under center-left governments from the late 1990s to the late 2000s to address the effects of the 1997 financial crisis. Table 7.23 reveals that Korea and Japan also introduced neoliberal tax-cuts policies in the early 1990s (Korea) and the late 1990s (Japan), during which the top marginal tax rate decreased greatly. China, as well, has had relatively low top marginal tax rates since the mid-1980s. Together, the top marginal tax rate index and the government transfers and subsidies index indicate that Korea and China have the smallest governments in the sample when it comes to income redistribution. It is very paradoxical that in terms of income redistribution, China, which has a socialist market economic system, has much smaller government than the United States, which is the representative country of liberal market economy.

One way to promote sustainable growth in Japan, Korea, and China is therefore to expand welfare systems in each country. Social policy in the East Asian Model was traditionally subordinated to industrial policy. In the developmental state, there was a productivist welfare regime or developmental welfare regime (Kwon, 2007), though Japan has been able to establish a welfare state with relatively high levels of social spending. In Korea, strong popular demand for welfare led to increases in social spending. However, the government opted for a selective welfare regime rather than a universal one.[15] When Korea's industrial policy started retreating in the 1990s, neoliberal policies focusing on investments in innovation took precedence over public social expenditures. Thus, Korea was the country where there was a high expenditure on R&D but a low expenditure on social welfare. Looking at Tables 7.21 and 7.24, for example, show that R&D expenditures as a percent of GDP is much higher in Korea than it is in the United States. On the other hand, public social expenditures as a percent of GDP is much lower in Korea than it is in the United States, where a typical liberal market economy prevails.

Although the growth in social spending in Korea from 1995 to 2015 was the highest in the OECD, the level of public social expenditures as a percent of GDP is still quite low. China also has very low, but gradually increasing levels of public social expenditures. As shown in Figure 7.3, in Korea R&D investment as a percent of GDP is relatively high while public social

Table 7.24 Public Social Expenditures as % of GDP

	1995	*2000*	*2005*	*2010*	*2015*
Japan	13.3	15.4	17.2	21.3	21.9
Korea	3.1	4.5	6.1	8.2	10.2
China	3.2	4.7	2.7	6.7	6.3
United States	15.1	14.3	15.6	19.4	18.8
Germany	25.2	25.4	26.2	25.9	24.9
Sweden	30.6	26.8	27.3	26.3	26.3

Source: OECD, Social Expenditures Database 2017, ILO, World Social Protection Report: 2017–2018.

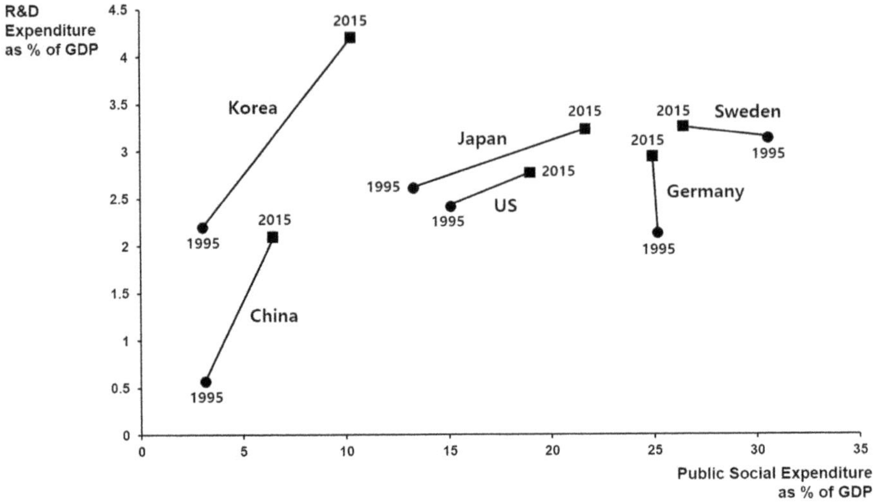

Figure 7.3 Changes in the Share of R&D Expenditures and Public Social Expenditures

Source: OECD (2017c), Social Expenditures Database, OECD (2018b), Main Science and Technology Indicators (MSTI).

expenditures (social investment) as a percent of GDP is relatively low. China is more biased toward R&D investment and falls short in social investment, while Japan strikes a balance between R&D investment and social investment. When it comes to changes in the share of R&D expenditures and public social expenditures from 1995 to 2015, Korea gained greatly in terms of both R&D expenditures and public social expenditures while Japan gained largely in terms of public social expenditures. China gained largely in terms of R&D expenditures. Thus, the trajectories of the changes are quite different among three countries. Meanwhile, the trajectories of the changes in Sweden, Germany, and the United States also showed completely different patterns. In Sweden, there was a relatively large reduction in public social expenditures with a small gain in R&D expenditures. In Germany, there was relatively large gain in R&D expenditure with a little reduction in public social expenditures. In the United States, there was relatively big gain in public social expenditures with a small gain in R&D expenditures.

The economic and social consequences of Korea's small government in terms of welfare expenditures can be observed by looking at elderly poverty in the country. At 49% in 2014, Korea's elderly poverty rate[16] is by far the highest in the OECD. Korea's high elderly poverty rate is negatively correlated with first-tier pension benefits which, as a percentage of average earnings, is the lowest (5% in 2014) in the OECD. Worse, Korea's crisis of elderly poverty is occurring as the population is rapidly aging. Another inconvenient truth is that the suicide rate of the elderly is the highest in Korea. Without active government policy, the living conditions of Korea's elderly are likely to deteriorate. In the short term, it may be necessary for the Korean government to reduce the coverage of the Basic Pension given to all the elderly. Instead, pension benefits should be concentrated on the elderly poor by covering a higher percentage of their previous earnings (OECD, 2015a). In the long term, social spending for the elderly should be expanded significantly by, for instance, creating jobs for them in both the public and private sectors. A rise in the fertility rate is also essential to eventually lower Korea's dependency ratio. Japan's elderly poverty rate (19% in 2014) is below the OECD average and its first-tier pension benefit (20%) is above the OECD average.

In order to finance the expanding public social expenditures, tax increase is inevitable. Tax increase to the rich and universal tax increase should be combined. However, reform of tax revenue structure is also essential. Table 7.25 shows that Japan and Korea have similar tax structure. It is remarkable that the shares of tax on personal income in GDP in Japan and Korea are much smaller than those in Sweden, the United States, and Germany. The share of tax on goods and services is also smaller than those in Sweden and Germany. When referred to the OECD average, it is recommendable that the direction of reform of tax revenue structure might be oriented toward significant increases in shares of tax on personal income and tax on goods and services as well as considerable decrease in the share of tax on corporate profits. This reform of tax revenue structure may contribute not only to reduction in income inequality but also to promotion of economic growth by encouraging corporate investments. It may be controversial whether the share of tax on property should be decreased since the OECD average may be too low when thinking about the share of tax on property in the United States, which is a representative country of the Anglo-American Model. Moreover, it would be rational to increase the share of tax on property in exchange for the reduction in the share of tax on corporate profits.

Let's now discuss labor market reform for sustainable growth in the East Asian Model. We saw earlier how flexibilization of the labor market in the East Asian Model brought about unemployment and the non-regularization

Table 7.25 Share of Tax Revenue by Type in GDP

	Tax on Personal Income	*Tax on Corporate Profits*	*Tax on Property*	*Tax on Goods and Services*
Japan	5.71	3.72	2.48	6.34
Korea	4.08	3.11	2.93	6.65
Germany	9.89	1.72	1.03	10.58
Sweden	12.53	2.91	1.03	12.08
United States	10.60	2.12	2.97	4.35
OECD Average	7.86	2.79	1.83	10.79

Note: Unit: %.

Source: OECD Database.

of workers, thus indicating that flexibility without security in the labor market is not sustainable. At the same time, it can also be argued that stability without flexibility in the labor market is unsustainable in a world of rapidly changing technologies and innovations.[17] Labor market flexicurity[18] is therefore needed for the East Asian Model to be sustainable. Labor market flexicurity can be realized by combining three elements: a flexible labor market, generous unemployment benefits, and active labor market policies[19] (Wilthagen and Tros, 2004). Together, these three elements offer an alternative to flexibility without security and stability without flexibility in the labor market by providing dynamic employment stability, rather than static employment stability. Moreover, flexicurity will contribute to a welfare regime promoting sustainable human development because it involves active labor market policies and generous unemployment benefits that can prevent the destruction of skills and livelihoods (Kim, 2012b).

Constructing a 'flexicurity triangle' is a useful way to analyze labor markets in terms of flexibility and security. As Figure 7.4 shows, the vertical axis represents the extent of labor market flexibility using the '6-EPL Index'.[20] The other two axes represent unemployment benefits as a percentage of previous earnings (also known as the replacement rate) and government expenditures

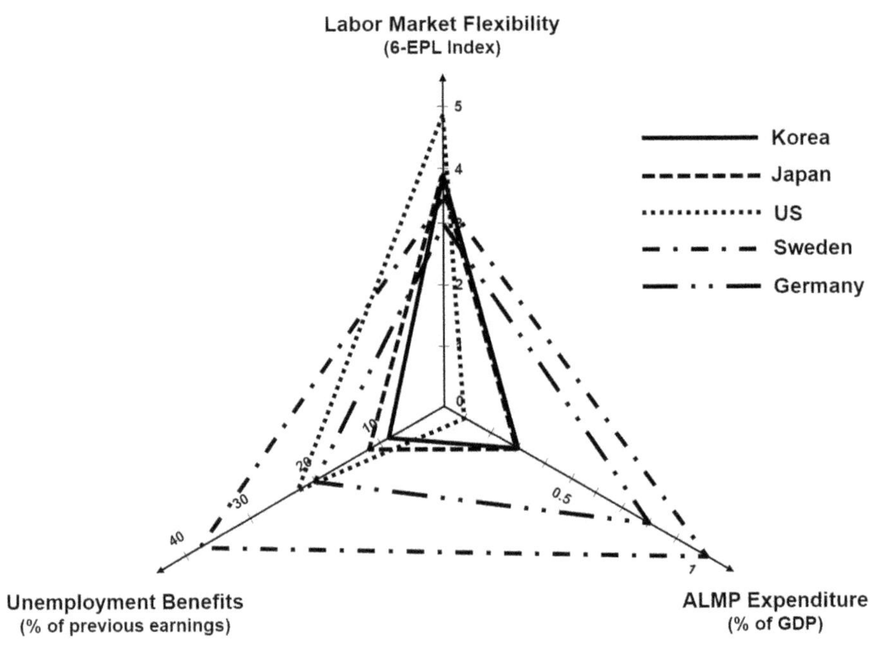

Figure 7.4 Flexicurity Triangles in Major Countries

Note: Labor Market Flexibility; 2013, UB Replacement Rates; 2011, ALMP Expenditure; 2011.

Source: OECD Database, Employment Outlook.

in the form of active labor market policies to retrain the unemployed. The shape and the size of a flexicurity triangle symbolize the degree of labor market flexicurity. The more equilateral the triangle is, the more flexibility and security are balanced. The larger the size of the triangle, the more the labor market is 'flexicure' (flexible and secure). Figure 7.4 thus indicates that labor markets in Korea and Japan are flexible but insecure like in the United States. Figure 7.4 also shows that Korea and Japan's flexicurity triangles are significantly smaller and less balanced than Sweden's and Germany's. According to the flexicurity triangle analysis, Sweden's labor market achieves higher flexicurity, while Korea's and Japan's labor markets achieve lower flexicurity. Based on this analysis, it can be argued that it is necessary for Korea and Japan to increase unemployment benefits and active labor market policy expenditures if they want to achieve sustainable growth.

Figure 7.5 also shows positions of labor market in each country in terms of labor market flexicurity. The OECD EPL Index on X-axis represents the extent of flexibility/rigidity of labor market, while the public spending on labor market as % of GDP on Y-axis indicates the extent of security/insecurity of labor market. As seen from the figure, Korea had rather high EPL index while it had much lower public spending on labor market in 2019.[21] This means that Korea should flexibilize labor market on the one hand with expanding public spending on labor market on the other hand if the country chooses realizing flexicurity of labor market. The table also reveals that even though Japan's labor market is more flexible than Korea's labor market, public spending on labor market is lower than that of Korea. For flexicurity of labor market, Japan should also increase public spending on labor market

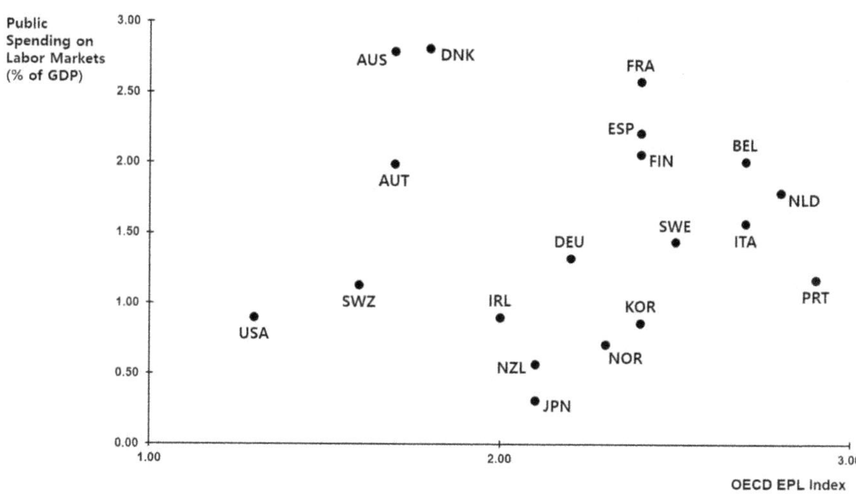

Figure 7.5 OECD EPL Index and Public Spending on Labor Market: 2019

Source: OECD Database.

while increasing flexibility of labor market. The United States, France, and Denmark are peculiar cases in view of flexicurity. The United States and France are far distant from the flexicuity of labor market. In the United States, labor market is very flexible and insecure due to rather low public spending on labor market. Conversely, France's labor market is rather rigid and very secure due to high public spending on labor market. Denmark and Australia's labor market belong to typical flexicurity, where labor market is both flexible and secure.

In addition to labor market flexicurity, the protection of workers' rights will contribute to sustainable growth. The Global Competitiveness Index (GCI) and labor protection data indicate that there needs to be no trade-off between flexible labor markets and the protection of workers' rights. According to the analysis of the Klaus Schwab and World Economic Forum (2019), two-thirds of countries with high levels of inequality have below-median protection of workers' rights, while two-thirds of countries with lower levels of inequality protect workers' rights more strongly. Moreover, 60% of states, which have high levels of workers' rights protection and labor market flexibility, achieve both high employment and low inequality. Norway, Sweden, Switzerland, the Netherlands, Germany, and especially Denmark have high levels of labor market flexibility and rights protection, with most of these countries having robust active labor market policies in place (Klaus Schwab and World Economic Forum, 2019).[22] These observations support the finding that workers' rights can well be protected in flexible labor markets, and that governments pursuing both objectives can have efficient labor markets as well as low levels of inequality. These countries, especially Denmark, realize flexicurity of the labor market. This suggests that the flexicurity of labor market can achieve both equity and efficiency and thus contribute to a sustainable growth. Labor market flexibility combined with protection of workers' rights may result in flexicurity of labor market.

The need for more government spending in areas such as social services brings issues surrounding the fiscal sustainability for sustainable growth to the fore. Seen from the fiscal position and government debts in Korea and Japan around 2016, Korea has a fiscal surplus and low gross government debt, while Japan has a large fiscal deficit and high gross government debts (OECD, 2017b). Though Korea now has a sound fiscal position, it is confronted with long-term fiscal challenges. For example, Korea's National Pension Fund (NPF) is predicted to record its first deficit in 2044, which is expected to grow rapidly thereafter (OECD, 2018a). Given the long-term fiscal challenges facing Korea, maintaining a sound fiscal position is a priority, which implies raising government revenue in line with expenditures. One way to prevent this deficit from occurring is to raise the NPF contribution rate, which has remained at 9% since 1998, well below the 20% OECD average. A contribution rate of 14.1% would be sufficient to keep the NPS in balance through 2083, assuming the replacement rate is cut to 40% as planned, and the pension eligibility age hikes from 61 to 65 by 2033. While there is no scope to further reduce the replacement rate, the eligibility age could be raised above 65, as was done in a number of OECD countries. Sources of revenue are also needed to finance other rising expenditures, notably in health and long-term care (OECD, 2018a).

Another issue Korea face is that of surging household debt. Korea's household debts climbed rapidly after the 1997 financial crisis, amounting to 180% of GDP in 2016. This increase in credit to households poses a serious threat to macro-financial stability in Korea, while credit growth to the corporate sector has been less buoyant, and fiscal and external macro-financial vulnerabilities are very low (OECD, 2018b). Japan and China also have serious debt problems. In Japan, gross government debts rose rapidly after the bursting of the asset bubble in 1991, reaching 220% of GDP in 2016. Japan's net government debts went up sharply after 1991 as well, growing to 120% of GDP. According to a long-run simulation, Japan's debt-to-GDP ratio will be 600% without improvement in the fiscal balance. However, if Japan's fiscal balance improves by 9.75% of GDP in fiscal year (FY) 2020, the debt-to-GDP ratio will decrease to 100% in 2060 (OECD, 2017b). In China, corporate debt,[23] of which 70% is from SOEs, soared from 97% of GDP in 2007 to 166% of GDP in 2016. On average, China's corporate debts is more than twice that of advanced countries (85%) and more than three times that of other emerging market economies (50%) (Duceux, 2018). Corporate leverage, defined as the debt-to-asset ratio, is particularly high in real estate, building materials, and metals industries due to excess capacity. The leverage of SOEs controlled by central government agencies increased very sharply, too, going from 45% in 2008 to 73% in 2013 amidst the Global Financial Crisis (OECD, 2017a). Korea, Japan, and China have their own serious debts problem like household debts, government debts, and corporate debts, respectively, which should be solved for the sustainable growth.

Finally, a new mode of regulation is necessary to realize a sustainable growth regime in Japan, Korea, and China. The type of state required to foster sustainable growth should be a welfare state that goes beyond developmental state and neoliberal state. For last two decades, there has been a shift from a developmental state to a neoliberal state. Now, there should be a transition from a neoliberal state to a welfare state. To achieve this transition, policy paradigms in all three countries must be changed from ones focusing on industrial policy or neoliberal policy to a sustainable development paradigm in which economic policy, social policy, and ecological policy for sustainability are complementary to each other. A new corporate system should be introduced as well in which corporate governance adopts stakeholder capitalism over shareholder capitalism, and where inter-firm relationships are rebuilt around open innovation. Financial liberalization should be prudentially controlled, too. Specifically, financial markets should be strictly regulated for financial capital to commit to industrial capital. Moreover, megabanks that have led to the 2008 financial crisis should not be promoted. Instead, a market-based financial system and a bank-based financial system should be developed in parallel (Park, 2002). Labor market flexicurity and participatory industrial relationships should also be established. An economic safety net as well as social safety net is needed (Kaneko, 1998). An economic safety net is composed of a financial safety net and an employment safety net (Kim, 2010). Flexicurity of labor market can play a role of an employment safety net. For a financial safety net, policy actions to prevent capital account crisis is required (Das, 2011).

At the international level, capital controls through mechanisms such as a financial transaction tax[24] should be introduced to redesign the international financial architecture. To this end, the 'Global Reserve Bank'[25] proposed by the Stiglitz Commission deserves to be discussed. It is necessary to establish the World Financial Organization,[26] WTO-type system for global financial regulation, proposed by Eichengreen (2009). A Global Glass-Steagall Act[27] should also be considered as a financial safety net (Das, 2011). Moreover, a New Bretton Woods system is needed to build a different global financial architecture to regulate international capital flows. A New Bretton Woods system should reform the 20th century international economic institutions to promote a more prosperous, just and sustainable world economic order fit for the 21st century (Gallagher and Kozul-Wright, 2022). At the regional level, Korea, China, and Japan should seek to establish an 'East Asian Community' in order to build a new regional financial architecture. Building the 'East Asian Community'[28] should be a key agenda in a new 'Seoul-Beijing-Tokyo Consensus' that goes beyond the Washington Consensus',[29] the core of which was a policy paradigm of the global neoliberalism.

Notes

1 According to Schumpeter, innovation is process of a creative destruction. Through innovation economy and society can achieve dynamic development. Social innovation seeks new innovative solutions to social issues such as working conditions, health, education, and community development. Since social innovation ultimately aim to improve the welfare and well-being of individuals and communities, it can facilitate inclusive and sustainable growth. Therefore, social innovation can contribute to social sustainability.

2 The Global Competitiveness Index (GCI) was designed by Klaus Schwab, Xavier Sala-i-Martí, and Richard Samans and reported by World Economic Forum. The GCI indicators are organized into 12 pillars: Institutions; Infrastructure; ICT adoption; Macroeconomic stability; Health; Skills; Product market; Labor market; Finance system; Market size; Business dynamism; and Innovation capability.

3 The index of goods market efficiency includes domestic competition, foreign competition, and taxation and regulation distortions. The index of labor market efficiency includes flexibility of labor market and talent utilization. The index of financial market development includes depth and stability of financial market.

4 The extent of market dominance is designated from the following question in the questionnaire: 'In your country, how do you characterize corporate activity? 1=dominated by a few business groups, 7=spread among many firms'.

5 The dependency ratio is defined by the population aged 14 and below and the population aged 65 and over as a percent of the population aged 15 to 64.

6 According to Marxian economics, the rate of surplus value(s) is S/V, where S = amount of surplus value and V = value of labor power. The value of labor power (Vt) equals quantity of means of living (wage goods) (Qt), multiplied by the unit value of means of living (Ut). Therefore, $V_{t+1} = (1 + \beta)Qt\cdot(1/(1 + \alpha))\cdot Ut = (1 + \beta)/(1 + \alpha) \cdot Qt\cdot Ut = (1 + \beta)/(1 + \alpha)\cdot Vt$, where α = labor productivity growth and β = real wage growth. Here, if $\alpha>\beta$, then s will increase. If $\alpha<\beta$, then s will decrease. And if $\alpha = \beta$, then s will be constant. We can thus infer the rate of surplus value from productivity growth and wage growth trends (Kim, 2001).

7 In 2020, for example, per capita GDP in Beijing was 164,889 yuan, while that of Ganshu was 35,995 yuan. People in Beijing earn 4.58 times more than people in Ganshu.

8 The Korean economy before 1997 had what can be described as a trickle-down mechanism for two reasons. First of all, economic growth created plentiful jobs for skilled and unskilled workers. Moreover, the growth in real wages was accompanied by productivity growth.

9 The vast majority of profits Chinese SOEs earn results from their monopoly situation and preferential treatment: easy access to bank loans at a third of market interest rate, massively subsidized rent on land, a tax rate less than half of that for private companies, tax breaks on energy resources, and direct injection of capital from the central government when required. Moreover, SOE profits are not redistributed through the financial system to help the rest of society but are instead largely retained (Breslin, 2012: 37–38).

10 According to Marxian economics, the relative surplus population is an industrial reserve army who waits the call of capital in labor market, that is, unemployed or underemployed.

11 The hukou system in China is a household registration system that gives the urban residents various benefits such as housing, education, health care, and pensions. It has been a major source of inequality between urban regions and rural regions.

12 According to the estimation of Piketty et al (2017), income share of top 10% in China increased from 27% to 42% in 2014, while income share of bottom 50% decreased from 27% to 15% in 2014.

13 The ecological debt refers to the ecological damage caused by a country to other countries or to ecosystems beyond its national jurisdiction through its production and consumption patterns. Moreover, it means the exploitation of ecosystems by a country at the expense of the equitable rights to these ecosystems by other countries.

14 Energy conversion from the nuclear energy to the renewable energy has been a very controversial issue in Korea. Former Moon Jae-In administration pursued radical energy conversion policy to stop some nuclear power plant without right administrative procedures. There is critic that radical reduction in nuclear power plant destructs the Korean nuclear energy industry that has strong global competitiveness. The gradual energy conversion policy with a very long-term time horizon from nuclear energy to renewable energy should be implemented. The new Yoon Suk-Yeol administration announced the abolition of the nuclear power phase-out policy of the former administration.

15 However, Korea has a universal health care system that is well institutionalized.

16 Elderly poverty denotes an individual aged over 65 with an income that is below 50% of the national median.

17 There are two types of innovation: radical innovation and incremental innovation. Radical innovation is driven by disruptive changes in technology, while incremental innovation is based on continuous improvements within an existing technological framework. Because radical innovation entails substantial shifts in production systems and the development of new goods, it requires rapid changes in the workforce within the firm to adapt to the new technology. Thus, radical innovation demands flexibility of the labor market (Hall and Soskice, 2001: 38–39).

18 Flexicurity is a compound of two words: flexibility and security.
19 An active labor market policy involves government's retraining the unemployed for reentry into the labor market. This differs from a passive labor market policy, in which government gives the unemployed unemployment benefits.
20 The EPL index is the employment protection legislation index, which ranges from 0 to 6. The EPL index measures the level of employment protection referring to regulations on hiring and firing workers. An EPL index of 0 denotes a perfectly flexible labor market, while an EPL index is 6 means that the labor market is perfectly rigid. Thus, the '6-EPL index' is a measure of labor market flexibility.
21 Public spending on labor market includes unemployment benefits (passive labor market policy) and active labor market policy such as public employment services (PES), training, hiring subsidies, and direct job creations in the public sector.
22 These countries adopt the Nordic Model (Sweden, Norway, Denmark, Netherlands) or the Rhine Model (Germany, Switzerland).
23 This refers to non-financial corporate debts, which accounts for over two-thirds of total debt in China.
24 A financial transaction tax was proposed to reduce the volatility of the global economy due to international capital flows. Major ideas proposed include a G20 financial transaction tax, a European Union financial transaction tax, and a Global Tobin Tax.
25 Stiglitz argued that a new global reserve system is essential to restore the world economy and promote sustained prosperity and stability. He added that Asian countries have an opportunity to reinforce existing regional arrangements, which would not only strengthen their economies, but also possibly be a critical building block in the creation of a new global reserve system (Stiglitz and Greenwald, 2010).
26 The WFO would establish principles for prudential supervision (capital and liquidity requirements, limits on portfolio concentrations and connected lending, adequacy of risk measurement systems and internal control) without attempting to prescribe the structure of regulation in detail. The WFO would define obligations for its members; the latter would be obliged to meet international standards for supervision and regulation of their financial markets and institutions (Eichengreen, 2009).
27 The Glass–Steagall Act was the United States Banking Act of 1933, which separated commercial banking from investment banking. The repeal of the Glass-Steagall Act in the United States in 1999 permitted banks to branch into risky lines of credit which precipitated the 2008 financial crisis. The idea of Global Glass–Steagall Act came in response to the 2008 financial crisis through re-imposing Glass-Steagall-like restrictions dividing the banking and financial system into two components.
28 After 1997 Asian financial crisis, the East Asian Vision Group proposed a report in 2001. The title of the report was 'Towards an East Asian Community: Region of Peace, Prosperity and Progress'. The report recommended some remarkable agenda. For example, the report recommended formation of East Asian Free Trade Area and East Asian Business Council as well as establishing East Asian Monetary Fund. In 2012, East Asian Vision Group II Report proposed to build East Asian Economic Community. Even though the two reports proposed to build East Asian Community, the latent tensions and conflicts in East Asian international political relations render the realization of the East Asian Community difficult.
29 The Washington Consensus, which was a policy paradigm to overcome the debt crisis of the early to mid-1980s in Latin America, recommended neoliberal policies such as privatization of public enterprises, deregulation, tax-cuts, austerity policy, liberalization of interest rates, and trade liberalization (Williamson and Kuczynski 2003).

8 Toward a Sustainable New East Asian Model

In the above chapters, we analyzed the transformation of state sector, corporate sector, financial sector, and labor sector in the East Asian Model while discussing the sustainability of the East Asian Model in terms of economic, social, and ecological sustainability. The major problems emerged from the transformation processes in Japan Model, Korea Model, and China Model were highlighted. The conditions for a sustainable development in the East Asian Model were clarified. During the last two or three decades, the East Asian Model transformed into a hybrid model. Even though the original East Asian Model exists no longer in Japan, Korea, and China, East Asian Model did not completely transit to other development model, for example, Anglo-American Model. The hybrid East Asian Model might not be sustainable due to not only the lack of institutional complementarity but also unsustainable growth regime and irrelevant mode of regulation. Especially, low growth potentials and polarization, very low fertility rates, and rapid population aging threaten sustainability of the Japanese, Korea, and Chinese economies and societies. Meanwhile, the three East Asian countries are also coping with Post-COVID 19 era and the Fourth Industrial Revolution. Therefore, a sustainable New East Asian Model for the recovery and rebuilding of the economy and society should be pursued in each country.

In this chapter, agenda for a sustainable New East Asian Model is suggested. We will focus on the agenda such as knowledge-led growth regime for a sustainable growth, a symbiotic market economy for sustainable shared growth, publicness for a new mode of regulation, and an alternative policy paradigm including a decentralized state for balanced regional development, an economic safety net for the stability of the national economy, bottom-up economics for reducing polarization between large firms and SMEs, a solidaristic knowledge policy for reducing knowledge differentials between workers, flexicurity of labor market for dynamic stability of employment, and a new welfare regime for sustainable human development.

DOI: 10.4324/9781003332725-8

8.1 Knowledge-Led Growth Regime for a Sustainable Growth

Beyond Finance-Led Growth Regime

As described in Chapter 7, a finance-led growth regime is unsustainable because it generates severe macroeconomic volatility and increases income inequality. Moreover, finance-led growth regime can be an obstacle to a smooth development of technological innovation due to its financial impatience (Boyer, 2004). Financial capital that seeks a short-term profitability is inherently impatient capital unlike the industrial capital that pursues long-term profitability. In addition, the finance-led growth regime is not sustainable because it might bring about a socio-political crisis.[1] Unlike Fordist wage-led growth regime based on industrial capital, a finance-led growth regime is one that includes the preponderance of financial capital in the national economy, the maximization of shareholder value in firms, and primacy of consumption based on financial income in the macroeconomic circuit. Finance-led growth regimes are characterized by four major processes: financialization, securitization, financial liberalization, and financial globalization (Chesnais, 1997; Boyer, 2000). Financial liberalization, as a core process for a finance-led growth, is associated with the deregulation of financial market, such as deregulation of interest rates, capital account liberalization, and the deregulation of financial institutions by, for example, abolishing the separation of investment banks from commercial banks. A finance-led growth regime emerged in a classic form around 1980s in the United States. Japan, and Korea attempted to establish this finance-led growth regime following the United States. As was discussed in Chapter 4, financial liberalization proceeded in the 1980s in Japan and in the 1990s in Korea. Financial 'Big Bang' in Japan Model and rapid financial liberalization in Korea Model attempted in part to introduce finance-led growth regime, even though the attempts have failed. As was clarified in the chapters above, financial liberalization ended up with Lost Decades in Japan and 1997 financial crisis in Korea.

The macroeconomic circuit of a finance-led growth regime is quite different from that of a Fordist growth regime. Fordist growth regimes are sustained by a macroeconomic circuit of 'mass production-high productivity-high wages-mass consumption' (Boyer and Saillard, 2002). Here, mass consumption fueled by high wages and stable labor markets that can guarantee quasi-full employment support a virtuous circle of growth. In contrast, finance-led growth regimes rely on stock prices and exchange rates, which are inherently volatile. Consumption based on financial incomes such as dividends and stock price earnings rather than wages further maintain the macroeconomic circuit of finance-led growth regimes (Kim, 2010). Likewise, asset bubbles generated from the speculative behavior of institutional investors and the herd behavior of individual investors make finance-led growth regimes volatile. This is because the boom-bust cycles that emerge from the formation and collapse of speculative bubbles bring about periodic financial crises (Soros, 2009). These financial crises mainly take the form of credit crunches which may bankrupt firms, sparking a drastic drop in production and a sharp increase in unemployment. Financial crises can therefore hurt decisively the real economy, as was seen during the 1997 financial crisis in Korea and the 2008 Great Recession in the global level world.

The Great Recession resulted in the reversal of financial liberalization and financial globalization. As we discussed in Chapter 4, the capital liberalization index decreased after the 2008 global financial crisis. There was massive deglobalization of finance (U.S. Government, 2010). Under finance-led growth regimes, the share of investment as a percentage of operating surplus has declined. The gross fixed investment as a share of operating surplus in major OECD countries largely decreased in 1980–2012 (Durand and Gueuder, 2016). Because a rising share of profits is used to pay dividends, fewer and fewer funds are channeled toward productive investments in the real economy. A reversal in financial liberalization and globalization through the strict regulation of financial markets may thus boost potential economic growth rates if productive investments increase as well.

The most influential actor in the finance-led growth regime is the institutional investor, such as the pension fund, the mutual fund, or the hedge fund. The institutional investor as a major shareholder, especially under shareholder capitalism, forces firms to adopt business strategies that focus on maximizing dividends[2] and shareholder value. To this end, firms attempt to realize labor market flexibilization, which allows them to get rid of inefficient processes in the organization and to fire redundant workers. Short-termism in business administration may thus sour industrial relations and make skill formation and the accumulation of social capital in the workplace difficult. Seen this way, long-term efficiency and growth by enhancing the capability of workers cannot be expected in a finance-led growth regime. As a result, the growth potential might fall in the finance-led growth regime. Because of the primacy of shareholder value and the subsequent bias toward the interests of shareholders at the cost of workers, finance-led growth regimes also have an inherent tendency to intensify inequality.[3] In the United States, for example, income inequality increased sharply in the 1990s due to skyrocketing CEO pay while real wages stagnated (Kim, 2010). Longer-term factors behind the 2008 Great Recession include financialization, which reduced the scope for development of the real economy. This is because mounting pressures for quick and better financial returns negatively impacted wages and job stability in the non-financial sector (ILO, 2009). Additionally, financial globalization contributed to an increase in the volatility of the national economy and brought about a rise in income inequality.

Then, East Asian Model also needs a new growth regime that goes beyond the finance-led growth regime with the strict regulation of financial markets for sustainable growth. A return to a Fordist growth regime in the era of globalization is unlikely since the globalization of production and markets undermines significantly the macroeconomic circuit of 'mass production and mass consumption' (Kim, 2010). A new growth regime should go beyond both Fordist growth regime and finance-led growth regime. A new growth regime will have a new productivity regime and a new demand regime. It will also have new sets of institutions to stabilize its regime. In terms of Regulation Theory, a new growth regime will have a new mode of regulation. The new development model based on a new growth regime and a new mode of regulation will likely have more progressive and more conservative variants. While more progressive variants will be based on a social market economy, more conservative variants will be based on a liberal market economy.

Knowledge-Led Growth Regime

As was stressed in the chapters above, instead of the finance-led growth regime, which is inherently unsustainable, innovation-led growth regime is required. For the achievement of the Fourth Industrial Revolution, which is promoted based on the creative knowledge, a knowledge-led growth regime as a kind of innovation-led growth regime should be established. A knowledge-led growth regime is a growth regime in which knowledge and innovation play major roles in value creation, income distribution, and economic growth (Kim, 2007). In knowledge-led growth regimes, flexible quality production systems are the foundation of the productivity regime and the diversified consumption of high-tech commodities is at the core of the demand regime. As shown in Figure 8.1, a virtuous circle in knowledge-led growth regime is completed through the nexus of 'flexible quality production-high value-added-high wages-and diversified consumption'. High value-added is created via innovation, the economies of variety,[4] and anti-Taylorist labor processes[5] with information technology. Moreover, high value-added is secured by high value-creating ability of the knowledge labor. The technological paradigm of knowledge-led growth regime is an ensemble of information, bio, and green technologies, which require knowledge workers empowered with job autonomy in the labor process.

In this macroeconomic circuit, the distribution of the high value-added is crucial. High value-added is shared out to high wages, high profits, and increase in free time (reduction in labor time). Institutional forms such as a collective bargaining focusing on skill bargaining[6] and skill pay or knowledge pay[7] can transform high value-added into high wages. With high wages, knowledge workers can purchase diverse high-tech goods, information goods, and educational/cultural services. Rather than the mass consumption of durables with less variety, diversified consumption of high-quality goods and services makes flexible quality production possible. Besides high wages, the value-added created by flexible quality production system are

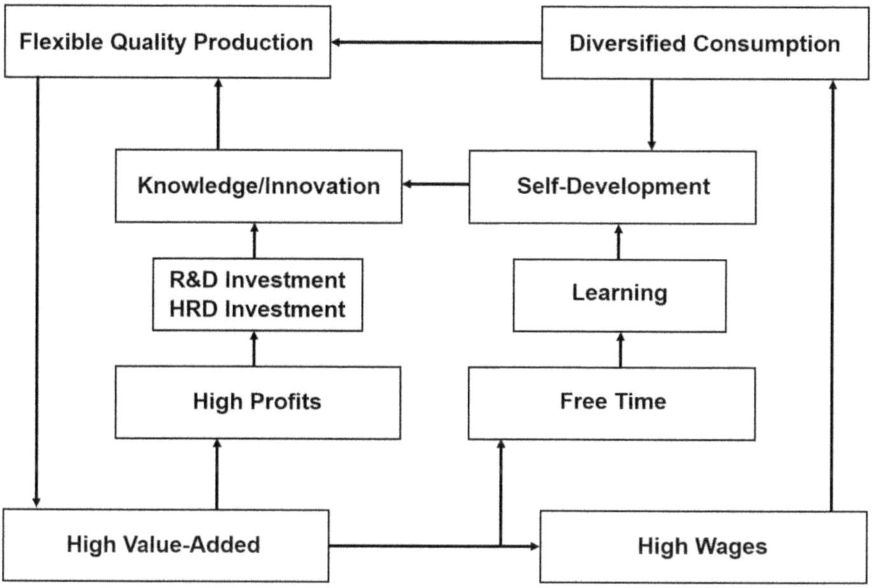

Figure 8.1 The Macroeconomic Circuit of a Knowledge-Led Growth Regime

Source: Kim (2007), p. 18. Figure 3.

shared out into high profits and increased free time. Here in the share out of the value-added, the ensemble of 'high wages-high profits-long free time' is crucial in macroeconomic circuit of knowledge-led growth regime. High profits gained by high value-added can finance high levels of knowledge investment, including R&D investment and HRD (human resources development) investment. Knowledge investment contributes to knowledge formation and innovation, which a flexible quality production system requires. High wages, coupled with the increase in free time due to the reduction in labor time that was possible based on high productivity, give workers opportunities for self-development through life-long learning. The expanding and deepening of life-long learning help transform unskilled labor into knowledge labor, unskilled workers into knowledge workers, and reproduces knowledge labor and knowledge workers, which is indispensable in the context of rapid technological change (Kim, 2007).

Both skill-biased technical change[8] and the internalization of knowledge by firms may polarize labor markets in knowledge-led growth regimes. The polarization of labor markets in knowledge-led growth regimes can be intensified because knowledge workers are generally paid higher wages than unskilled workers. Moreover, the higher wages knowledge workers receive allows them to invest more in personal development than unskilled workers can, creating a positive feedback mechanism between knowledge formation and income distribution. Especially the fact that knowledge-led growth regimes require 'high skill-high participation' workers make them compatible with stakeholder capitalism unlike finance-led growth regimes, which are associated with shareholder capitalism. In this respect, knowledge-led growth regimes are well suited for progressive development models. Yet as with finance-led growth regimes, knowledge-led growth regimes can be polarizing because of the knowledge gap between skilled and unskilled workers and skill-biased technical change.[9] Moreover, since there is positive feedback between knowledge level and wages level, polarization tendency becomes stronger.

In order for knowledge-led growth regimes to be progressive in the 21st century, they must be embedded in a social market economy and a green economy. In a social market economy,[10] the government intervenes in the market to reduce macroeconomic instability and income inequality, establish a welfare state, and make the participation of workers in management possible (Pontusson, 2005). A social market economy can thus create a knowledge-led growth regime that minimizes polarization, while knowledge-led growth regimes in liberal market economies (LMEs) are likely to generate more polarized growth. A green economy is an ecologically sustainable economy that can lower pollution and GHG (notably CO_2) emissions. Greening economies requires the enhancement of energy efficiency and the energy conversion from fossil energy to renewables (UNEP, 2008a). Green technology, green institutions, and green culture are needed for the green economy. A transition from a high-carbon mass production economy to a low-carbon green economy is essential for the progressive development model. This transition is especially needed in the East Asian Model where carbon intensity is high, as we discussed in Chapter 7. In short, a knowledge-led growth regime, a social market economy, and a green economy are the core elements of a new progressive development model that is more stable, more egalitarian, and more ecological (Epstein, 2009). This new progressive development model might be a benchmark of the New East Asian Model.

8.2 Symbiotic Market Economy as a New Economic Order

Hall and Soskice (2001) classified market economies into liberal market economies (LMEs) and coordinated market economies (CMEs). As we specified in Chapter 3, Japanese economy belonged to CME, while Korean economies might be classified as regulated market economies (RMEs) rather than LMEs and CMEs. Chinese economy was officially defined as socialist market economy (SME). However, as we analyzed in Chapter 4, in the transformation processes during the last two or three decades, hybridization has proceeded in the East Asian Model (Japan Model, Korea Model, and China Model): hybridization between CME and LME in Japan, between RME and LME in Korea, and between SME and LME in China. This hybridization may not be sustainable since it renders the East Asian Model inefficient and unstable due to the deficiency in institutional complementarity. Thus, we can't expect that the situation of hybridization in the East Asian Model will last long with good performances. Then, for a sustainable growth, a new economic order beyond LMEs, CMEs, RMEs, and SMEs should be pursued. Here, we suggest a symbiotic market economy as a new economic order in the East Asian Model.

A symbiotic market economy is defined as a market economy in which the principles of liberty, equality, and reciprocity are realized through equal power among economic agents who participate in the market (Kim, 2018b: 111). A symbiotic relationship can be realized only when the symmetry of power among economic agents exists in the market economy. For the symmetry of power, the weak economic agents such as small and medium-sized enterprises (SMEs), self-employed, employees, and peasants who are powerless can organize themselves into associations or unions through which they conclude collective bargaining with the strong economic agents like large firms and employers. The cooperatives and labor unions are essential socio-economic organizations for a symbiotic market economy. The state can intervene in the market through laws and policies such as Anti-Trust Act or Fair Trade Act, three labor rights (right to organize, collective bargaining right, and right to strike), employment and unemployment protection policies. State interventions in the market, if they are implemented rationally, can help to realize a symbiotic market economy. Enhancing collective bargaining power of the weaker economic agents by institutional reforms is necessary for a symbiotic market economy. Moreover, a symbiotic market economy is a market economy in which not only symbiosis between human beings within the economic system but also symbiosis between man (economic system) and nature (ecological system) is realized. Now in the East Asian Model, symbiosis between large firms (Keiretsus in Japan, Chaebols in Korea, and SOEs in China) and SMEs (non-SOEs in China), as well as symbiosis between regular workers and non-regular workers are especially top priority agenda, especially for a symbiotic market economy.

Creative Economy: First Category of Symbiotic Market Economy

A symbiotic market economy is comprised of three economic categories like a creative economy, a cooperative economy, and a clean economy. A creative economy is an economy where creativity of the people is a major engine of economic growth. Since creativity of the people brings about innovation, endless innovation sustains economic growth in a creative economy. The mass production economy, where economic growth is based on natural resources, experiences slow-down of growth due to the limited resources. The catching-up growth based on imitation of imported technology also slows down as an economy nears the technological frontier set by advanced countries. As described above, the recent slow-down of growth in Korea and China is partly attributable to the exhaustion of catching-up growth.

Table 8.1 The Global Creativity Index Rankings: 2015

	Global Technology Index		*Global Talent Index*		*Global Tolerance Index*		*Global Creativity Index (Rankings)*
	R&D Investment	*Patents per Capita*	*Creative Class*	*Educational Attainment*	*Racial & Ethnic Minorities*	*Gays & Lesbians*	
Japan	5	2	64	36	54	37	24
Korea	3	1	78	1	58	82	31
China	17	11	—	77	90	83	62
United States	8	5	34	2	20	9	2
Germany	7	10	16	38	30	21	14
Sweden	4	19	7	19	13	12	7

Note: Technology Index-R&D investment and patents per capita; Talent Index-Share of adults with higher education and workforce in the creative class; and Tolerance-Treatment of immigrants, racial and ethnic minorities, gays, and lesbians.

Source: Florida et al (2015).

In order to overcome the limits of catching up growth, a creative economy should be realized. 'From imitation to creation' is really needed for a sustainable growth in the East Asian Model.

Harrison (1985) argued that creative capacity of citizens is the main source of economic growth. Moreover, he even argued that underdevelopment is a state of mind. According to his argument, ultimately creative mind is a major engine of growth. Florida et al (2015) constructed the Global Creativity Index based on technology index, talent index, and tolerance index. Richard Florida assume that creativity comes from so-called 3Ts (Technology, Talent, and Tolerance). Technology Index is based on R&D investment and patents per capita. Talent Index is based on share of adults with higher education and workforce in the creative class.[11] And Tolerance Index is based on treatment of immigrants, racial and ethnic minorities, gays, and lesbians. As Table 8.1 shows, when compared to the United States, Sweden, and Germany, where the Global Creativity Index rankings are in the top level, the Global Creativity Index rankings in China, Korea, and Japan are low largely due to lower share of workforce in the creative class and less tolerance to racial and ethnic minorities and gays and lesbians. According to Florida's argument, China, Korea, and Japan should have much more tolerant societies and more workforces in the creative class in order to achieve a creative economy.

Cooperative Economy: Second Category of Symbiotic Market Economy

A cooperative economy is an economy in which shared growth and social integration are realized through the cooperation between the economic agents (Kim, 2018b). The cooperation based on trust can reduce social costs and enhance productivities in a society. The trust and cooperation are social capitals since they create the flow of returns in the future through enhancing productivity. Especially, trust promotes cooperation among firms and cooperation between labor and management. Trust reduces transaction costs and coordination failures during economic exchanges. Thus, generalized trust can affect economic growth by facilitating investment and innovation through reducing uncertainty on account of moral hazard and difficulties of contract enforcement (Algan and Cahuc, 2014). Moreover, countries with higher levels of trust have higher levels of cooperative relations between labor and management, which is associated with factors that favor GDP growth. When a cooperative economy is realized through trust and cooperation, shared growth between large firms and SMEs and between labor and management, as well as between regular workers and non-regular workers can be realized. And shared growth is essential for social integration. Especially in order to cope with the intensifying polarization in the East Asian Model, cooperation between large firms and SMEs in terms of technology and managerial skills is imperative.

Moreover, for a cooperative economy, a high-trust society should be built. According to survey results of World Values Survey, Japan, Korea, and China belong to low-trust society. As Table 8.2 shows, Sweden is a high-trust society in terms of trust in people, while Japan, Korea, and China are low-trust societies. Though Chinese respondents are less likely to trust others, they do have a high level of confidence in government and parliament. In Japan, respondents exhibit not only very low trust in others but also very low confidence in public institutions. Since trust comes largely from fairness in the behaviors of people and public institutions, to build a fare society is essential. Especially, fair competition and fair-trade order should be established firmly in economic activities. In short, a fair market economy alongside a

Table 8.2 Levels of Trust in People and Public Institutions

	Trust in People			*Confidence in Public Institutions*		
	Neighborhood	*People You Know Personally*	*People You Meet for the First*	*Government*	*Courts*	*Parliament*
Sweden	3.070	3.386	2.455	2.085	2.836	2.543
Germany	2.821	3.045	2.1	2.363	2.789	2.340
United States	2.714	3.167	2.177	2.435	2.696	2.067
Japan	2.369	2.829	1.493	1.872	2.672	1.861
Korea	2.784	2.913	1.899	2.18	2.52	1.961
China	2.894	2.66	1.689	3.049	2.674	2.83

Note: Points were given as follows: 'Trust completely' = 4, 'Trust somewhat' = 3, 'Do not trust very much' = 2, and 'Do not trust at all' = 1. Germany 2013, Japan 2010, Korea 2010, Sweden 2011, and United States 2011.

Source: World Values Survey Association (2014).

free market economy should be embedded in fair institutions in a country. The penalties on the opportunistic behaviors of individual economic agents should be imposed properly, while enough incentives should be given to the cooperative behaviors. The state, as a neutral third party, should play a role of the enforcer of fair competition orders. The trust in public institutions of the state sector is imperative in cooperative economy. Breaking the vested interests and removing the unjustifiable privileges of the public institutions are required. Through these institutional reforms, Japan, Korea, and China will be able to move from a low-trust society to a high-trust society.

Within a high-trust society, social dialogues between different interest groups can be promoted. Thus, social compromise or social consensus to the conflicting interests among social groups, for example, between labor and management, can be concluded easily based on the cooperation in a high-trust society. This contributes to ensure the political and social stability that are necessary for a sustainable economic growth.

Clean Economy: Third Category of Symbiotic Market Economy

A Clean economy is an economy in which man and nature have symbiotic relations through protecting ecosystem and preventing global warming (Kim, 2018b). Therefore, a clean economy is not only a green economy that protects ecosystem but also a clean energy economy that prevents global warming. Since reducing CO_2 for curbing global warming is an urgent global agenda, a clean economy should be a low-carbon economy. The green technologies that reduce CO_2 and enhance energy efficiency is a fundamental of a clean economy. The gradual energy conversion from fossil energy to renewable energy (such as solar energy, wind energy, hydropower, and bioenergy) is needed. Until foreseeable future, the safe use of nuclear power is indispensable for curbing global warming. In order to realize a clean economy, de-materialization and de-toxification of the production systems should be promoted intensively. The institutions for throughput innovation, which reduces the entropies that increase in production and consumption, should be built (Cho, 2009).

The institution building for the transition from a high-carbon economy to a low-carbon economy is essential for realization of the clean economy. The introduction of carbon-tax instead of the existing cap-and-trade system is necessary for effective reduction in CO_2 emissions. To build a local energy system that supplies the self-reliant energy to the small size local community is also needed. The electricity supply system should be transformed partly from a high-carbon centralized one-way network to a low-carbon decentralized interactive network (Morotomi and Asaoka, 2011). Moreover, innovation to introduce sustainable manufacturing methods and construction methods, which enhance ecological efficiency and prevent creation of the waste materials, are necessary (McDonough and Braungart, 2002). An ecological way of life or eco-friendly living of the people helps to realize a green economy or clean economy.

Table 8.3 The Green Growth Index 2019: Four Sub-Indices

	Efficient and Sustainable Resource Use	*Natural Capital Protection*	*Green Economic Opportunities*	*Social Inclusion*	*Green Growth Index (Score)*
Japan	41.39	73.53	33.23	83.23	53.86
Korea	34.48	61.09	54.06	76.41	54.31
China	34.49	70.15	55.41	70.17	55.41
United States	38.88	62.61	44.14	80.44	54.22
Germany	55.02	81.52	60.55	88.65	70.04
Sweden	75.79	77.26	57.96	93.70	75.09

Source: Global Green Growth Institute (2019).

Because of the imperative of reducing CO_2 emissions to cope with climate change, green growth will probably be an essential component of new growth regime, no matter their ideological inclination (UNEP 2008a). The Green Growth Index constructed by the Global Green Growth Institute is useful to highlight the policy agenda for a green economy in the East Asian Model. Table 8.3 shows that Japan, Korea, and China get nearly the same scores in terms of the Green Growth Index that are comparable to the score of the United States but are much lower than those of Sweden and Germany. From the sub-indices of the Green Growth Index, the relatively strong and weak points of each country can be clarified. Japan showed lower performance in green economic opportunities and efficient and sustainable resource use, while Korea and China showed lower performances in efficient and sustainable resource use. Germany showed higher performance in natural capital protection, while Sweden showed higher performance in efficient and sustainable resource use. According to the data, Japan's top priority policy agenda would be to expand green economic opportunities and the efficient sustainable resource use. Korea's and China's top priority policy agenda might be efficient and sustainable resource (Global Green Growth Institute, 2019).

From the sub-indices of the 'efficient and sustainable resource use index', we can see that Japan and China are getting very low score in 'sustainable land use', which is comparable to the United States. Korea is getting very low scores in 'efficient sustainable water use' and 'efficient sustainable energy'. For 'natural capital protection' index, Korea and Japan get lower score in 'cultural and social value', while Korea and China get lower score in 'biodiversity and ecosystem protection'. Therefore, for natural capital protection, Korea and China should strengthen biodiversity and ecosystem protection, while Korea and Japan should cultivate cultural and social values of the people. For 'green economic opportunities' index, Japan showed lower performance in 'green innovation' and 'green employment', while Korea showed lower performance in 'green innovation'. China showed lower performance in 'green trade'. Therefore, for expanding green economic opportunities, Japan's top priority policy agenda would be to create more green jobs and to promote green innovation. Top priority policy agenda of Korea should be to promote green innovation, while that of China might be to expand green trade.

In order to realize a symbiotic market economy which is comprised of the 3Cs economy (creative economy, cooperative economy, and clean economy), sufficient knowledge investment for a creative economy, investment to social capital for a cooperative economy, and green investment for a clean economy are required. In addition to this, three values of autonomy, solidarity, and ecology[12] should be prevailed as an alternative societal paradigm. The value of autonomy is the principle of a creative economy, while the value of solidarity is the principle of cooperative economy. And the value of ecology is the principle of clean economy (Kim, 2018b).

8.3 Publicness as a New Mode of Regulation

Publicness can be defined as the quality of institutions and culture that, together, contribute to realizing the universal interests of society. As a major rule of game, publicness plays a role as mode of regulation that provides regularity and consistency to the growth regime. Publicness in most capitalist countries, including in East Asia, weakened greatly following thirty years of deregulation, privatization, and tax-cuts since the 1980s. For example, Stiglitz (2014) showed how publicness in US policymaking was adversely influenced by the private interests of capitalists.[13] In the transformation process of the East Asian Model, publicness was greatly weakened since marketization, privatization, liberalization, and flexibilization themselves undermined the public domain. This damage done to publicness should be addressed to mitigate the severe instability and inequality caused by neoliberalism. Specifically, politics should be restored for the state to take back the power yielded to the market'.[14] In the midst of the Great Recession after the 2008 global financial crisis, the voices appealing for the enhancement of publicness also favored the expansion of the public domain over the private domain. And the need to reduce selfishness and greed for a more eco-friendly lifestyle rose. Improving publicness is one of the necessary conditions to achieve sustainable development in the East Asian Model.

Capitalism is based on two fundamental institutions: private property and the market economy, which guarantee the pursuit of private interests. On the one hand, publicness in capitalism can be realized when the government restricts properly the rights of private property and intervene in markets to act in the public interests. On the other hand, publicness can be achieved by promoting a publicness-oriented culture, as seen through measures of societal paradigms such as the World Values Survey,[15] which is performed by the World Values Survey Association (WVSA). Societal paradigm is a dominant worldview (Weltansachung) of the people in a society. And World Values Survey shows the societal paradigm in a country (Kim, 2018b).

Government can realize publicness through taxes and spending to provide public goods such as defense, police, education, and welfare. The role of government in realizing publicness may reach from the passive public expenditures for compensating market failures to the active public social expenditures for universal welfare. In this aspect, publicness of a country will be different whether it has 'small government and big market' or 'big government and small market'. Thus, an indicator of publicness can be measured by the economic role of the government that is identified by government size. Size of Government Index shown in chapter 4 represents that countries with lower levels of government expenditures as a share of GDP, a smaller public enterprise sector, and lower marginal tax rates earn the higher ratings, which means lower level of publicness.

Table 8.4 shows the indicators of publicness in four types of development models. First of all, publicness in terms of government size is the highest in the Nordic Model and the lowest in the Anglo-American and East Asian Models. Second, publicness in terms of the OECD Employment Protection Legislation (EPL) Index, which measures the level of employment protection referring to regulations on hiring and firing workers, is the lowest in the Anglo-American Model. Third, publicness in terms of public social expenditures as percentage of GDP is the highest in the Nordic Model and the lowest in the East Asian Model. These differences in publicness across development models may have an influence on the extent of income inequality, as seen with the Nordic Model's high levels of publicness and low level of income inequality (low Gini coefficient). It is remarkable that high Gini coefficient, high Size of Government Index, and low public social expenditures as % of GDP in the East Asin Model[16] is comparable to Anglo-American Model's high Gini coefficient, high Size of Government Index, and low public social expenditures as % of GDP.

Table 8.4 Indicators of Publicness in Selected Development Models

Development Model	*Size of Government Index (2019)*	*OECD EPL Index (2019)*	*Public Social Expenditure as % of GDP (2017)*	*Gini Coefficient (2017–2019)*
Anglo-American	6.7	1.58	18.4	0.361
Rhine	5.8	2.20	23.0	0.318
Nordic	5.1	2.25	27.5	0.281
East Asian	6.3	2.25	16.2	0.340

Notes

1. The countries represented in each development model are as follows: Anglo-American Model (Australia, Canada, UK, United States), Rhine Model (Austria, Belgium, France, Germany, Ireland, Netherlands, Switzerland), Nordic Model (Denmark, Finland, Sweden, Norway), East Asian Model (Japan, Korea)
2. The higher OECD EPL Index means the stronger employment protection.
3. Gini Coefficients of Canada and the UK are for 1997. Those of Australia, France, Germany, Ireland, Korea, and Switzerland are for 2018. Those of the other countries are for 2019.

Source: Gwartney et al (2020) OECD Database, OECD(2020).

Publicness can further be decomposed into four aspects: public interest orientation, fairness, civil spirit, and openness. Table 8.5 presents these sub-indices of publicness in the selected OECD countries, as analyzed by the Seoul National University's Institute for Social Development and Policy Research (2014). Among 33 OECD countries, publicness is overall the highest in Norway and the lowest in Korea. Examining Table 8.5 in detail reveals that public interests orientation is the lowest in Korea and the highest in Norway. Looking at the rankings for fairness shows that Korea also places last in this category, while Norway places first. Standings for civil spirits show that Sweden performs the best and Korea the worst. Finally, openness is the highest in Norway and the lowest in Korea. In sum, publicness is the highest in Norway and the lowest in Korea.

Another trend observed in the publicness rankings is the correlation between the type of development model and the level of publicness. Indeed, countries that adopt the Nordic Model (Norway, Sweden, Finland, and Denmark) are shown to rank the highest in terms of publicness. Rhine Model countries (Ireland, Switzerland, Netherlands, Germany, Belgium, and Austria) also have relatively high levels of publicness. At the other end of the publicness spectrum, countries belonging to the Anglo-American Model (the UK and the United States) and the East Asian model (Japan and Korea) exhibit low publicness.

Table 8.5 Publicness Rankings in Selected OECD Countries

Country	*Public Interests Orientation*	*Fairness*	*Civil Spirits*	*Openness*	*Publicness*
Norway	3	1	3	1	1
Sweden	6	2	1	3	2
Finland	5	3	4	2	3
Denmark	4	6	2	5	4
Ireland	7	9	18	12	8
Switzerland	27	7	10	6	9
Netherlands	12	8	14	14	11
Germany	16	18	6	10	12
Belgium	11	11	12	19	13
Australia	22	17	8	15	15
Austria	8	24	16	22	16
Canada	25	16	11	18	18
UK	24	22	17	16	22
France	18	15	24	26	23
United States	32	31	5	8	24
Japan	29	27	30	27	31
Korea	33	33	31	29	33

Source: Institute for Social Development and Policy Research (2014).

Besides looking at public interest orientation, fairness, civil spirits, and openness, analyzing indicators from the World Values Survey can help show the impacts of diversity of institutions and cultures on the level of publicness in different countries. It can be said that institutions in Nordic Model tend to have high publicness and institutions in Anglo-American and East Asian Model tend to have low publicness. Difference in cultures in the world can be clarified by the World Values Survey. Publicness in terms of ways of thinking and modes of behavior from people in different countries can be analyzed through some indicators of the World Values Survey. Table 8.6, for example, presents results for a part of the survey in which respondents were asked whether 'tolerance and respect for other people' and 'unselfishness' are important qualities to teach children. The share of people who think tolerance and respect for other people is important quality to the child is highest in Sweden between the 1995–1999 and 2010–2014, while that is lowest in Korea. Because tolerance and unselfishness are associated with higher levels of publicness, these results suggest that Sweden is the best when it comes to enhancing publicness in terms of those two qualities, while Korea is the worst. In contrast, the share of people who think unselfishness is important quality for the child is highest in Japan between 1995–1999 and 2010–2014, while that is lowest in Germany.[17] Anyway, Korea needs child education reforms for enhancing publicness through nurturing the tolerant and unselfish attitudes of the child within the school and family.

People's opinions on their experiences with political activism help us further understand why levels of publicness vary across regions. Popular political participation may further enhance publicness when public or private institutions and corporations behave unfairly against public interests. The proportion of people who reported involvement in political activities such as signing petitions, joining boycotts, attending peaceful demonstrations, joining strikes, or partaking in any other act of protest is relatively high in

Table 8.6 Opinions on Important Child Qualities: Tolerance & Respect for Other People and Unselfishness

	Tolerance and Respect for Other People		*Unselfishness*	
	1995–1999	*2010–2014*	*1995–1999*	*2010–2014*
Sweden	90.4	87.0	23.7	30.4
Germany	88.3	66.7	5.4	5.9
United States	75.0	71.8	36.0	32.7
Korea	46.8	40.8	10.6	10.5
China	61.1	52.2	28.2	29.2
Japan	58.3	64.6	37.8	45.1

Note: Unit: %.

Source: World Values Survey Association (1999), World Values Survey Association (2014).

Table 8.7 People's Experience with Political Action

	Sweden	*Germany*	*United States*	*Korea*	*China*	*Japan*
Signing a petition	68.0	42.7	60.1	26.4	4.5	28.0
Joining in boycotts	21.9	12.9	15.5	5.4	2.6	1.4
Attending peaceful demonstrations	20.8	21.1	13.7	9.5	1.7	3.6
Joining strikes	16.0	11.9	7.4	5.3	1.4	3.5
Any other act of protest	14.0	10.9	5.6	4.0	1.2	1.7

Note: These numbers denote the proportion of people who took political action.

Source: World Values Survey Association (2014).

Sweden and Germany. In contrast, the degree of political activism is much lower in Korea, Japan, and especially China (see Table 8.7). These observations suggest that the possibility of enhancing publicness through direct political action by citizens is high in the Nordic and Rhine Models and low in the East Asian Model.

The societal views presented so far are further reflected in people's materialist and post-materialist inclinations. According to Inglehart (1981), those who have materialist values give priority to order and stability and to economic and military strength. Contra materialists, post-materialists place a higher value on ideas, equality of opportunity, citizen involvement in decision-making at government and community levels, and environmental protection (Inglehart, 1981; Braithwaite et al, 1996). Materialist inclinations thus tend to impede on publicness, whereas post-materialist inclinations enhance it. As Table 8.8 shows, post-materialist inclinations are stronger in Sweden and Germany, while materialist inclinations are more salient in Korea and China. A post-materialist way of life will help promote values of solidarity and ecology that are important to achieving sustainable development.

Publicness should also be based on individual liberty. To avoid totalitarianism, individual liberty shall not be opposed in the name of publicness. Enhancing publicness through individual liberty requires embracing emancipative values: personal autonomy, equality of opportunities, freedom of choice, and the ability to voice opinions. Because these values constitute the key cultural component of human empowerment, they are the best available

Table 8.8 Materialist or Post-Materialist Inclinations

	Sweden	*Germany*	*United States*	*Korea*	*China*	*Japan*
Materialist	7.6	19.6	23.2	44.2	53.0	19.3
Post-materialist	30.0	22.4	16.7	5.1	2.5	6.6

Note: The post-materialist index contains four items: (1) Maintaining order in the nation, (2) Giving people more say in important political decisions, (3) Fighting rising prices, and (4) Protecting freedom of speech.

Source: World Values Survey Association (2014).

Table 8.9 Emancipative Values: Sub-Indices

	Sweden	*Germany*	*United States*	*Korea*	*China*	*Japan*
Autonomy	0.68	0.63	0.52	0.55	0.60	0.65
Equality	0.85	0.72	0.76	0.55	0.53	0.52
Choice	0.79	0.51	0.50	0.30	0.20	0.48
Voice	0.56	0.55	0.37	0.35	0.18	0.38

Source: World Values Survey Assocaition (2014).

predictors of a state's effective level of democracy and of other indicators of good governance (Kim, 2018b). Autonomy, equality, choice, and voice also provide social capital that makes the public more self-expressive and vitalizes civil society (Welzel, 2013). In short, emancipative values can help promote sustainable development by enhancing publicness. According to the World Values Survey, people in Sweden—a Nordic model state—espouse emancipative values the most compared to the rest of the countries in our sample (see Table 8.9). Respondents in a Rhine Model country such as Germany are, too, more likely to endorse autonomy, equality, choice, and voice. By contrast, all major East Asian Model societies (Korea, China, and Japan) are shown to take up emancipative values less than they are elsewhere. For a sustainable East Asian Model, people of the East Asian countries should have emancipative values.

Important policy implications can be derived based on the above observations. As we saw above, different development models have varying levels of publicness. Specifically, the Nordic Model or social democratic model is shown to have the highest level of publicness, followed closely by the Rhine Model or social market economy model. Meanwhile, the Anglo-American Model or LME model, and especially the East Asian Model, have relatively low levels of publicness. To enhance publicness in countries such as Japan, Korea, and China, the economic role of the state should be expanded by, for instance, strengthening its income redistribution function. Governments should also be able to implement institutions that can increase fairness and equal opportunities in every aspect of people's economic and social lives. 'Responsive government' rather than 'small government' is needed. Politically, participatory democracy and deliberate democracy should be bolstered as well.

In order to enhance publicness as a new mode of regulation, some institutional and cultural reforms are required. In the realm of business, corporate social responsibility (CSR) should be promoted by introducing stakeholder capitalism rather than shareholder capitalism in corporate governance. As we saw in previous chapters, corporations under shareholder capitalism aim to maximize shareholder value since only shareholders are involved in decision-making. Unlike shareholder capitalism, corporations that adopt stakeholder capitalism try to realize the mutual interests of stakeholders such as shareholders, employees, consumers, and residents, which advances publicness. For example, workers' participation in management through practices such as *Mitbestimmung* (co-determination) in Germany enhance publicness because they tend to promote CSR. Cooperative inter-firm linkages should also be incentivized by fostering symbiotic relationships between large firms and SMEs. Thus, 'from subcontracting to partnership' should be a major agenda for inter-firm relations. To establish these symbiotic relations, the asymmetric power between large firms and SMEs must be reduced by, for instance, allowing SMEs to form strong associations, which will help them better engage in collective bargaining with large firms. To this end, Fair Trade Acts or Anti-Trust Acts in the countries should include an exception clause that grants SMEs the right to negotiate collectively.[18] Together, these measures will strengthen publicness in the corporate sectors of East Asian economies by creating more grounds for partnership between large firms and SMEs rather than the prevailing dominant-subordinate relationship (Kim, 2012).

It is also necessary to expand the social economy that has the principle of publicness as well as profitability. The capitalist market economy has three economic sectors: the private economy, the public economy, and the social economy. Publicness can be realized via CSR in private economy. Public economy, in which government is a major economic agent, has, by definition, an obligation to safeguard publicness. However, because the public economy in capitalism might be captured by the private interests of business elites or other interest groups, monitoring government policies through democracy should be strengthened to protect and enhance publicness. Capitalist state tends to be inherently class-biased toward capitalist class. However, when democracy is broadened and deepened, class-biasedness will be weakened and publicness can be increased (Kim, 2001).[19] Indicators of publicness should thus be prioritized over other indicators when government evaluates the performance of public institutions. Moreover, social consensus among capitalists, the working class, and the state on economic and social policies further serves to cultivate publicness. The social economy, which is comprised of cooperatives, social enterprises, and community businesses, will contribute to the advancement of publicness as well. This is because the social economy plays a key role in providing jobs to disadvantaged workers and delivering welfare to the poor. State support of the social economy through measures such as the promotion of social entrepreneurship may therefore help reduce unemployment and expand welfare. In the cultural sector, innovation of way of life should be achieved. Principles of communitarianism should prevail in every level of social organization. Community consciousness should be encouraged instead of selfish individualism and participation consciousness should be strengthened. A voice option, rather than an exit option, should also be chosen as the behavioral norm for concerned citizens.[20] A post-materialist ecological way of life should be promoted as well, and social capital such as trust and cooperation should be accumulated. Additionally, tolerance and unselfishness among children should be nurtured in education processes within the family and at school. In short, three values of new progressivism, that is, autonomy, solidarity, and ecology (Lipietz, 1992), should be a societal paradigm.

We saw above that publicness is the highest in the Nordic Model, in which there is a responsive government and a vibrant civil society. A responsive government means that government plays an active role in correcting market failures and in realizing fairness and equality in socio-economic processes. A vibrant civil society means that the majority of citizens actively participate in political and social processes to serve the public interest. Here, the government should be able and transparent. And the government should have autonomy from the interest groups. As we analyzed above, Sweden, the representative country of Nordic Model, has both a responsive government and a vibrant civil society. Indeed, Sweden is a high-trust and tolerant society that embraces emancipative values and whose people participate actively in political action. These cultural factors must have contributed to the state achieving top levels of publicness globally. As Stiglitz (2014) argued, a deficiency in publicness endangers the future of capitalism as it may bring about a divided society. If we anticipate a sustainable development in the East Asian Model, we should achieve institutional and cultural reforms to enhance publicness. In order to enhance publicness in the East Asian Model, Nordic Model or Rhine Model rather than Anglo-American Model should be referred in designing a new East Asian Model.

8.4 An Alternative Policy Paradigm for a New East Asian Model

Alongside with a knowledge-led growth regime, a symbiotic market economy, publicness as a new mode of regulation, an alternative policy paradigm for a new East Asian Model should be implemented. Here we suggest an alternative policy paradigm such as a decentralized state for balanced regional development, an economic safety net for the stability of the national economy, bottom-up economics for intensive R&D and human development investment to the SMEs and their workers, a solidaristic knowledge policy for reducing knowledge differentials between workers and between firms, flexicurity of labor market for dynamic stability of employment, and a new welfare regime for sustainable human development. These policies will reduce systemic risk and polarization that have emerged in the East Asian Model since the 1990s and can revitalize the economies from the COVID pandemic that stroke the East Asian economies strongly.

A Decentralized State for Balanced Regional Development

The East Asian development state in Japan, Korea, and China has been a highly centralized state where the central government only has rights of legislations and rights of taxation at a national level. There were no local governments that had such rights. The local governments have a very limited local autonomy. The ordinances of the local governments can be introduced within (or within the scope of not violating) the law acted by the central government. Tax rates also are determined by the central government. The constitution defines such power relationships between the central government and local governments. In Japan and especially in Korea, highly centralized state systems have been existed long time from modernization and industrialization processes. Meanwhile, the concentration of resources (man and money) upon capital cities like Tokyo and Seoul, proceeded greatly. Thus, Japan and especially Korea evolved toward politically, economically, and culturally hyper-centralized countries. Even though China has been less centralized than Korea and Japan, the country also has a strong centralized state under the monolithic power of the Chinese Communist Party.

Under the centralized state system, a regional disparity has been intensified significantly. The gap between capital cities and provinces has been widened hugely. Thus, the words like 'Tokyo one-pole regime' in Japan and 'Seoul one-pole regime' in Korea were coined. Especially in Korea, there is a cynical argument that the Republic of Korea became the 'Republic of Seoul'. All in all, the population concentration in Tokyo/Seoul Metropolitan region is a definite indicator of unbalanced development between Tokyo/Seoul Metropolitan region and the provinces. Half the population live in Seoul Metropolitan region and a third of the population live in Tokyo Metropolitan region. The consequence was the deplorable 'extinction of the provinces', which was originally specified by Mazda (2014). The 'extinction of provinces' is occurring due to moving of the young people from the provinces to Tokyo metropolitan region. This phenomenon is emerging more rapidly and extensively in Korea. According to the estimation by Lee (2018), about 40% of total 228 primary local authorities (cities and counties) entered into a stage of extinction risk. In a rapidly population aging, the risk of 'extinction of the provinces' in Korea and Japan may be the most serious challenge to the sustainability of the countries.

According to Mazda (2014), the population concentration upon Tokyo brought about a low fertility rate in Japan since it forced young people to postpone or give-up marriage due to the difficulties of finding decent jobs and having a comfortable house. Mazda argued that in order to enhance the fertility rate, the population concentration in Tokyo should be reduced, and thus extinction of provinces should be prevented. His argument is much true of Korea. Now, Korea's total fertility rate is the lowest in the world. It was 0.84 in 2020, which was far lower than 1.34 in Japan. Henderson (1968) argued that in Korea highly centralized political system brought about concentration in Seoul Metropolitan city through 'the politics of vortex' summoning man rapidly. When the two arguments of Mazda and Henderson are combined, it can be concluded that ultimately a hyper-centralized state system in Korea and Japan brought about a very low fertility rate.

If then, the fundamental system reforms that transform the centralized state system into the decentralized state system are essential to prevent the extinction of provinces and to recover the fertility rate. Especially such fundamental reforms need the revision of the constitution that defines the hyper-centralized state system. Under the decentralized state system, the local governments who have the right of legislation and the right of taxation should implement regional innovation system to create growth potentials in the regions. In the knowledge-led growth regime, decentralization can be facilitator of value creation beyond value distribution (Kim, 2002). The growth potentials nurtured through the regional innovation system can be realized in creation of high value-added, which is a factor of the regional economic growth and job creation. Here, if welfare community is established under the decentralized state system, a care economy may emerge as a new economic sector, which will serve as a new engine of regional economic growth. More regional decent jobs creation is possible through the regional innovation system and a care economy. In this way, a decentralized state system can contribute to balanced regional development.

An Economic Safety Net

An economic safety net, which is comprised of a financial safety net and an employment safety net, is needed to reduce systemic risk stemming from volatility in the global economy. The financial safety net will aim to protect national economies from financial crises. This can be achieved by introducing financial transaction taxes, such as a global Tobin tax,[21] to regulate the international movement of short-term capital. Strengthening the regulation of short-term foreign debts and financial derivatives can act as another important financial safety net. Through these measures, financial markets will be better embedded in governments and other social institutions to work efficiently and serve the needs of society (Epstein, 2009). Financial regulation must also be coordinated on a global scale. The IMF and the World Bank should abandon the principle of high conditionality and free capital mobility embodied in neoliberalism. Instead, they should promote an alternative approach to economic development that gives developing countries more policy autonomy and resources to bolster domestic demand and capacity. As Epstein (2009) argues, international economic structures should be reformed to increase the role of developing countries in global economic governance by expanding the policy space available to them through altering the neoliberal policy apparatus. Empowering developing countries can further be accomplished via a reduction of the reliance on the United States as the global buyer of last resort. This can be achieved by urging countries with trade surpluses to reorient their economies away from exports and toward domestic demand.

Alongside a financial safety net, an employment safety net is composed of institutions that can enhance dynamic employment stability and maintain jobs. This safetynet can take the form of EPL(employment protection legislation) imposing legal restraints on dismissing workers, active labor market policies providing the unemployed with vocational training, job sharing through the reduction in working hours, creation of social enterprises to provide jobs for the unemployed and the poor, and social compacts between employers and labor unions for employment stability. As countries seek to green their economies, it is needed to establish an employment safety net that can transform the existing jobs in high carbon-intensive sectors to green jobs in low carbon-intensive sectors (UNEP, 2008b). An economic safety net serves as an ex-ante stabilizer of the national economy. A social safety net for the loser and disadvantaged groups in the market should—as an ex-post stabilizer—be strengthened as well. For example, universal basic income as a welfare system can contribute to enhancing the quality of life of the poor and improving their productivity. An ex-ante economic safety net and an ex-post social safety net should therefore be coupled to achieve sustainable growth (Kim, 2018b).

Bottom-Up Economics

There may be two opposing strategies for achieving economic growth, whether the government policies focus on the top or the bottom of the economy. One is top-down economics, and the other is bottom-up economics. The logic of top-down economics is that tax-cuts and deregulation for the rich and large firms will encourage them to consume and invest more, generating economic growth in the process. Top-down economics then expects a trickle-down effect, through which the fruits of economic growth from the top (the rich and large businesses) transfers to the bottom (the poor and small businesses). In this respect, top-down economics can be classified as a conservative economic philosophy like neoliberalism. A more progressive model, the logic of bottom-up economics, as a progressive economic philosophy, criticizes the top-down economics or top-down approach to the economic policies (Kim, 2018b).

Bottom-up economics argues that investments don't trickle-down in a global economy. Instead, they trickle-out to wherever in the world the wealthy can get the highest returns (Reich, 2007). Indeed, without trickle-down effects, top-down economics has resulted in greater income inequality and polarization, as was shown in the United States under the Bush administration (2001–2009). Bottom-up economics, instead, argues the necessity of intensive investment for the poor and small businesses for a sustainable and shared growth. Bottom-up approach to economic policies has a special importance in the East Asian Model since productivity and wage differentials between large firms/SOEs and SMEs/non-SOEs are huge and even widening. Through the bottom-up economics, the huge productivity and wage differentials should be reduced significantly. Through the intensive R&D and HRD investments in the bottom, the productivities of workers and small businesses should be enhanced greatly. In order to cope with polarization, bottom-up approach to economic policies should be adopted in a New East Asian Model.

Contra top-down economics, bottom-up economics is based on the proposition that the engine of economic growth is the productivity of workers (Talbott, 2008). If the high productivity of workers translates into high wages, domestic markets will expand as rising wages fuel increases in consumption. Higher productivity is also associated with larger profits, which may boost investment. Moreover, in the age of globalization, capital flows into countries where the productivity of workers is higher, *ceteris paribus*. Committing to human resources development (HRD) through education and job training is therefore vital, as is social spending in areas such as healthcare and childcare. These bottom-up approaches to economic policies require a strict regulation of financial markets, without which the security of labor markets is at risk. In the absence of labor market security, the development of skills that enhance the productivity of workers cannot be expected. Without strong regulation of the financial market, which inherently tends to create volatility of the economy, productive investment rather than speculation might not be encouraged. Together, these factors make capital controls essential to a bottom-up approach to economic policy.

Solidaristic Knowledge Policy

A solidaristic knowledge policy is a kind of solidaristic policy in knowledge-led growth regime. The goal of the solidaristic knowledge policy is to address the knowledge differentials between workers (Kim, 2007). Unlike solidaristic wage policies, which aim to lower ex-post inequality through the 'equal pay for equal work' principle, solidaristic knowledge policies target the reduction in ex-ante inequality by helping finance R&D investments in low knowledge-intensive firms and HRD investments for low-wage workers. A solidaristic wage policy as an egalitarian strategy pursued by LO in Sweden operates best in a mass production economy in which homogenous unskilled workers compose the bulk of the labor force. However, solidaristic wage policies lose relevance in knowledge-based economies where the proportion of knowledge workers with heterogenous skills is high. In short, a solidaristic wage policy can't solve the problem of 'unequal pay for unequal work' that can be effectively addressed by a solidaristic knowledge policy. Seen from the equity principle, a solidaristic knowledge policy is an example of assets-based egalitarianism (Bowles and Gintis, 1995) rather than the income-based egalitarianism that is associated with solidaristic wage policies. Assets-based egalitarianism is a new approach to curb inequality by increasing the knowledge and skills of low-wage workers, the unemployed, and marginal groups, which is needed to establish a knowledge-led growth with equity. While solidaristic wage policy pursues an equality in results, solidaristic knowledge policy pursues an equality in opportunities.

Knowledge investments (R&D investments and HRD investments) in low knowledge-intensive SMEs are also necessary for implementation of solidaristic knowledge policy.

Since knowledge differentials between workers largely come from education inequality, to reduce education inequality is a fundamental condition for the implementation of a solidaristic knowledge policy. Moreover, since education inequality originates initially from the discrimination in nurturing the child, a supply of high quality childcare programs from the government to the poor people and households is essential. The inequality in a higher education is another important factor in education inequality. Especially in Korea, differentials in private education expenditures among households determine the differentials in higher education, which in turn creates differentials in earnings. Since the differentials in household income and wealth largely determine the differentials in private education expenditures by the households, vicious circle of poverty from education inequality is sustained. A high-quality life-long education, through which workers and citizens adapt to the rapidly changing technologies in the production systems and social lives, should be given equally by the local governments and universities. Because the sharing of the tacit knowledge is crucial in knowledge information, it is necessary for the broader workers to be included in the various knowledge networks extended by universities, research institutes, corporations, and government (Progressive Policy Institute, 1999). In the labor sector, knowledge bargaining, which aims to enhance knowledge level of workers equally, should be concluded alongside wage bargaining. Since increasing knowledge investments to the workers through knowledge bargaining can increase simultaneously wages and productivities, it can be a win-win bargaining between labor and management. Since another goal of the solidaristic knowledge policy is to make all the workers knowledge workers, to build 'science-technology-skill' linkage system is also essential to reach the goal. On the one hand, a top-down ladder of 'science → technology → skill' path, which facilitates transmission of the scientific knowledge created from the universities to the technologies development in the industries and far to the skill formation in the firms, should be established. On the other hand, bottom-up ladder of 'skill → technology → science' path, through which empirical skills of the production workers on the workplace can be upgraded to technology and ultimately to scientific knowledge, should also be established. Building the top-down ladder of 'science → technology → skill' path and the bottom-up ladder of 'skill → technology → science' path will be a new paradigm of R&D and HRD policies (Kim, 2018b).

Labor Market Flexicurity

Labor market flexicurity is needed for dynamic employment stability.[22] Flexicurity means the combination of both labor market flexibility and job security of workers. Dynamic stability of employment is realized through the flexicurity of labor market. In order to realize the dynamic stability of employment, active labor market policies like retraining of the unemployed are necessary. This was best practiced in Demark, where labor market flexicurity was attained through a so-called 'golden triangle' with a flexible labor market, a generous social security system, and an active labor market policy (Wilthagen and Tros, 2004). Low employment protection with high unemployment protection and high expenditure on vocational training for the unemployed are a core of the flexicurity policy. Since flexible labor markets fit a knowledge-led growth regime in which rapid technological change occurs, labor market flexicurity is essential for employers and knowledge workers. Especially in industries where the radical innovation rather than incremental innovation occurs, flexible labor markets, in which employment adjustment is easy, are imperative to the firms. Another characteristic of labor market flexicurity is that it goes beyond both rigid (secure) labor markets common in corporatist or social democratic models and flexible (insecure) labor markets associated with neoliberalism. As we analyzed in Chapter 4, labor markets in Japan, Korea, and China were flexibilized and became insecure as the East Asian Model underwent its transformation processes. A New East Asian Model must therefore have flexicurity of labor markets for all three countries to achieve sustainable growth.

As analyzed through a 'flexicurity triangle' in Chapter 7, labor markets in Korea and Japan are rather flexible but insecure like in the United States. Korea and Japan's flexicurity triangles are significantly smaller and less balanced than Sweden's and Germany's. According to the flexicurity triangle analysis above, Korea's and Japan's labor markets achieve lower flexicurity. Based on the analysis, it can be argued that it is necessary for Korea and Japan to increase unemployment benefits and active labor market policy expenditures if they want to achieve sustainable growth. Moreover, especially in Korea, in order to break down the strong labor market dualism between large firms and SMEs as well as between regular workers and non-regular workers, flexicurity of labor market is essential. Over-protection of regular workers and under-protection of non-regular workers should be redressed. Excessive employment protection for regular workers has prompted firms to hire non-regular workers to increase employment flexibility. In other words, the difficulties and high costs incurred from laying-off regular workers increase incentives for firms to hire non-regular workers (OECD, 2016). This resulted in labor market dualism and the increase in the proportion of non-regular workers among workers. Therefore, reducing excessive employment protection for regular workers is essential to break down labor marker dualism, which is not only unfair but also inefficient. Instead, more generous unemployment benefits and higher public spending on unemployment are necessary. This is the goal of labor market flexicurity policy.

A New Welfare Regime for Sustainable Human Development

Even though there are controversies over the concept of the welfare, welfare should ultimately be approached by the viewpoint of sustainable human development that means the situations in which economic, social, and ecological sustainability are realized in order for all the people to enjoy a decent human lives (Anand and Sen, 1994). The key point of sustainable human development is that the socio-economic conditions for building capabilities, through which all the people can enjoy decent human lives with freedom, are created. A sustainable human development is, in short, a free human development. Based on this concept, welfare can be defined as social security for a free human development (Kim, 2011). In the free human development, not only material aspects but also moral aspects are important. The emancipative values such as autonomy, equality, choice, and voice, as we discussed above, should be pursued for a free human development. The existing welfare regime such as a welfare state ignored these moral aspects with only focusing on the material aspects. Post-materialist inclinations in the way of lives should be strengthened for a new welfare regime. Materialist inclinations that have been strong in the East Asian Model should be reduced. From this viewpoint, a welfare community as a new welfare regime can be suggested.

A welfare state[23] is that the central government gives benefits in cash such as unemployment benefits unilaterally to the welfare recipients. With reference to the experiences of the Western welfare states, realization of solidarity through benefits in cash exposed some serious problems. First, the inefficiency due to centralized bureaucracy and the welfare recipients' dependency to the state were prevalent in most countries. Second, since, in the welfare state based on benefits in cash, welfare expenditures are largely social consumptions rather than social investments, economic growth and social welfare can't assume a virtuous circle. Third, since, in the welfare state, local governments simply deliver welfare benefits to the residents, they can't design their own welfare policies relevant to their regions. It goes without saying that this welfare state could not reach the social security for a free human development. Instead, it brought about the crisis of welfare state in the 1970s' growth slow-down.

In order to cope with these problems, a paradigm shift from a centralized welfare state to a decentralized welfare community is necessary. A welfare community is that local governments provide benefits in kind, such as childcare, elderly care, and healthcare to the local recipients through public-private partnership among local government, labor and management, and NGOs under the fiscal support from the central government (Lipietz, 1992; Naohiko, 2000; Kim, 2006). Unlike a centralized welfare state, a welfare community operates in decentralized system, since in order to provide region-specific benefits in kind the local governments should have legal and fiscal autonomy to design their own welfare programs. The merits of welfare community may be as follows. First, through the welfare community, regional residents can receive childcare, elderly care, education care, and healthcare relevant to their own needs from the local government. This contributes to enhance the quality of lives of the residents. Second, welfare community helps to create jobs in childcare, elderly care, education care, and healthcare. Here, a care economy emerges as a new economic sector. Third, in the welfare community, social enterprises, which pursue both public interests and profitability, emerge as major agents of realizing welfare community (Borzaga and Defourny, 2004). Therefore, welfare community can achieve virtuous circle between growth and welfare and job-rich growth through the combination of 'welfare-employment-growth'. It is recommendable that the East Asian Model, in which welfare state is less developed, proceed toward welfare community without going toward a mature welfare state.

Notes

1 The financial crisis from the failure of the finance-led growth regime created a socio-political crisis of the Bush government in the United States, which was one of the main causes of power shift from the Republican party to the Democratic party. Obama administration tried to reform the financial system toward strong regulation of the financial market. At global level, G20 discussed about the establishment of a new global financial system with stronger regulation of global financial market.

2 Dividends as a percentage of total profits in the United States doubled from 22.8% in 1946–1979 to 46.3% in 1980–2008 (ILO, 2009).

3 The share of wages in the five most financialized countries declined by 3.6% between 1989 and 2005, while the share of wages in the five least financialized countries declined by 2% (ILO, 2009).

4 In Fordist growth regimes, economies of scale through mass production systems are the basis of productivity. In contrast, economies of variety in flexible quality production systems are the basis of productivity. These economies of variety come from diversified production systems in which various models of the same goods are produced within a factory.

5 Anti-Taylorist labor processes feature the unity of conception and execution, which goes beyond the separation of conception from execution that characterizes Taylorist labor processes.

6 Skill bargaining is different from wage bargaining. In the former, employees demand skill upgrading, while in the latter, employees demand wage increases.

7 Skill pay or knowledge pay is a type of wage system in which wages are determined on the basis of a worker's skill level or knowledge level.

8 The hypothesis of skill-biased technical change stresses the complementarity between technology and skills. According to this hypothesis, new technologies demand more skilled workers than unskilled workers.

9 In the event of jobless growth, for example, unskilled workers will be disproportionately impacted in a negative way.

10 Pontusson classified market economies into social market economies and liberal market economies. Hall and Soskice (2001) categorized market economies into coordinated market economies and liberal market economies. Pontusson's social market economy is equivalent to Hall and Soskice's coordinated market economy.

11 The concept of the creative class is suggested by Florida (2002). The creative class includes scientists, researchers, engineers, artists, and creative professionals in education, business, and healthcare. Florida argued that the creative class facilitates regional economic development through their creative activities. Even though there

is controversy over the concept of the creative class and the real impacts of the creative class on the regional economic development, the creative class can contribute to enhance the growth potentials in the regional economy through their creativity. Moreover, creativity of the creative class can be a core engine of growth of the knowledge-led growth regime.

12 The values of autonomy, solidarity, and ecology are three values that have been pursued by the new progressives for a new economic order beyond both Fordist growth regime and finance-led growth regime (Lipietz, 1992)

13 Stiglitz argued that the capture of public officials by the private interests of capitalists is a common phenomenon in capitalist societies where the level of democracy is low.

14 After the 2008 global financial crisis, 'restore the politics!' became a major slogan of advocates for progressive policy alternatives.

15 The World Values Survey questionnaire is structured along 14 thematic subsections, including social values, social capital, political participation and culture, demography, ethical values, economic values, and post-materialist index, among others.

16 China's public social expenditures as % of GDP in 2016 was 8.0% (OECD, 2016), which was lower than those of Japan (22.3%) and Korea (10.1%) in 2017.

17 These results need a deeper analysis on the cultures including societal paradigms (the prevalent Weltansachung) in Germany and Japan.

18 Germany's Act Against Unfair Competition (UWG) allows SMEs organized in an association to negotiate collectively with large firms.

19 Class biasedness in the capitalist state has a negative relationship with democracy, while publicness in the capitalist state is positively correlated with democracy (Kim, 2001).

20 Hirschman states that three options exist for employees who are dissatisfied with their job: the exit option, the voice option, and the acquiescence option. The acquiescence option means that though a problem is perceived, no action is taken. Unlike acquiescence, the exit option and the voice option can improve an organization. If we apply Hirschman's voice-exit paradigm to society at large, it can be argued that using the voice option through active participation can benefit society more than the exit option, which implies non-participation (Hirschman, 1970).

21 The Tobin tax is a kind of financial transaction tax in which a duty is proposed on spot currency trades to penalize short-term currency trading in order to stabilize markets and disincentive speculation. If all the countries around world introduce simultaneously Tobin Tax, the Global Tobin Tax can be an effective financial safety net.

22 In a knowledge-based economy in which technological change is rapid, achieving static employment stability with one fixed lifetime job is less realistic than achieving dynamic employment stability with variable lifetime jobs.

23 Here, the concept of welfare state is not a kind of state type. It means that the agent of welfare policy is the central government rather than local governments. It is differentiated with a welfare community.

9 Conclusion

In this study, the core of the East Asian Model and its variants, such as Japan Model, Korea Model, and China Model, were specified based on Five Sector Model for analyzing a development model. The great transformations that occurred in the East Asian Model since the 1980s were analyzed. The major changes in the great transformations were the marketization and privatization of the public sector, the liberalization of financial markets, the introduction of shareholder capitalism in corporate governance, and the flexibilization of labor markets. These developments resulted in hybridization, rather than a transition away from the East Asian Model, as elements of neoliberalism seen in the Anglo-American Model have been introduced to the East Asian Model. Specifically, there were hybridizations between the coordinated market economy (CME) and the liberal market economy (LME) in Japan, between the regulated market economy (RME) and the LME in Korea, and between the socialist market economy (SME) and the LME in China. The great transformations occurred during two or three decades in the East Asian Model were followed by long-term stagnation during the Lost Decades in Japan, low growth and polarization in Korea, and polarization and an ecological crisis in China. Indeed, the jobless, finance-led, polarized, and high carbon-based growth regimes that emerged in the transformation processes in the East Asian Model were economically, socially, and ecologically unsustainable. Moreover, the export-led growth, especially in China, has created serious global imbalances that will provoke trade frictions and stoke protectionism,[1] which may bring about widespread deflation.

To build a sustainable East Asian Model, a growth regime, which is job-rich, innovation-led, knowledge-led, shared, and low carbon intensity, should be established. To cope with the Fourth Industrial Revolution, special importance should be put on a knowledge-led growth regime beyond a Fordist growth regime and a finance-led growth regime. For a knowledge-led growth regime, institutional reforms to introduce both a collective bargaining system focusing on skill bargaining and a wage system which is regarding highly skill pay or knowledge pay are needed in the labor sector. The life-long learning in order to transform unskilled labor into knowledge labor, unskilled workers into knowledge workers, and reproduces knowledge labor and knowledge workers should

DOI: 10.4324/9781003332725-9

be expanded and deepened. A solidaristic knowledge policy for upgrading the knowledge level of the workers equally should be promoted. A knowledge-led growth regime should be embedded in a social market economy and a green economy that constitute the core elements of a new progressive development model, which is more stable, more egalitarian, and more ecological than the other development models.

Beyond an LME and RME, a symbiotic market economy with principles of liberty, equality, and reciprocity should be established. The 3C's economy—creative economy, cooperative economy, and clean economy—should be emerged. Knowledge investment for a creative economy, investment to social capital for a cooperative economy, and green investment for a clean economy should be increased significantly. The value of autonomy for a creative economy, the value of solidarity for a cooperative economy, and the value of ecology for a clean economy should be prevailed as alternative societal paradigms. Since the recent slowdown of growth in Korea and China is partly attributable to the exhaustion of catching-up growth, a creative economy should be realized in order to overcome the limits of catching-up growth. 'From imitation to creation' should be a catchword for the creative economy. China, Korea, and Japan should have much more tolerant societies and more workforces in the creative class in order to achieve a creative economy. For a shared growth between large firms and SMEs and between labor and management as well as between regular workers and non-regular workers, a cooperative economy should be realized through trust and cooperation. In order to cope with the intensifying polarization within the corporate sector of the East Asian Model, cooperation between large firms and SMEs in terms of technology and managerial skills is imperative.

For a cooperative economy, a high-trust society should be built. Through the institutional reforms such as establishing fair competition and fair-trade orders in the markets, breaking the vested interests, and removing the unjustifiable privileges of the public institutions, Japan, Korea, and China can move from a low-trust society to a high-trust society. In order to realize a clean economy, de-materialization and de-toxification of the production systems, the throughput innovation, which reduces the entropies rising from the production and consumption, and institution building for the transition from a high-carbon economy to a low-carbon economy are required. In order to reduce CO_2 emissions, introduction of carbon-tax, building a local energy system that supplies the self-reliant energy to the small size local community, transformation of the electricity supply system from a high-carbon centralized one-way network to a low-carbon decentralized interactive network, and innovation to introduce sustainable manufacturing methods and construction methods that enhance ecological efficiency and prevent the creation of the waste materials, are needed. Moreover, an ecological way of life of the people should be encouraged.

It is essential to enhance publicness as a new mode of regulation through institutional and cultural reforms. Publicness, which can be decomposed into public interest orientation, fairness, civil spirits, and openness, was lowest in Korea and Japan among the OECD countries. Korea and Japan need institutional and cultural reforms to enhance especially public interest orientation and fairness in a society. Moreover, according to World Values Survey, the share of people who think tolerance and respect to other people as well as unselfishness are important qualities for the child is low in Korea. Because tolerance and unselfishness are associated with higher levels of publicness, enhancing the publicness in Korea needs child education reforms for nurturing the tolerant and unselfish attitudes of the child within the school and family. Post-materialist inclinations, which promote values of solidarity and ecology that are important to achieving sustainable development were very low in Korea and China. Thus, a post-materialist way of life should be nurtured. To avoid totalitarianism, enhancing publicness with guaranteeing individual liberty requires embracing emancipative values: personal autonomy, equality of opportunities, freedom of choice, and the ability to voice opinions. Since autonomy, equality, choice, and voice also provide social capital that makes the public more self-expressive and vitalizes civil society, emancipative values can help promote sustainable development by enhancing publicness. Korea, China, and Japan are shown to take up emancipative values less than they are elsewhere. For a sustainable East Asian Model, people of these countries should have emancipative values. To enhance publicness in Japan, Korea, and China, governments should be able to implement institutions that can increase fairness and equal opportunities in every aspect of people's economic and social lives. 'Responsive government' rather than 'small government' is needed.

Based on knowledge-led growth regime, symbiotic market economy, and strong publicness, an alternative policy paradigm is needed as follows: a decentralized state for balanced regional development, an economic safetynet for the stability of the national economy, bottom-up economics for intensive R&D investment and human development investment to the SMEs and their workers, a solidaristic knowledge policy for reducing knowledge differentials between workers and between firms, flexicurity of labor market for dynamic stability of employment, and a new welfare regime for sustainable human development.

Since a highly centralized state system in Korea and Japan brought about concentration upon the capital city of Seoul/Tokyo and a very low fertility rate, fundamental reforms that transform the centralized state into a decentralized state are imperative in order to realize balanced regional development and to increase fertility rate significantly. In order to reduce systemic risk stemming from volatility in the global economy, a financial safety net as an economic safety net is needed. Protecting national economies from global financial crises can be achieved by introducing financial transaction taxes such as the Tobin tax to regulate the flow of short-term international capital. Strengthening the regulation of short-term foreign debts and financial derivatives can function as a financial safety net. An employment safety net as another economic safety net is also required. Moderate employment protection legislation imposing rational legal restraints on dismissing workers, active labor market policies providing the unemployed with vocational training, job sharing through the reduction in working hours, social enterprise creation to provide jobs for the unemployed and the poor, social compacts between employers and labor unions for employment stability, and jobs creation through expanding green economy and care economy can function as employment safety net.

Since productivity and wage differentials between large firms/SOEs and SMEs/non-SOEs are huge, bottom-up approach to economic policies or bottom-up economics is required in the East Asian Model. Through the bottom-up economics that focus on intensive R&D and HRD investments in the bottom, productivity and wage differentials between firms can be reduced significantly. In order to cope with polarization, bottom-up approach to economic policies should be adopted in a sustainable New East Asian Model. In order to cope with the problem of 'unequal pay for unequal work' in the knowledge-led growth regime, solidaristic knowledge policies that target the reduction in ex-ante inequality by helping finance R&D investments in low knowledge-intensive firms and HRD investments for low-wage workers are necessary. A solidaristic knowledge policy as a kind of assets-based egalitarianism that aims to reduce ex-ante inequality is a new policy paradigm in contrast to an existing solidaritic wage policy as a kind of income-based egalitarianism that targets the reduction in ex-post inequality. In order to weaken the polarization tendency in the Easy Asian Model, solidaritic knowledge policy is essential.

Since labor markets in Japan, Korea, and China were flexibilized and became insecure as the East Asian Model underwent its transformation processes, a New East Asian Model for a sustainable growth must achieve flexicurity of labor markets. From the analysis of a 'flexicurity triangle', it is clarified that Korea and Japan's flexicurity triangles are significantly smaller and less balanced than Sweden's and Germany's, which means that Korea's and Japan's labor markets achieve lower flexicurity. Thus, it is necessary for Korea and Japan to increase unemployment benefits and active labor market policy expenditures. Moreover, especially in Korea, in order to break down the labor market dualism between large firms and SMEs as well as between regular workers and non-regular workers, flexicurity of the labor market is essential. A new welfare regime for sustainable human development, in other words, a free human development, the emancipative values such as autonomy, equality, choice, and voice should be pursued. Existing welfare regime such as a welfare state ignored these moral aspects with only focusing on the material aspects. Post-materialist inclinations in the way of lives should be strengthened for a new welfare regime. A decentralized welfare community rather than a centralized welfare state should be established as a new welfare regime. In contrast to a centralized welfare state that the central government gives benefits in cash such as unemployment benefits unilaterally to the welfare recipients, a decentralized welfare community is that local governments provide benefits in kinds such as childcare, elderly care, and healthcare to the local recipients through public-private partnership among local government, labor and management, and NGOs under the fiscal support from the central government.

Recently, governments in Japan, Korea, and China has been tried to reform their development models to achieve sustainable growth. In Japan, the former Prime Minister Abe Shinzo implemented 'Abenomics' in an attempt to help the Japanese economy recover from the long-term stagnation of the Lost Decades. The core of Abenomics is to give a demand-side stimulus to the Japanese economy through a depreciation of the yen and quantitative easing. However, a simple demand-side policy without fundamental institutional reforms for a sustainable growth is unlikely to create a new growth trajectory for reviving the Japanese economy. Even though Abenomics is evaluated to have some positive impacts on the recovery from the long-lasted recession (OECD, 2017b), the recovery was weak and fragile.[2] Without creation of a new mode of regulation with coherent sets of institutions, the robust recovery from the long stagnation of the Japanese economy cannot be expected by quantitative easing and expansion of public expenditures (Boyer, 2012). A New Japan Model that orients toward a coordinated market economy (CME) with an open innovation system is needed.

In Korea, the former President Moon Jae-In suggested three types of economic policies to overcome polarization and low growth. These were an income-led growth, a fair economy, and an innovative growth. An income-led growth strategy was finally implemented as the Korean version of wage-led growth. As we mentioned in Chapter 6, income-led growth aimed to raise growth rates through increases in household income. To this end, the Korean government raised minimum wages by 27.3% in two years. An academic and political controversy existed surrounding the impact of the sharp rise in minimum wages, though it was certain that employment in SMEs and among the self-employed has been negatively affected by this policy to a significant degree. Income distribution policies without strong industrial policies to enhance the innovation capabilities of SMEs and regional policies to improve the competitiveness of provincial economies amplified these adverse effects. Therefore, The new Yoon Suk-Yeol administration should adopt an 'innovation-led shared growth' strategy instead of an income-led growth strategy of the former government in order to cope with low growth and polarization.

In China, Xi Jinping's government has plans to shift the country's growth regime from export-led growth to domestic market-led growth and from unsustainable growth to sustainable growth. The core of 'Xikonomics'[3] in China is to achieve structural reforms for sustainable growth. To accomplish these goals, China should not pursue excessive marketization and privatization of the public sector, rapid capital liberalization in financial sector, and excessive labor market flexibilization in labor sector. Especially the marketization and privatization of social services such as health care and education should be avoided. Instead, the top priority when designing policies should be given to social and ecological sustainability, thus orienting China toward a kind of 'social market economy', rather than a present hybridization between an socialist market economy (SME) and an liberal market economy (LME).

It is highly recommendable that Japan, China, and Korea act cooperatively to establish a New East Asian Model for sustainable growth. For example, a progressive 'Seoul-Beijing-Tokyo Consensus' that goes beyond the neo-liberal Washington Consensus in the 1980s should be concluded between the three countries to build up a regional financial architecture and a new regional division of labor. To establish an 'East Asian Community' initiated by Japan, Korea, and China is needed for the goals. However, the recent trade and technology war between the United States and China threaten the possibility to open the window of opportunity to build an East Asian Community since Japanese and Korean economies are deeply linked in terms of trade and technology with both the US economy and Chinese economy. Therefore, to solve the trade conflicts and technology war between the United States and China is necessary in order to build an East Asian Community for a sustainable East Asian Model. The geo-political and geo-economical risks in the East Asian region should be reduced through the cooperative US-China relationship.

Notes

1 The trade war between the United States and China resulting from President Trump's 'America First' policy is an example of these frictions.
2 During the years of the Abe administration, annual average real GDP growth in 2012–2019 was only 1.1%, which is nearly the same growth rate of 1.0% during the Koizumi administration (2001–2006).
3 It refers to the economic policies of President Xi Jinping.

References

Abiad, A., Detragiache, E., Tressel, T. (2008), "A New Database of Financial Reforms", IMF Working Paper.

Acemoglu, Daron and James A. Robinson (2012), Why Nations Fails: The Origins of Power, Prosperity and Poverty, New York: Crown.

Aglietta, Michel and Gou Bai (2013), China's Development: Capitalism and Empire, New York: Routledge.

Alexander, Arthur (2003), Korea's Capital Investment: Returns at the Level of the Economy, Industry, and Firm, Special Studies Series 2, Seoul: Korea Economic Institute.

Alexander, Arthur (2008), The Arc of Japan's Economic Development, London and New York: Routledge.

Algan, Y. and P. Cahuc (2014), "Trust, Growth and Well-Being: New Evidence and Policy Implications", In Aghion, P. and S. Durlauf (eds), Handbook of Economic Growth, Vol. 2, Amsterdam: Elsevier.

Amable, Bruno (2003), The Diversity of Modern Capitalism, New York: Oxford University Press.

Amin, Samir (1976), Unequal Development: An Essay on the Social Formations of Peripheral Capitalism. New York: Monthly Review Press.

Amsden, Alice H. (1989), Asia's Next Giant: South Korea and Late Industrialization, Oxford: Oxford University Press.

Anand, Sudihir and Amartya Sen (1994), "Sustainable Human Development: Concepts and Priorities", http://www.undp.org/hdro/oc8a.htm

Aoki, Masahiko (2001), Toward a Comparative Institutional Analysis, Cambridge: MIT Press.

Aoki, Masahiko (2012), "The Five Phases of Economic Development and Institutional Evolution in China, Japan, and Korea", In Aoki, M, T. Kuran and G. Roland Aeds, Institutions and Comparative Economic Development, IEA, Conference Volume No. 150-1. 13-47

Bae, Kyusik and Jung Woo Kim, (2012), The Status Quo of Korean Employment Relations: Results of Analysis of Panel Survey on Firms, Seoul: Korea Labor Institute.

Bai, Moo-Ki (1982), "The Turning Point in the Korean Economy", *The Developing Economies* Vol. 20, No. 2: 117–140.

Bai, Chong-En, Chang-Tai Hsieh, and Yingyi Qian (2006), "The Return to Capital", Working Paper 12755, National Bureau of Economic Research. http://www.nber.org/papers/w12755

Barth, James R., Gerard Caprio, Jr., Ross Levine (2013), "Bank Regulation and Supervision in 180 Countries from 1999 to 2011", NBER Working Paper. National Bureau of Economic Research.

Blasi, Joseph R., Maya Kroumova, and Douglas Kruse (1997), Kremlin Capitalism: Privatizing the Russian Economy, Ithaca: Cornell University Press.

Borzaga, Carlo and Jacques Defourny (eds) (2004), The Emergence of Social Enterprise, London: Routledge.

Bowles, Samuel and Gintis, Herbert (1995), "Productivity-Enhancing Egalitarian Policies", *International Labor Review*, Vol. 134, No. 4–5: 559–585.

Boyer, Robert (2000), "Is a Finance-Led Growth Regime a Viable Alternative to Fordism? A Preliminary Analysis", *Economy and Society*, Vol. 29, No. 1: 111–145.

Boyer, Robert (2004), The Future of Economic Growth: As New Becomes Old, Cheltenham: Edward Elgar.

Boyer, Robert (2012), "The Chinese Growth Regime and the World Economy", In Robert Boyer et al., Diversity and Transformation of Asian Capitalism, New York: Routledge.

Boyer, Robert and Yves Saillard (2002), Regulation Theory: The State of the Art, London: Routledge.

Boyer, Robert, Hiroyasu Uemura, and Akinori Isogai (eds) (2012), Diversity and Transformations of Asian Capitalisms, New York: Routledge.

Boyer, Robert and Toshio Yamada (eds) (2000), Japanese Capitalism in Crisis: A Regulationist Interpretation, New York: Routledge.

Braithwaite, Valerie, Toni Makkai, and Yvnne Pittelkow (1996), "Inglehart's Materialism—Post-Materialism Concept: Clarifying the Dimensionality Debate Through Rokeach's Model of Social Values", *Journal of Applied Social Psychology*, 1996: 1536–1555.

Breslin, Shaun (2012), "Government-Industry Relations in China: A Review of the Art of the State", In Andrew Walter and Xiaoke Zhang (eds), East Asian Capitalism: Diversity, Continuity, and Change, Oxford: Oxford University Press.

Burawoy, Michael (1985), The Politics of Production: Factory Regimes Under Capitalism and Socialism, London: Verso Books.

Byun, Hyung-Yoon (1995), Introduction to the Korean Economy, Seoul: Yupoong Publishing Company (in Korean).

Cai, Fang and Zhao Wen (2012), "When Demographic Dividend Appears: Growth Sustainability of China", In Masahiko Aoki and Wu Jinglian (eds), The Chinese Economy, International Economic Association Series, London: Palgrave Macmillian. http://doi.org/10.1057/97811370344298_5n

Cargill, Thomas F. and Elliott Parker (2001). "Financial Liberalization in China-Limitations and Lessons of the Japanese Regime," *Journal of the Asia Pacific Economy*, Vol. 6, No. 1: 1–21.

Carney, Richard (2012), "Political Hierarchy and Finance: The Politics of China's Financial Development", In Andrew Walter and Xiaoke Zhang (eds), East Asian Capitalism: Diversity, Continuity, and Change, Oxford: Oxford University Press.

Chang, Ha-Joon (2007), The East Asian Development Experience: The Miracle, the Crisis and the Future, New York and Penang: Zed Books and TWN.

Chavance, Bernard (2017), "Ownership Transformation and System Change in China," Revue de la Régulation—Capitalisme, institutions, pouvoirs, Association Recherche et Régulation, vol. 21.

Chen, Edward K.Y. (1979), Hyper-Growth in Asian Economies: A Comparative Study of Hong Kong, Japan, Korea, Singapore and Taiwan. London: Macmillan.

Chen, Shiyi, Gary Jefferson, and Jun Zhang (2011), "Structural Change, Productivity Growth and Industrial Transformation in China, *China Economic Review*, Vol. 22: 133–150.

Chen, Yun (2009), Transition and Development in China: Towards Sustainable Growth, Burlington: Ashgate.

Chesnais, Francois (1997), "L'emergence d'un Regime d'accumulation a Dominante Financiere", *La Pensee*, Vol. 309: 1-32.

Chi, Wei, Richard B. Freeman, and Hongbin Li (2012), "Adjusting to Really Big Changes: The Labor Market in China, 1989–2009", NBER Working Paper No. 17721.

Cho, Young Tak (2009), "Sustainable Development and Throughput Innovation: Traditional New Deal, Green-Colored New Deal, and Ecological New Deal", Paper Presented to a Seminar at Institute of Economics and Management, Kyungpook National University (in Korean).

Choi, In Chul (2006), "Change in Economic System in Korea after 1987", mimeo, Symposium for 20th Anniversary of the Samsung Economic Research Institute (in Korean).

Chowdhury, Anis and Iyanatul Islam (1993), The Newly Industrializing Economies of East Asia, London and New York: Routledge.

Colpan, Hikino, and Yoshikawa 2011, "Changing Ownership and Governance Innovation: Japanese Enterprises in Transition", In Hiroaki Miyoshi and Yoshifumi Nakata (eds), Have Japanese Firms Changed? The Lost Decade, Hampshire: Palgrave Macmillian.

Conrad, Harald (2010), "From Seniority to Performance Principle: The Evolution of Pay Practices in Japanese Firms Since the 1990s", *Social Science Japan Journal,* Vol. 13, No. 1: 115–135.

Das, Dilip K. (2011), The Asian Economy: Spearheading the Recovery from the Global Financial Crisis, New York: Routledge.

Dong, Jinyue and Le Xia (2018), "China's Financial Liberalization: Time to Restart", China Economic Watch, May 2018.

Duceux, Alice Jetin (2018), "China's Corporate Debt: On the Way to Crisis? Part 1: An Overview of Chinese Debt", Committee for the Abolition of Illegitimate Debt.

Durand, Cédric and Maxime Gueuder (2016), "The Investment-Profit Nexus in an Era of Financialisation and Globalisation. A Profit-centred Perspective", Post Keynesian Economics Study Group, Working Paper 1614.

Eichengreen, Barry (2009), "Out of the Box Thoughts about the International Financial Architecture". WP/09/116. International Monetary Fund.

Eichengreen, Barry, Dwight H. Perkins, Kwanho Shin (2012), From Miracle to Maturity: The Growth of the Korean Economy, Cambridge: Harvard University Press.

Epstein, Gerald (2009), "Obama's Economic Policy: Achievements, Problems and Prospects", *Revue de la régulation*, Vol. 5. https://doi.org/10.4000/regulation.7459

Fan, L.K., Li, X.P. and S.S. Ying (2015), "The Realistic Bases and Formation Mechanism of Excess Capacity Based on Incremental Reform". *China Industrial Economies* 1. 19–31.

Fan, Rui (2015), "China's Excess Capacity: Drivers and Implications", Law Offices of Stewart and Stewart. Haley, U.C.V.

Fields, Karl J. (2012), "Not of a Piece: Developmental States, Industrial Policy, and Evolving Patterns of Capitalism in Japan, Korea, and Taiwan", In Andrew Walter and Xiaoke Zhang (eds), East Asian Capitalism: Diversity, Continuity, and Change, Oxford: Oxford University Press.

Florida, Richard (2002), The Rise of Creative Class, New York: Basic Books.

Florida, Richard, Charlotta Mellander, and Karen King (2015), The Global Creativity Index, Toronto: Martin Prosperity Institute, Toronto University.
Frank, Andre Gunder (1966), The Development of Underdevelopment, New York: Monthly Review Press.
Fukao, Kyoji, YoungGak Kim, and Tatsuji Makino (2010), "The Structural Causes of Japan's Lost Decades", Policy Discussion Papers, Research Institute of Economy, Trade and Industry.
Gallagher, Kevin P. and Richard Kozul-Wright (2022), The Case for a New Bretton Woods, Cambridge: Polity.
Global Green Growth Institute (2019), Green Growth Index: Concept, Methods, and Applications. GGGI Technical Report No. 5.
Goldstein, Morris (1998), The Asian Financial Crisis: Causes, Cures, and Systemic Implications, Institute for International Economics.
Green, Fergus and Nicholas Stern (2015), "China's 'New Normal': Structural Change, Better Growth, and Peak Emissions", Policy Brief, Center for Climate Change Economics and Policy, London: Grantham Research Institute on Climate Change and Environment, London School of Economics and Political Science.
Gwartney, James, Robert Lawson, and Joshua Hall(2013), Economic Freedom of the World 2013 Annual Report, Fraser Institute.
Gwartney, James, Robert Lawson, Joshua Hall, and Ryan Murphy (2018), Economic Freedom of the World 2018 Annual Report, Fraser Institute.
Gwartney, James, Robert Lawson, Joshua Hall, and Ryan Murphy (2020), Economic Freedom of the World 2020 Annual Report, Fraser Institute.
Haggard, Stephan (1990), Pathways from the Periphery: The Politics of Growth in the Newly Industrializing Countries. Itaca: Cornell University Press.
Hall, Peter. A and David Soskice (2001), Varieties of Capitalism: The Institutional Foundations of Comparative Advantage, New York: Oxford University Press.
Hamaaki Junya, Masahiro Hori, Saeko Maeda, and Keiko Murata (2012), 'Changes in the Japanese Employment System in the Two Lost Decades', ILR Review Vol. 65, No. 4: 810-846
Harrison, Lawrence E. (1985), Underdevelopment Is a State of Mind, Cambridge: Harvard University Press.
Henderson, Gregory (1968), Korea: The Politics of the Vortex, Cambridge: Harvard University Press.
Henderson, Jeffery (2011), East Asian Transformation: On the Political Economy of Dynamism, Governance and Crisis, New York: Routledge.
Heston, Alan, et al. (2012), Penn World Table Version 7.1, Center for International Comparisons of Production, Income and Prices at the University of Pennsylvania, July 2012.
Hirschman, Albert O. (1970), Exit, Voice, and Loyalty: Responses to Decline in Firms, Organizations, and States, Cambridge: Harvard University Press.
Hofstede, G. (1991), "Empirical Models of Cultural Differences". In N. Bleichrodt and P. J. D. Drenth (eds), *Contemporary Issues in Cross-Cultural Psychology*, Amsterdam: Swets & Zeitlinger Publishers.
Holz, Carsten A. (2017), "China's Investment Rate: Implications and Prospects", CESifo Working Papers, Munich Society for the Promotion of Economic Research.
Hsu, S. Philip, Yu-Shan Wu, and Suisheng Zhao (eds) (2011), In Search of China's Development Model: Beyond Beijing Consensus, New York: Routledge.
Huang, Zixan and Nicholas R. Lardy (2016), "China's Rebalance Reflected in Rising Wage Share of GDP", China Economic Watch, Washington, DC: Peterson Institute for International Economics.

Hunter, WC., Kaufman, GG., Krueger, TH., (1999), The Asian Financial Crisis: Origins, Implications and Solutions, New York: Springer.

IEA (2013), CO2 Emissions from Fuel Combustion, IEA, Paris. https://doi.org/10.17871/CO2_fuel-2013-en

IMF Staff (1998), "The Asian Crisis: Causes and Curses", *Finance and Development,* Vol. 35, No. 2: 18–21.

Inglehart, Ronald (1981), "Post-Materialism in an Environment of Insecurity", *American Politicla Science Review,* Vol. 75: 880–900.

Institute for Social Development and Policy Research (2014), Disaster of Dual Risk Society and Publicness, Seoul: Seoul national University (in Korean).

International Labor Organization (2009), World of Work Report 2009: The Global Jobs Crisis and Beyond. Geneva: International Institute for Labor Studies.

International Labor Organization (2013), World Employment Outlook: Repairing the Economic and Social Fablic. Geneva: International Institute for Labor Studies.

Isogai, Akinori (2012), "The Transformation of the Japanese Corporate System and the Hierarchical Nexus of Institutions", In Boyer et al (eds), Diversity and Transformations of Asian Capitalisms, New York: Routledge.

Isogai, Akinori (2014), "Transformation of the Japanese Corporate System and Possibility of the "New J-type Firm" Reexamined", Department of Economics Kyusu University, Discussion Paper, No.2014-1.

Jackson, Gregory (2009), "The Japanese Firm and Its Diversity", *Economy and Society,* Vol. 38 No. 4: 606–629.

Jain-Chandra, Sonali, Niny Khor, Rui Mano, Johanna Schauer, Philippe Wingender and Juzhong Zhuang (2018), "Inequality in China—Trends, Drivers and Policy Remedies", IMF Working Paper. No.2018/127

Jingu, Takeshi, (2009), "Property Rights Exchanges in China", *Nomura Journal of Capital Markets,* Vol. 1. No. 1.

Johnson, Chalmers (1982), MITI and the Japanese Miracle: The Growth of Industrial Policy. California: Stanford University Press.

Kagono, Tadao, Jkujiro Nonaka, Kiyonori Sakakitara and Akihiro Okumura (1983), Strategic Adaptation to Environment: Japanese and U.S. Firms Compared'. *Japanese Economic Studies,* Vol. 13, No. 2: 33–80.

Kambayashi, Ryo and Takao Kato (2011), "The Japanese Employment System after the Bubble Burst: New Evidence", In Koichi Hamada, Anil K. Kashyap, and David E. Weinstein (eds), Japan's Bubble, Deflation, and Long-Term Stagnation, Cambridge and London: MIT Press.

Kaneko, Masaru (1998), "The Political Economy of the Safety Net", *Journal of International Studies,* Vol. 12: 1–22.

Kang, Dongsoo (eds) (2011), Development and Challenges of the Chinese Financial System, Seoul: Korea Development Institute.

Kang, Yong, Lu Shi, and Elizabeth D. Brown(2008), Chinese Corporate Governance: History and Institutional Framework. Santa Monica, CA: RAND Corporation.

Kapsos, Stern (2005), "The Employment Intensity of Growth: Trends and Macroeconomic Determinants", Employment Strategy Papers, International Labor Organization.

Kim, Hyungkee (1988), Monopoly and Wage Labor in Korea, Seoul: Khachi (in Korean).

Kim, Hyungkee (2001), New Political Economy, Seoul: Hanul Academy (in Korean).

Kim, Hyungkee (2002), "Decentralization and Regional Development: A New Vision of Regional Development", In Kim Hyungkee (eds), Policy Alternatives for Decentralization, Seoul: Hanul Academy (in Korean).

Kim, Hyungkee (2003), "Labor Reform for an Alternative Development Model of the Korean Economy", In Lee Won Duck et al. (eds), The Future of Work and a New Order, Seoul: Korea Labor Institute (in Korean).
Kim, Hyungkee (2006), The Third Way of Korean Economy, Seoul: Hanul Academy (in Korean).
Kim, Hyungkee (2007), "The Knowledge-Led Accumulation Regime: A Theory of Contemporary Capitalism", Working Paper No.158-07, Institute for Research on Labor and Employment, University of California, Berkeley.
Kim, Hyungkee (2010), "Capitalism after the Great Recession: A New Progressive Development Model", *World Review of Political Economy*, Vol. 2: 226–237.
Kim, Hyungkee (2011), "A Solidaristic Knowledge Policy for Sustainable Human Development", *International Critical Thought*, Vol. 1, No. 3: 267–279.
Kim, Hyungkee (2012a), "The Great Transformation of the Korean Economy since 1962: Processes and Consequences", In Boyer et al (eds), Diversity and Transformations of Asian Capitalisms, New York: Routledge.
Kim, Hyungkee (2012b), "Symbiotic Market Economy: A New Economic Order for Sustainable Human Development", Paper presented to WAPE 2012 Forum, World Association for Political Economy.
Kim, Hyungkee (2016), "Financial Liberalization and Transformation of the East Asian Development Model", *Asia Review*, Vol. 6 No. 2: 63–87.
Kim, Hyungkee (2018a), "How Financial Liberalization Transformed the East Asian Model", In Lim, Hyun-Chin, Jan Nederveen Pieterse, and Suk-Man Hwang (eds), Capitalism and Capitalisms in Asia: Origin, Commonality and Diversity, Seoul: Seoul National University Press.
Kim, Hyungkee (2018b), A New Korea Model: Beyond Park Jung Hee Model, Seoul: Hanul Academy (in Korean).
Kim, Chul Ju and Michael C. Huang (2019), "The Privatization of Japan Railways and Japan Post: Why, How, and Now", ADBI Working Paper 1039, Asian Development Bank Institute (in Japanese).
Kim, Do Wan, Jin Hyun Han, and Eun Kyung Lee (2017), "Estimation of Korea's Potential Growth Rate", *Monthly Survey Statistics*, Bank of Korea (in Korean).
Kim, Dong Suk, Min Soo Kim, Young Jun Kim, and Sung Ju Kim (2012), An Analysis on Factors of Growth in the Korean Economy: 1970–2010, Seoul: Korea Development Institute (in Korean).
Kim, Hyungkee and Aekyung Kim (2005), "The 1997–1998 Korean Economic Crisis and Economic Reform: An Appraisal and Policy Agenda", *Review of Economic Development*, Vol. 11, No. 1: 51–77 (in Korean).
Kim, J. I. and L.J. Lau (1994), "The Sources of Economic Growth in the East Asian Newly Industrialized Countries", *Journal of Japanese and International Economies* Vol. 8, No. 3: 235–271.
Kim, Taigi and Byung You Cheon (2003), "Restructuring and Industrial Relations", *Korean Economic Review*, Special Issue for the 50th Anniversary of the Korean Economic Association: 73–102 (in Korean).
Klaus Schwab and World Economic Forum (2018), The Global Competitiveness Report: 2017-2018, Geneva: World Economic Forum
Klaus Schwab and World Economic Forum(2019), The Global Competitiveness Report 2019. Geneva: World Economic Forum.
Kohsaka, Akira (eds) (2013), Aging and Economic Growth in the Pacific Region, New York: Routledge.
Krugman, Paul (1994), "The Myth of Asia's Miracle", *Foreign Affairs*, Vol. 73, No. 1: 62–78.

Krugman, Paul (1997), What Ever Happened to the Asian Miracle? *Fortune*, Vol. 136, No. 4: 26-29.

Kusida, Kenji E. and Philip Y. Lipsey (2013), Japan Under the Democratic Party of Japan: The Politics of Transition and Governance, Washington, DC.: Shorenstein APARC/ Brookings Institution Press.

Kwon, Huck-Ju (2007), "Transforming the Developmental Welfare State in East Asia", DESA Working Paper No. 40, Department of Economic and Social Affairs, United Nations.

Kwon, O. Yul (2011), "Does Culture Matter for Economic Development in Korea?". *Journal of East Asian Affairs*, Vol. 25. No. 2: 163–182.

Labor Policy Research and Training Institute (2007), The Report of Survey Research on Corporate Governance, CSR, and Personnel Strategies of Japanese Firms (in Japanese)

Lam, W. Raphael, Xiaoguang Liu, and Alfred Schipke (2015), "China's labor Market in the 'New Normal'", IMF Working Paper, 15/151.

Lee, Byung-Chun (2003), "The Political Economy of Developmental Dictatorship and the Experience of Korea", In Lee, Byung-Chun (eds), Developmental Dictatorship and the Age of Park Chung Hee: Seoul: Changbi Publishers (in Korean).

Lee, Ching Kwan (2012), "Durable Subordination: Chinese Labour Regime through a South Korean Lens", In Andrew Walter and Xiaoke Zhang (eds), East Asian Capitalism: Diversity, Continuity, and Change, Oxford: Oxford University Press.

Lee, Keun (2013), "The Past, Present, and Future of Korean Capitalism and Policy Choices", Paper Presented to a Symposium of the Seoul Institute of Economic and Social Studies (in Korean).

Lee, Kyu-Sung (2011), The Korean Financial Crisis of 1997: Onset, Turnaround, and Thereafter, World Bank and Korea Development Institute. Washington, DC: Worldbank Pubications.

Lee, Sang Ho (2018), "The Extinction of the Provinces in Korea 2018: 2013–2018", Employment Trends Brief, Korea Employment Information Service (in Korean).

Lewis, Arthur (1954), "Economic Development with Unlimited Supplies of Labour". *The Manchester School*, Vol. 22, No. 2: 139–191.

Lin, Chun (2008), "China: Changing the Rules of the Game", *Soundings*, Vol. 39: 7–19.

Lincoln, James and Masahiro Shimotani (2009), "Whither the Keiretzu, Japan's Business Networks? How Were They Structured? What Did They Do? Why Are They Gone?" Institute for Research on Labor and Employment, Working Paper Series, University of California, Berkeley: 134–139.

Lipietz, Alian (1987), Mirages and Miracles: Crisis in Global Fordism, London: Verso.

Lipietz, Alain (1992), Towards a New Economic Order: Postfordism, Ecology and Democracy, London: Polity Press.

Lu, Ming, Zhao Chen, Yongqin Wang, Yan Zhang, and Chanyuan Luo, (2013), China's Economic Development: Institutions, Growth and Imbalances, Northampton: Edward Elger.

Maddison, Angus (2006), "The World Economy in the Second Half of the Twentieth Century", In The World Economy: Volume 1: A Millennial Perspective and Volume 2: Historical Statistics, OECD Development Centre. Paris: OECD Publishing. http://doi.org/10.1787/9789264022621-en

Mahoney, James and Kathlen Thelen (2010), Explaining Institutional Change: Ambiguity, Agency, and Power, New York: Cambridge University Press.

Marglin, Stephen A. and Schor, Juliet B. (eds) (1990), The Golden Age of Capitalism, Oxford: Clarendon-Oxford University Press.

Mazda, Hiroya (2014), The Extinction of the Provinces, Tokyo: JuoKoronShinSia (in Japanese).

McDonough, William. and Michael Braungart (2002), From Cradle to Cradle: Remaking the Way We Make Things, New York: North Point Press.

Meng, X. (2012), "Labor Market Outcomes and Reforms in China", *Journal of Economic Perspectives*, Vol. 26, No. 4: 75–102.

Min, Byung-Seong (2016), "Corporate Governance Reform: The Case of Korea", *Asian Journal of Political Science*, Vol. 24, No. 1: 21–41.

Minami, Ryoshin (1968), "The Turning Point in the Japanese Economy", *The Quarterly Journal of Economics*, Vol. 82, No. 3: 380–402.

Miyamoto, Mitsuharu(2019), "Change and Continuity in Japanese Corporate Governance", In Miyamoto Mitsuharu eds(2019) The New Japanese Firm as a Hybrid Organization, New York: Springer.

Miyoshi, Hiroaki and Takeo Nakao (2011), "Why Do Japanese Companies Issue Stock Options?: Behind the Introduction of Stock Options in Japan: Theory of Shareholder Sovereignty vs. Theory of Managerial Sovereignty", In Hiroaki Miyoshi and Yoshifumi Nakata (eds). Have Japanese Firms Changed?: The Lost Decade, Hampshire: Palgrave Macmillan.

Morotomi, Touru and Mye Asaoka (2011), The Road to a Low Carbon Economy, Seoul: Environment and Civilization (Korean Version).

Muchhala, Bhumika (eds) (2007), Ten Years After: Revisiting the Asian Financial Crisis. Washington, DC: Woodrow Wilson International Center for Scholars Asia Program.

Naohiko, Jinno (2000), The Political Economy of Regime Reforms, Seoul: Hanul Academy (Korean Version).

OECD (2015a), Pensions at a Glance 2015. https://doi.org/10.1787/pension_glance-2015-en

OECD (2015b), OECD Economic Surveys: China 2015. Overview

OECD (2016), "Social Spending", In Society at a Glance 2016: OECD Social Indicators, Paris: OECD Publishing. https://doi.org/10.1787/soc_glance-2016-19-en

OECD (2017a), Economic Surveys: China 2017. www.oecd.org/eco/surveys/economic-survey-china.htm

OECD (2017b), Economic Surveys: Japan 2017. www.oecd.org/eco/surveys/economic-survey-japan.htm

OECD (2017c), Social Expenditure Database.

OECD (2017e), Employment Outlook 2017. http://dx.doi.org/10.1787/empl_outlook-2017-en

OECD (2017f), OECD Economic Outlook: Statistics and Projections. https://doi.org/10.1787/eo-data-en

OECD (2018a), OECD Economic Surveys: Korea 2018. OECD Publishing.

OECD (2018b), Main Science and Technology Indicators, 211–226. https://jstor/org/stable/25063173

OECD (2020), OECD Economic Outlook. https://doi.org/10.1787/eo-data-en

Pack, Howard (2001), "Technical Change and Growth in East Asia: Macro vs. Micro Perspectives", In Stiglitz, Joseph. E. and Shahid Yusuf (eds), Rethinking the East Asian Miracle, New York: Oxford University Press.

Pagano, M.S. (2002), "Crises, Cronyism, and Credit", *The Financial Review*, Vol. 37: 227–256.

Park, Albert, Wu, Yaowu, and Du, Yang(2012). Informal Employment in Urban China: Measurement and Implications. World Bank, Washington, DC. https://openknowledge.worldbank.org/handle/10986/27218 License: CC BY 3.0 IGO."

Park, Yung Chul (2002), "Does East Asia Need a New Development Paradigm?", *Brookings Trade Forum*, vol.2002, 211-226. doi:10.1353/btf.2003.0009.

Peking University (2014), China Welfare Development Report, Beijing: Institute of Social Science Survey.

Pempel, T. J. (1999), The Politics of the Asian Economic Crisis. Ithaca: Cornell University Press.

Perkins, Dwight (2013), East Asian Development: Foundations and Strategies, Cambridge: Harvard University Press.

Perkins, Dwight H. and T. G. Rawski (2008), "Forcasting China's Economic Growth to 2025", In Loren Brant and Thomas G. Rawski (eds), China's Great Economic Transformation. New York: Cambridge University Press.

Piketty, Thomas (2013), Capital in the Twenty-First Century, Cambridge: The Belknap Press of Harvard University Press.

Piketty, Thomas, Li Yang, and Gabriel Zucman (2017), "Capital Accumulation, Private Property and Rising Inequality in China, 1978–2015", WID, Working Paper Series No. 2017/6.

Pirie, Iain (2008), The Korean Developmental State: From Dirigisme to Neo-Liberalism, New York: Routledge.

Pontusson, Jonas (2005), Inequality and Prosperity: Social Europe vs. Liberal America, A Century Foundation Book, Ithaca and London: Cornell University Press.

Progressive Policy Institute (1999), Rules of the Road: Governing Principles for the New Economy, Washington, DC: Progressive Policy Institute.

Przeworski, Adam and Fernando Limongi (1993), "Political Regimes and Economic Growth", *Journal of Economic Perspectives*, Vol. 7, No. 3: 51–69.

Pye, Lucian W. (2000), "'Asian Values': From Dayamos to Dominoes?", In L.E. Harrison and Samuel P. Huntington (eds), Culture Matters: Values Shape Human Progress, New York: Basic Books.

Radelet, Steven, Jeffrey D. Sachs, Richard N. Cooper, and Barry P. Bosworth (1998), "The East Asian Financial Crisis: Diagnosis, Remedies, Prospects", *Brookings Papers on Economic Activity*, Vol. 1998, No. 1: 1–90.

Reich, Robert (2007), "Trickle Down or Bottom Up", *Robert Reich's Blog.*

Richter, Frank-Jurgen (eds) (2000), The East Asian Development Model: Economic Growth, Institutional Failure and the Aftermath of the Crisis, New York: St. Martin's Press.

Rodrik, Daniel and Andres Velasco (1999), "Short-Term Capital Flows", NBER Working Paper 7364, National Bureau of Economic Research.

Sako, Mari and Masahiro Kotosaka (2012), "Institutional Change and Organizational Diversity in Japan", In Christel Lane and Geoffrey T. Wood (eds), Capitalist Diversity and Diversity within Capitalism, New York: Routledge.

Schumpeter, Joseph A. (2008), Capitalism, Socialism and Democracy, New York: HarperCollins Publishers.

Song, Lei (2001), "The Limit of Gradual Reform without Long Term Perspective: Instability of Institutional Arrangements in Mainland China", mimeo, Nagoya University.

Soros, George (2009), The Crash of 2008 and What It Means, New York: Public Affairs.

Statista (2019), Gini Index, Inequality of Income Distribution in China from 2008 to 2018. Statista's Research and Analysis Service.

Stiglitz, Joseph E. (2001), "From Miracle to Crisis to Recovery: Lessions from Four Decades od East Asian Experience", In Joseph E. Stiglitz and Shahid Yusuf (eds), Rethinking the East Asian Miracle, New York: Oxford University Press

Stiglitz, Joseph E. (2002), Globalization and Its Discontents, New York: W. W. Norton & Company.

Stiglitz, Joseph E. (2008), "China: Towards a New Model of Development", *China Economic Journal*, Vol. 1, No. 1: 33–52.

Stiglitz, Joseph E. (2014), The Price of Inequality: How Today's Divided Society Endangers Our Future, New York and London: W. W. Norton & Company.

Stiglitz, Joseph E. and Bruce Greenwald (2010), "Towards a New Global Reserve System", *Journal of Globalization and Development*, Vol. 1, No. 2: 1–24.

Stiglitz, Joseph E. and Shahid Yusuf (eds) (2001), Rethinking the East Asian Miracle, New York: Oxford University Press.

Takahashi, Wataru (2012), "The Japanese Financial Sector's Transition from High Growth to the Lost Decades" In Hiroaki Miyoshi and Yoshifumi Nakata (eds), Have Japanese Firms Changed?: The Lost Decade, Hampshire: Palgrave Macmillan.

Takeda, Masahiko and Philip Turner (1992), "The Liberalisation of Japan's Financial Markets", BIS Working Papers No. 34. November 1992, Bank for International Settlements.

Talbott, John R. (2008), Obamanomics: How Bottom-Up Economic Prosperity Will Replace Trickle-Down Economics, New York: Seven Stories Press.

Tohyama, Hironori (2000), "The Capital-Labour Compromise and the Financial System", In Boyer and Yamada (eds) (2000), Japanese Capitalism in Crisis: A Regulationist Interpretation, New York: Routledge.

Uemura, Hiroyasu (2012), Institutional Changes and the Transformations of the Growth Regime in the Japanese Economy, In Boyer, Robert, Hiroyasu Uemura, and Akinori Isogai (eds) (2012), Diversity and Transformations of Asian Capitalisms, New York: Routledge.

UNEP (2008a), "A Global Green New Deal", Report Prepared for Economics and Trade Branch, Division of Technology, Industry and Economics, United Nations Environment Programme.

UNEP (2008b), Green Jobs: Towards Decent Work in a Sustainable, Low-Carbon World, United Nations Environment Programme. www.unep.org/civil/society/publications/index.asp

Uni, Hiroyuki (2012a), "Increasing Wage-Inequality in Japan since the End of 1990s: An Institutional Explanation", In Boyer et al (eds), Diversity and Transformations of Asian Capitalisms, New York: Routledge.

Uni, Hiroyuki (2012b), "Institutional Changes and the Transformations of the Growth Regime in the Japanese Economy: facing the Impact of the World Economic Crisis and Asian Integration", In Boyer et al (eds), Diversity and Transformations of Asian Capitalisms, New York: Routledge.

U.S. Government (2010), Economic Report of the President, Washington, DC: US Government Printing Office.

Wade, Robert (1990), "Industrial Policy in East Asia: Does It Lead or Follow the Market?", In Gary Gereffi and Donald L. Wyman (eds), Manufacturing Miracles: Path of Industrialization in Latin America and East Asia, Princeton: Princeton University Press.

Walter, Andrew and Xiaoke Zhang (eds) (2012), East Asian Capitalism: Diversity, Continuity, and Change, Oxford: Oxford University Press.

Weber, Max (1930), The Protestant Ethic and the Spirit of Capitalism, London and Boston: Allen and Unwin.

Weber, Max (1951), The Religion of China: Confucianism and Taoism, New York: Macmillan.

Wei, Q. (2009), A Study of Pay for Performance in China's Non-Public Sector Knowledge-Intensive Industry. Unpublished Doctoral Thesis. City University London.

Welzel, Christian (2013), Freedom Rising: Human Empowerment and the Quest for Emancipation, New York: Cambridge University Press.

WID (2017), World Inequality Database. WID.WORLD.

Williamson, John and Pedro-Pablo Kuczynski (eds) (2003), After the Washington Consensus: Restarting Growth and Reform in Latin America, Washington, DC: Peterson Institute for International Economics.

Wilthagen, T. and F. Tros (2004), "The Concept of 'Flexicurity': a New Approach to Regulating Employment and Labour Markets" Transfer. *European Review of Labour and Research*, Vol. 10, No. 2. https://doi.org/10.1177/102425890401000204

Wolf, Charles(1988), Markets or Governments: Choosing between Imperfect Alternatives. Cambridge, Mass: MIT Press

Woo-Cummings, Meredith(2001), "Miracle as Prologue: The State and the Reform of the Corporate Sector in Korea", In Joseph Stiglitz and Shahid Yusuf(eds). Rethinking the East Asian Miracle, New York: Oxford University Press.

Woo-Cumings, Meredith (eds) (2019), The Developmental State, Ithaca and London: Cornell University Press.

World Bank (1993), The East Asian Miracle: Economic Growth and Public Policy, New York: Oxford University.

World Economic Forum (2018), The Global Gender Gap Report 2018.

World Values Survey Association(1999), World Values Survey Wave 3: 1995-1999.

World Values Survey Association(2014), World Values Survey Wave 6: 2010-2014.

Yamada, Toshio (1993), "Japanese Type of Capitalism and Companyist Regulation", *Gendai Shiso*, Vol. 21, No. 13: 166–175.

Yamada, Toshio and Yasuro Hirano (2012), "How Has the Japanese Mode of Regulation Changed? The Whereabouts of Companyism", In Boyer et al. (eds), Diversity and Transformations of Asian Capitalisms, New York: Routledge.

Yan, Isqabel K., Chan, Kenneth S., and Dang, Vinh Q.T. (2011), Financial Liberalization and Financing Constraints: Some Evidence from Panel Data of Listed Chinese Firms, *Munich Personal RePEc Archive*.

Yang, Mingming (2020), "Analysis of the Current Situation of Asset Securitization of State-Owned Enterprises in China', *Financial Forum*, Vol. 9, No. 2: 48–51.

Yamada, Toshio (2000), "Japanese Capitalism and the Companyist Compromise", In Robert Boyer and Toshiom Yamada (eds), *Japanese Capitalism in Crisis*, London: Routledge.

Young, Alywn (1994), "Lession from the East Asian NICs: A Contrarian View", *European Economic Review*, Vol. 38, No. 3–4: 964–973.

Yusuf, Shahid (2001), "The East Asian Miracle at the Millennium", In Joseph E. Stiglitz and Shahid Yusuf (eds), Rethinking the East Asian Miracle, New York: Oxford University Press.

Zhu, Min, Longmei Zhang, and Daoju (2019), "China's Growth Potential—A Stocktaking and Reassessment", IMF Working Paper, WP/19/263.

Index

Note: Page references in *italics* denote figures, in **bold** tables and with "n" endnotes.

For Product Safety Concerns and Information please contact our EU representative GPSR@taylorandfrancis.com
Taylor & Francis Verlag GmbH, Kaufingerstraße 24, 80331 München, Germany

www.ingramcontent.com/pod-product-compliance
Ingram Content Group UK Ltd.
Pitfield, Milton Keynes, MK11 3LW, UK
UKHW020004200926
475702UK00015B/2474

* 9 7 8 1 0 3 2 3 6 5 7 7 0 *